You2Uni

Decide. Prepare. Apply.

Stella Cottrell

palgrave
macmillan

Aberdeen | Abertay | **Aberystwyth** | Adam Smith College | **Anglia Ruskin** | **Arts UC** | **Aston** | **Bangor** | **Bath** | **Bath Spa** | Bedfordshire | Belfast Met | Birkbeck | **Birmingham** | Birmingham City | **Bishop Grosseteste UC** | **Blackburn College** | **Bolton** | **Bournemouth** | **Bournemouth and Poole College** | **BPP UC** | Bradford | **Bradford College** | Brighton | **Bristol** | Bristol College | **Brunel** | **Buckingham** | **Buckinghamshire New** | **Burnley College** | **Cambridge** | **Campus Suffolk** | Canterbury Christ Church | **Cardiff** | Cardiff and Vale College | **Chester** | Chichester | **City** | **Colchester College** | **Cornwall College** | **Courtauld Institute** | **Coventry** | **Creative Arts** | Cumbria | **De Montfort** | Derby | **Doncaster College** | Dublin | **Dundalk College** | **Dundee** | **Dundee College** | **Durham** | **East Anglia** | **East London** | Edge Hill | Edinburgh | Edinburgh Napier | **Essex** | Exeter | **Falmouth UC** | **Farnborough College** | **Galway-Mayo** | **Glamorgan** | **Glasgow** | **Glasgow Caledonian** | Glasgow College of Art | Gloucestershire | Glyndwr | **Goldsmiths** | Greenwich | **Grimsby Institute** | **Guildford College** | **Harper Adams UC** | **Hartpury College** | **Havering College** | **Heriot-Watt** | Hertfordshire | Highlands and Islands | Huddersfield | **Hull** | Hull College | **Imperial** | **Keele** | **Kent** | **King's** | **Kingston** | **Lancaster** | Leeds | **Leeds City College** | Leeds Met | **Leeds Trinity UC** | Leicester | **Letterkenny College** | **Limerick** | **Lincoln** | **Liverpool** | **Liverpool College** | **Liverpool Hope** | Liverpool John Moores | **London** | London Met | **LSE** | **London South Bank** | Loughborough |

Loughborough College | Manchester | **Manchester College** | **Manchester Met** | **Maynooth** | **Middlesex** | **Newcastle** | **Newcastle College** | **New College Durham** | **New College Nottingham** | Newham College | Newman UC | Newport Wales | **Northampton** | Northbrook College | **Northumbria** | **Norwich City College** | **Norwich UC** | **Nottingham** | **Nottingham Trent** | **NRC** | NUI Galway | OU | Oxford | **Oxford Brookes** | Pembrokeshire College | **Plymouth** | **Plymouth College of Art** | **Portsmouth** | **Queen Margaret** | **Queen Mary** | **Queen's Belfast** | Ravensbourne | Reading | Robert Gordon | **Roehampton** | Rose Bruford | **Royal Agricultural** | **Royal Holloway** | **Salford** | **Scottish Agricultural College** | SERC | **Sheffield** | Sheffield College | **Sheffield Hallam** | SOAS | **Southampton** | Southampton Solent | **South Tyneside College** | **Sparsholt College** | **SRC** | **Staffordshire** | **St Andrews** | **St Helens College** | St Mary's UC | **Stirling** | Stockport College | **Strathclyde** | Sunderland | **Surrey** | **Sussex** | **Swansea** | **Swansea Met** | **Tallaght College** | **Teesside** | **Trinity Dublin** | **Trinity Laban** | Trinity St David | **UC Birmingham** | UC Cork | **UCL** | **UCLAN** | **UCP Marjon** | **Ulster University** | **University of the Arts** | **UWE** | UWIC | **Wakefield College** | **Warwick** | **Warwickshire College** | West London | **West Nottinghamshire College** | **West of Scotland** | **Westminster** | **West Suffolk College** | **Wigan and Leigh College** | **Winchester** | Wolverhampton | **Worcester** | Worcester College | **Writtle College** | York | **York College** | **York St John**

Contents

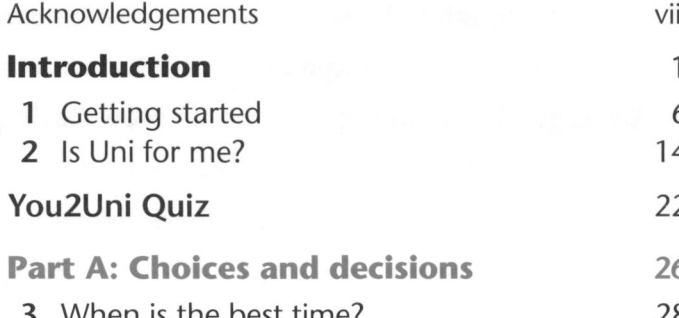

Acknowledgements

To all those who help students prepare and apply for higher education.

To all those students who follow their dreams, whether into higher education or elsewhere.

Thanks to Claire Dorer for inspiration, input, and administration of the book from inception to completion and, in particular, for the chapters on shopping and cooking. Thanks to everyone at Palgrave Macmillan for their support and input, especially Suzannah Burywood, Tina Graham, Della Oliver, Jocelyn Stockley and Jim Weaver. Finally, thanks to all the colleges and universities who kindly supplied the photographs included in the book.

Introduction

Hundreds of thousands of students go to Uni every year. Most people who make that decision have a fantastic time, and find the experience to be life changing.

Each year, hundreds of thousands of other students are just setting out on that journey, deciding whether Uni is for them. You may be one of these. If so, this book is for you.

If you are thinking of going to Uni, you may be wondering now about such things as what to study, whether you would get a place and whether you would enjoy life as a student.

The range of options open to you is enormous. That is wonderful in one way, but it can also be bewildering when juggling such a vast array of choices. This book is designed to help you work your way through the process and arrive at the best decisions for you.

This short introduction provides some initial information to set the scene and to help you to make best use of the book.

- It tells you briefly about why the book was written.
- It explains some of the terminology.
- It gives you an overview of the book as a whole.
- It describes some of the book's key features.

Action Plan

The Action Plan on pages 280–3 provides a step-by-step guide to the overall process. You may find it helpful to read through that early.

Understanding the jargon

A glossary is provided on pages 304–8 so that you can look up any terminology with which you are not familiar.

Enjoy the journey

Whatever final decision you make about applying to Uni, make the most of this chance to think about and plan your future. This is an exciting time, with lots of opportunities for visiting Unis, seeing different parts of the country, meeting new people, learning new skills and taking on new challenges. Have a great time.

About this book

Who?

This book is written for those who are thinking about going on to higher level study at university or college – or who haven't ruled it out.

Why?

> **The majority of students arrive at Uni or college unprepared for what lies ahead ...**
>
> Surveys undertaken by Cambridge Assessment of first years in higher education and also of sixth formers, found the following.
>
> *"94% of first year students felt that secondary education could have prepared them much better for the academic rigour of university."*
>
> *"50% of first years felt that they lacked the necessary independent research and study skills."*
>
> *"37% of the sixth formers we talked to said they didn't have the necessary essay writing skills."*
>
> (Lebus, S. (2011), 'Higher Education ensuring access through partnerships with schools', *Higher Education Futures Forum, London, 11 May 2011*.
>
> From the video of the conference at www.policyreview.tv/video/561/3621)

What?

The book gives you a sense of what to expect if you choose to go to Uni or college and gives pointers to things that you can do now that will:

- help you decide whether you want to continue your studies and, if so, to choose the right place for you;
- prepare you for the academic challenges of higher education;
- help you develop life skills that make it much more manageable and enjoyable if and when you go to Uni.

When?

Use at any time before you apply to, or start in, higher education. The book is designed for those currently studying for A levels or equivalent level 3 qualifications (e.g. International Baccalaureate, BTEC, etc.) or who are about to do so. The earlier you start, the more time you have to prepare for Uni at a reasonable pace.

How?

You don't need to read every page. Select sections that best match where you are in your current studies, your life skills and the stage you are at in the process of applying for higher education.

Terminology: Unis, HEIs, HE in FE

'Uni'

Uni is an abbreviation of the word 'university' but it is also used sometimes as a short-hand for higher education in general.

In this book, the term 'Uni' is used in that more generalised sense to mean higher education, whether at Uni or college. This is because most people have heard of university, but not everyone is familiar with the term 'higher education' or aware that you can study at that level in a range of institutions apart from universities.

At times in the book, you will see the terms 'HEI' or Uni/College used in full as reminders that this material is relevant to all higher education. At other times, Uni is used as a short-hand.

Higher Education Institutions (HEIs)

It used to be the case that you could only study for higher level qualifications such as degrees at a university. However, for many years, it has been possible to study for degrees and other higher level qualifications at a range of institutions, such as at university colleges, at colleges, and with private providers.

Many colleges and private providers that offer degrees do this in collaboration with one or more universities or university colleges. If you are thinking of applying to study at a college, find out which university or university college awards the qualification.

HEIs with similar names

Check the names of HEIs carefully as there are several universities or university colleges that share similar names. Typically, large cities tend to have several HEIs and these might sound very similar.

Liverpool
- The University of Liverpool
- Liverpool John Moores
- Liverpool Hope

Leeds
- The University of Leeds
- Leeds Metropolitan University
- Leeds Trinity University College
- Leeds City College (for HE in FE).

Higher education in further education (HE in FE)

Universities can also award degrees through local colleges. Some students prefer this as they are already familiar with their local college or it is convenient for where they live. Typically, the university is responsible for ensuring that the qualification is of the right standard.

In such cases, you would be a member of the university that awarded the qualification, but the teaching and support would be provided on the college site, generally by college staff. In some instances, your course might transfer to the university site after the first or second year. In either case, you would usually be able to use all the facilities of both the college and the university.

Overview of the book

Getting started

The 'Getting Started' chapter helps you to familiarise yourself with the book.

Choices and decisions

Your choice of subject, programme and Uni will have a big impact on your life – on the people you will meet, the money you will spend, the places where you will live, how you will spend your time, the view, the food, the nightlife, opportunities open to you and, in many cases, the kind of job you will get or career you will enter. Clearly, there are a great many different things to decide and these should not be rushed.

Managing the information

There is a great deal of information available to help you to make up your mind – so much that it may feel overwhelming at times. Chapter 4 provides you with guidance on how to manage the range of information available. A list of key sources of information about higher education is provided on pages 291–4.

Making your application

This chapter helps you to draw together your thinking. It takes you through key aspects of applying to Uni, including writing personal statements, so that you can present yourself to best effect.

Academic skills

If you are using the book over a year before going to Uni, then starting with the academic skills chapters gives you a long lead-in for developing gradually the skills and study habits needed in higher education. These are also likely to help your current study, even if you decide not to go on to university or college.

Life as a student

Students often find that the hardest part of being at Uni is managing the basics of day-to-day living that, previously, had been strongly supported or directed by parents, carers, teachers and others.

It may seem strange to have chapters about topics such as travel or cooking in a book about preparing for Uni. However, it is not unusual for students to arrive at Uni with no experience of travel outside of their immediate area and little idea how to cook, even with a cook book.

Whilst the university or college on your doorstep may be brilliant, it is better not to select it primarily on the grounds of inexperience in travel and other life skills. These skills can be fun to learn. Developing them now means that you have a wider range of Unis to choose from and that you can focus on having a good time once at Uni.

In-between sections

Between the main parts and at the end of the book there is further material to help you gain a feel for life in higher education. Have a go at the quiz: see how much you already know and whether you can tell the true from the false.

Activities, checklists and reflection

Activities

You will find many activities suggested throughout the book. The final page of each chapter draws together those referred to within that chapter or related to it. Be selective. It is unlikely that you would need to undertake every activity.

> ### Priorities
>
> At the end of each chapter, you are encouraged to pick a limited number of priorities as your starting points. Unless you are set tasks to do by your tutors, it is up to you which activities you follow up and in what order.

Checklists and self-evaluations

For those aspects of higher education that matter the most to you, you may find the relevant self-evaluation or checklist helps you to work through the issues and choices. Adapt these to suit you:
- Highlight the questions that matter to you.
- Cross out those that are not of interest.
- Use the spaces provided to add in questions or items relevant to you.

Reflection and questioning

At various stages throughout the book you are encouraged to pause and reflect. This gives you a chance to consider the implications of the information or the decisions that you might need to make, to jot down questions and to follow these up later. In some places, you can jot down your thoughts and questions straight away.

Other reflections would benefit from more detailed or ongoing thought. For these, it is a good idea to carry round a light notebook to capture your thoughts. Alternatively, you could set up a file on your computer to do this electronically.

Working alone or with others?

You can use this book on your own, but it is likely that you will get more out of the process if you work with others going through the same experience.

Your tutors may set certain activities as group exercises or discussions. If not, you may find it helpful to form your own group or ask a teacher to set one up at your school or college. In particular, you may find it useful to:
- hear different perspectives on the issues;
- share out information-gathering activities to save time;
- discuss your findings and thoughts;
- share information that you find out about particular universities, colleges, subjects, or financial support available.

1 Getting started

Why think about Uni now? | What is it really like? | **What are you supposed to do in lectures?** | What if I am not sure what I want? | **What are my priorities for preparing for Uni?** | How would I go about making friends? | **What is the big deal about essays?** | **There are so many courses to choose from – how do I decide?** | **What about clean clothes – how does all that laundry business work???** | **There's so much to decide, where do I begin?** | What can I do now so I am ready when I get there?

This chapter

This chapter provides a starting point for using the book and thinking about Uni. It:

→ raises some initial questions about what it is like to be a student in higher education;

→ encourages you to think forward about your own future life as a student at Uni;

→ provides an opportunity for you to consider your priorities for preparing for higher education.

1.1 What students wish they had known ...

Most students in their first year at Uni say that they wish they had known more about what to expect and had been better prepared before they arrived. Although Uni may seem a long way off, there are many things that you can do now to start to prepare.

Three years ago, Uni seemed a long way away to this intrepid four.

Now they are at Uni – and what a bad, sad set they are!

◁ **Jasmine** *Uni! That's years away! What's the point of thinking about that now?*

◁ **Jasmine** *I can manage but it would have been much easier if I had got to grips with everything before coming to Uni.*

◁ **Arun** *I can read. I can write. I can talk. I'm cool all round.*

◁ **Arun** *Read how much? Duh! Nobody can do that!*

◁ **Alisha** *I already get really good marks.*

◁ **Alisha** *I wish someone had told me how different it all was at Uni.*

◁ **Jack** *What's to know?*

◁ **Jack** *I want my mum!*

1.2   Is this book for me?

This book is for anyone who could achieve at Uni, whether or not they have made a definite decision to go. If the following questions are relevant to you, then the book is for you.

What if I already know I want to go to Uni?

If you do, then this book is likely to be for you. It can help you to:

- check that you are making the right decisions for the right reasons;
- clarify the difference between skills needed at school and at Uni;
- think and prepare ahead so that you are better able to hit the ground running when you get to Uni.

What if I don't know what I want yet?

The book can help you decide whether higher education is for you. By working through the activities, it is likely that you will:

- become excited at the prospect of going to Uni – and engaged in the preparation process;
- *or* – realise that the process is not interesting you and that higher education may not be right for you in the near future;
- *or* – work out what is putting you off higher education, and consider whether that is something that might change in the short or long term.

If you decide that higher education is for you, then at least you will have a head start in thinking through the issues and getting ready.

What if I don't want to go to Uni?

If you don't want to continue on to higher education, then it is important to honour your decision. Going to Uni is a big commitment, in terms not just of money but also of time and emotional energy. If you cannot make that commitment, then higher education is probably not right for you – at least not now.

However, this book may still be useful for you if:

- you haven't really given full consideration to higher education or if you ruled it out for the wrong reasons;
- you want to develop your academic skills to help your current studies;
- you want to develop skills that help you become more independent after school /college;
- you want to know what Uni is about – for your own general knowledge or in case you want to go there at some point in the future.

1.3   What is the purpose of this book?

Overnight, when you get to Uni, you are in charge of your study and everyday life in ways that you probably will not have experienced before.

This book helps you to plan towards higher education so that you:

- understand the nature of the choices that face you;
- make the right choices for you about going to Uni;
- know what to expect so that it doesn't come as too great a surprise when you get there;
- think in a constructive way about life at Uni, and the skills you will need to cope with both study and everyday life;
- start to plan your journey towards becoming a student in higher education;
- know where to look for information;
- consider the actions you can take now, well in advance of entering higher education, so that you are well-placed to look after yourself, manage your studies and have a good time as a student.

Think forward! Don't wait until the last minute to decide whether you want to go to Uni – or you may find it becomes more difficult to study what you want, when and where you want.

Be informed! Know what to expect – and use that information to make your decisions.

Prepare ahead! Think through what you will need to know and do when you arrive at Uni. Before you get there, start to develop the skills that will support your independence as well as your study.

Identifying what options are out there | Finding out what I need to know | **Hearing what current students wish they had known in advance** | Knowing what to expect | **Developing my academic skills** | **Making decisions for myself** | **Preparing for life away from home**

1.4 What will it be like?

What is it like in higher education?

Jot down a few thoughts here or in your blog about how your study and day-to-day life might be different at Uni/college than it is now.

Share your thoughts

Depending on where you are reading this, share the thoughts you jotted down, either with the rest of your group in class or online. Consider the following questions together.

1. How accurate are your views of Uni likely to be and why?
2. What kinds of things do you think you would like about Uni?
3. What are likely to be the early challenges for you at Uni?
4. What kinds of things could you work on now so that you start life at Uni as prepared as possible?

Set your priorities

Browse through the book quickly to gain a feel for the issues that you might want to start to address.

Use the next page to set your priorities for preparing for Uni.

1.5 My priorities for preparing for Uni

Use column (a) to identify all the areas that you need to consider. (✓ Tick those that apply)
Use column (b) to identify your top 5 priorities. Number these 1–5, 1 being the item most important to you, 2 for the next most important, etc. Start with these priorities.

Things to consider	(a) Need to consider	(b) My priority
1 Clarifying my own thinking about whether to go on to higher education.		
2 Finding out what information is available about higher education and how to work my way round this.		
3 Understanding more about the costs of being a student, the financial support available and how to apply for it.		
4 Choosing what subject and programme to study, at which Uni, to support my career plans.		
5 Drawing all the information together so as to make the right decisions about which Uni or college to go to.		
6 Finding out how to apply for a place in higher education.		
7 Starting to develop myself outside of my studies so that I have a better chance of gaining a place.		
8 Writing a strong personal statement so as to have a good chance of being considered by the HEIs that I like best.		
9 Developing the academic skills I will need as a student in higher education.		
10 Getting a better sense of what life is like as a student in higher education.		
11 Developing the kinds of skills that I will need in order to live independently when I get to Uni/college.		
12 Understanding how to manage my money when I am a student.		

1.6 Following up on my priorities

Start with the items that you identified as your priorities on page 11.

Things to consider	Where to look for more information
1 Clarifying my own thinking about whether to go on to higher education.	Chapters 2 and 3
2 Finding out what information is available about higher education and how to work my way round this.	Chapter 4 and Appendix 4
3 Understanding more about the costs of being a student, the financial support available and how to apply for it.	Chapter 9 and Appendix 3
4 Choosing what subject and programme to study, at which Uni, to support my career plans.	Chapters 5, 6, 7 and 8
5 Drawing all the information together so as to make the right decisions about which Uni or college to go to.	Chapter 10
6 Finding out how to apply for a place in higher education.	Chapter 11; Appendices 1 and 2
7 Starting to develop myself outside of my studies so that I have a better chance of gaining a place.	Chapters 11 and 25
8 Writing a strong personal statement so as to have a good chance of being considered by the HEIs that I like best.	Chapters 11 and 25
9 Developing the academic skills I will need as a student in higher education.	Chapters 12–19
10 Getting a better sense of what life is like as a student in higher education.	Chapter 20; 'What they wish they had known' page in each chapter
11 Developing the kinds of skills that I will need in order to live independently when I get to Uni/college.	Chapters 21–6
12 Understanding how to manage my money when I am a student.	Chapters 21 and 22

1.7 Make it happen

Follow up on your priorities

On page 12, you identified the aspects that you most want to consider. Work through these in your order of priority. Even if you are working through the chapters in a different order in class, that does not prevent you from following up your priorities either on your own or with friends and family.

Plan it!

Don't leave it as a good intention to follow up on your priorities. Start to develop the planning skills that you will need once you are a student in higher education by making more specific plans now.

Set yourself a time scale for investigating or addressing the priories that you identified.

- Write these into your diary or planner.
- If you do not use a diary or planner, then make this an additional priority.

Ask for different opinions

You are making big decisions which are exciting, but that can sometimes feel a bit overwhelming. It can really help to work through some of the issues both with:

- other people who are going through the same process *and*
- those who are more detached and objective.

Support your classmates

You and your friends may have very different opinions about the best thing to do after school or college. These decisions aren't always easy to make. Be prepared to help each other by being understanding and supportive of the decisions that others make.

Share information

You will find that there is a great deal of information available about higher education. You may find it easier if you share out tasks such as the following:

- making a list of the resources that are available to help you research different aspects of going to Uni – such as information about student finance, which universities are best for which subject or facilities, the qualifications you will need, and how to apply to Uni;
- deciding which resources are best for various purposes;
- finding out which universities are best for the kinds of programmes that interest people in the group.

Find out what interests people in your group

This will make it easier for you to spot information that might be relevant to someone else. This will help ensure that none of you miss out on information that would have helped you.

2   Is Uni for me?

What kind of people go to Uni? | Would I really like it? | **What about all the reading – how would I get through it?** | How will I cope without my family? | **Will the work be too hard?** | **Will there be anyone like me there?** | **Do people like me really get in?** | **What about my girlfriend – will I miss her too much?** | **I don't want to leave my boyfriend.** | **What do I need to know?** | Do I really want to go to Uni anyway? | What if I don't go to Uni now – will I miss my chance for ever? | Am I rushing into this? | **Would I regret it more if I didn't go to Uni – or if I did?** | My friends are all going but what is best for me?

This chapter

This chapter helps you to:

→ clarify where you are now in your thinking about going on to higher education after your current studies;

→ consider why you do, or don't, want to go on to higher education;

→ identify what, at present, is influencing your decision-making about whether to go to Uni or not.

2.1 What they wish they had known ...

Six years ago, this cool four were biting their nails in a not so cool fashion about what their futures would bring.

Six years on – little has changed. The future now looks a whole lot closer and some still have problems with their nails.

 ◁ **Erin** *I want to go to Uni to do drama but my dad says I should get a proper job.*

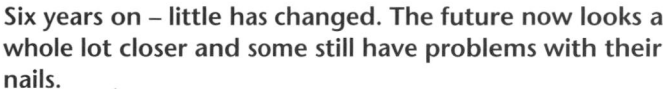 ◁ **Erin** *I qualified as an electrician and work in a TV studio. I am still thinking about going to Uni – maybe part-time. I get envious of the actors, though I am glad that I have a solid trade behind me.*

 ◁ **Amelia** *My teachers say I should go to Uni but I am fed up of studying.*

 ◁ **Amelia** *I ended up at Uni studying history and hated the first year. I took a year out and then really missed study, would you believe? I came back to train as a teacher.*

 ◁ **Kwame** *I think my parents had decided when I was in the womb that I would go to Uni. I don't want to disappoint them but am not sure what I want for me.*

 ◁ **Kwame** *I went to Uni and it was OK. In retrospect, it would have been better to take time out to decide what I really wanted.*

 ◁ **Jack** *To go or not to go? That is the question. I guess I'll do whatever my mates do.*

 ◁ **Jack** *I have a degree and still don't know what I want to do, but now I am expected to do something! Meanwhile, I'm living with mum. I thought she would be much happier to have me around than she appears to be ...*

2.2   What do I really want?

Not everyone is clear in their own mind about whether they really want to enter higher education or not. This book aims to help you to work through your inner thoughts, so that you make a decision that is right for you.

Higher Education isn't for everyone – even if they have good grades. Studying at that level at either university or college can be a fantastic experience. It can also open up opportunities that will benefit you throughout your life.

Many people rule themselves out of going to university for the wrong reasons. They may assume that they won't be accepted, won't be able to afford it, or won't succeed if they get there. They may just ignore the option because it isn't the route taken by anyone they know, or assume that there will be nobody there like them.

On the other hand, there are people who don't think through fully the many opportunities available outside of higher education. Some of the most successful individuals, from leading entrepreneurs to artists, performers and sports-people either didn't go to Uni, or did so later in life. It is worth pausing before jumping onto the band-wagon, and really weighing up your options.

To help clarify your own thinking, take a look at the table on page 17. Consider which of these statements apply to you. Then, select the one you decide best fits the current state of your thinking.

I really want to go to Uni. It will be exciting and help me get the jobs I want.

I want to study for a degree but I don't want to go away to study.

I would go if I thought there were other people like me there.

I would need to know more before I made up my mind whether to go to Uni or not.

Not for me! No, not ever! Well, maybe …

Everyone goes to Uni so I suppose I have to.

2.3   Do I want to go to Uni – where am I at?

- Which of the following statements best describes the current state of your thinking about Uni? Use column (a) to tick **all** that apply.
- Then use column (b) to decide which **one** statement fits you best at present.

Statement	(a) Applies to me to some extent	(b) The one that fits me best
1 I'm definitely going to study in higher education.		
2 I want to go on to higher education straight from school.		
3 I want to go to Uni – but I think I want to have a gap year first.		
4 I want to go to Uni one day but probably not for a few years.		
5 I want to go on to higher education but still have to decide what to study and which Uni to choose.		
6 I am interested but they probably wouldn't take me.		
7 I have to go – there's a lot of pressure to go on to higher education straight from school.		
8 Probably, but I need to know more before I can make up my mind.		
9 Possibly. I think I want to go to Uni but other things interest me too so I keep changing my mind.		
10 Don't know. I haven't a clue whether I want to go to Uni.		
11 Don't know – I might like it but it sounds like a lot of work and I don't know if I would cope.		
12 I do want to go but I probably won't try as I'd probably fail anyway.		
13 Uni? Don't know much about it. You don't think about things like that round here.		
14 No. I absolutely do not want to go to Uni.		

See page 291 for feedback on your responses. Give thought to whether you have rushed to any decisions before thinking through all of the implications and options.

2.4 Why I do – or don't – want to go to Uni

If you have decided that you do want to go on to higher education, be clear why you are doing this and for whom. It is such a big commitment that it pays to be sure about your motivations.

- Use column (a) to tick any reason that applies to you.
- Use column (b) to decide which fits you best.

Statement	(a) True of me	(b) The reason that fits me best
Because of other people		
1 Because other people say it is great.		
2 Because most of my friends are going.		
3 Because it is expected in my family.		
4 Because it is expected at my school.		
5 Because I don't want to disappoint my parent(s).		
6 Because I don't want to disappoint my teacher(s).		
7 Because I have to be a role model to my brother(s) and/or sister(s).		
8 Because everyone goes to Uni these days.		
For study reasons		
9 Because I enjoy studying.		
10 Because I love the subject(s) I want to take at Uni.		
11 Because I want to study a subject in depth.		
For career reasons		
12 Because it will help me get a good job.		
13 Because it will broaden my career options.		
14 Because I'll earn more money if I have a degree.		
15 Because I can't enter the profession I want without a degree.		
16 Because I want to go on to postgraduate study or a research career, and need a degree first.		

Statement	(a) True of me	(b) The reason that fits me best
For personal reasons		
17 I don't know what else to do after school.		
18 It's like a 'rite of passage' when you leave school.		
19 I am doing this for me – because I feel it is something that I will enjoy.		
20 I want to prove I can do it.		
21 I want the student lifestyle for a few years.		
22 There will be lots of opportunities to try new things.		
23 I'll get to meet interesting people.		
24 Other reasons:		

Reasons I don't want to go to Uni

Statement	(a) True of me	(b) The reason that fits me best
1 I don't want to leave my family/boyfriend/girlfriend.		
2 I don't want to spend all that money on a qualification.		
3 I want to get a job straight after school.		
4 I have had enough of studying.		
5 It doesn't interest me.		
6 I don't know anyone who has been to university.		
7 I don't think there will be anyone else like me there.		
8 I am scared I won't be clever enough.		
9 Other reasons:		

See page 293–6 for feedback on your responses to 2.4 and 2.5.

2.6   Deciding for yourself

Who is influencing your choice?

Other people's opinions and attitudes can sometimes influence you more than you think. This can be true whether they express these aloud or through hints, behaviour or body language. Give some thought to the ways that other people's attitudes could be influencing your own opinions about higher education and whether this is helpful. Decide whether you really agree with their views.

What do your teachers think?

Do you think that they feel you should, or shouldn't, go on to higher education? How is that affecting your thinking?

What does your family think?

Would they be disappointed if you did – or if you didn't – go on to higher education? How is that affecting your thinking?

What do your friends think?

What would they think of you if you did, or didn't, go to Uni? How is that affecting your thinking?

What about your boyfriend/girlfriend?

- Do you think they want you to go to Uni?
- What would happen if you did/didn't?
- How is that affecting your thinking?

What do you really think?

In your own opinion, do you think you would benefit from going to Uni?

© Stella Cottrell (2012) *You2Uni*, Palgrave Macmillan

2.7   Make it happen

Which strategies will I use?

Decide which of the strategies below could help you to clarify your thinking about whether higher education is for you. Tick all that apply.

1 ☐ Take a rain check from time to time to consider where I am in my own thinking about going to Uni. (2.3)

2 ☐ Work out my own reasons for why I do, or don't, want to continue on to higher education. (2.4 and 2.5)

3 ☐ Put time aside to talk to someone I trust about whether I should or shouldn't go to Uni.

4 ☐ Talk to my teacher(s) about what I would need to do if I wanted to go to Uni.

5 ☐ Talk to my family about what it would mean for them if I went to Uni.

6 ☐ Talk to my friends about what I really want to do next.

7 ☐ Talk this through with my boyfriend/ girlfriend.

8 ☐ Talk to a careers adviser about my options.

9 ☐ Talk to someone who is at Uni now in order to get a feel for what is involved.

10 ☐ Put time aside to think through carefully what I would do if I decided not to go to Uni.

11 ☐ Draw up a list of the pros and cons of going to Uni.

12 ☐ Keep a reflective diary to help me to see what is influencing changes in my thinking about going to Uni.

Prioritise

Choose between one and three of the strategies listed opposite to try out first. Enter the number given beside each strategy into the box below.

First 3 choices	
First choice	
Second choice	
Third choice	

Plan

Decide exactly when you will make use of each strategy. Set times that help you to build up a routine and that won't clash with other things you want to do.

- Jot down the times into your planner or diary – or your timetable for planning towards Uni.
- Jot down a date within the next month to check what is working.

Experiment

Once you have used your first set of strategies, have a go with a new set. See which ones are most helpful for you in practice.

Give and receive support

Share your ideas with others in your group. For example, if you and your friends have blogs or use social networking, post comments about your current thinking about the pros and cons of continuing on to higher education.

You2Uni Quiz

True or false?

For each of the statements below, circle the answer you think applies.

1 You can take other qualifications at Uni apart from a degree.

True / False

2 You can study for a higher qualification at a college as well as at a university.

True / False

3 Some students start studying for a degree at college and then complete it at a university.

True / False

4 British students can only study for a higher qualification in Britain.

True / False

5 You can study for a degree at almost any age, even if you are 80.

True / False

6 If you don't complete your degree, then you can't come back to finish it later.

True / False

7 People from state schools don't go to Uni.

True / False

8 There is no longer financial support available for students from low income families.

True / False

9 Universities make arrangements to support students with disabilities.

True / False

10 Most students rate their time at Unis in Britain as good or excellent.

True / False

11 A degree course always lasts for three years.

True / False

12 You don't have to pay for your study at Uni up front – you only pay later and if you personally earn over a certain income.

True / False

Multiple choice questions

13 According to the Sodexo University Lifestyle Survey (2008), which of the following is the top reason people give for going to university?

(a) To improve job opportunities
(b) To obtain an additional qualification
(c) To have a good social life
(d) To improve knowledge in an area of interest

14 What does UCAS stand for?

(a) Universities Collaborative Admissions Survey
(b) Universities and Colleges Advice and Support
(c) Universities and Colleges Admissions Service
(d) Universities and Colleges Admissions Support

15 Which subject received the most applicants to Uni through UCAS in 2011 (by February 2011)?

(a) Nursing
(b) Medicine
(c) Social work
(d) Fine Art

16 Which subject had the highest ratio of applications to acceptances in 2010?

(a) Social work
(b) Nursing
(c) Drama
(d) Dentistry

You2Uni Quiz

17 Which Uni had the highest ratio of applications to places in 2010?

(a) Brighton and Sussex Medical School
(b) Oxford
(c) Edinburgh
(d) Cambridge

18 Which Uni received the highest number of applications for degree programmes in 2010?

(a) Manchester   (c) Birmingham
(b) Leeds   (d) Edinburgh

19 The Russell Group Universities are all universities that:

(a) are located in the South-East of England
(b) were set up by Bertrand Russell
(c) are research-intensive universities
(d) specialise in maritime subjects

20 For the following four subjects, match the subject with the % that goes on to graduate jobs within 6 months of graduating (according to the HESA Survey for 2009/10)?

(a) Law   %
(b) Social work   %
(c) Italian   %
(d) Mathematics   %

21 What proportion of graduates are unemployed 6 months after graduating (according to the HESA Survey for 2009/10)?

(a) 2%   (c) 14%
(b) 9%   (d) 23%

22 What is the NSS?

(a) National Student Survey
(b) National Student Support
(c) National Students Society
(d) Naughty Students Society

You2Uni Quiz

23 What proportion of students live at home with parents or family (according to the HEFCE report *Living at Home* 2009)?

(a) 1%   (c) 26%
(b) 20%   (d) 37%

24 What is the most popular subject for international students?

(a) Art and Design   (d) Business and
(b) Medicine   Administrative
(c) Civil Engineering   Studies

Fact finding

25 What proportion of students in each of the following subjects is unemployed 6 months after graduating (according to the HESA Survey for 2009/10)?

(1) History
(2) Law
(3) Architecture
(4) Aeronautical and Manufacturing Engineering
(5) Celtic Studies
(6) Accounting and Finance

26 According to the current National Student Survey ratings, which universities got the highest overall satisfaction ratings of any university for each of the following subjects?

(1) Electronic and Electrical Engineering
(2) Art and Design
(3) Food Science
(4) Business Studies
(5) History
(6) Other Subjects Allied to Medicine
(7) Social Work
(8) Sports Science

See pages 296–8 for the answers.

You2Uni Quiz

Part A

Choices and decisions

© University of Birmingham 2012

Introduction to Choices and decisions

When you are deciding about what to do after school or college, you are faced with some big choices.

Which Uni would be best for me?

How independent do I want to be?

Will it be worth it?

Would I be happier at Uni or college?

Which part of the country do I want to be in?

Do I want to study part-time and work whilst I learn?

Should I take a break after school first?

What would I study?

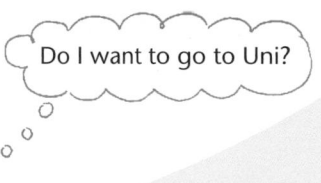

Do I want to go to Uni?

Here, you have the opportunity to think more deeply about the key decisions that you will need to make.

The earlier you start to think about these, the more time you have to:

1 find out the information you need to make good choices;
2 consider the potential consequences of decisions you could make;
3 decide wisely for yourself.

Each of the earlier chapters in Part A focuses on one set of decisions that you will need to make. Chapters 4, 10 and 11 help you to find the information you need and to draw together your thinking on a wide range of issues so that you can:

- choose the right Uni or college for you *and*
- express this well in your application; this will increase your chance of gaining a place at the institution you prefer.

3   When is the best time?

Straight away | Gap year | **Work first** | Preparation | **Wait** | **Go** | **Pros** | **Cons** | **Commitment** | **Finances** | Adventure | **Career** | Now | **Foundation level** | Later | **Relationships** | **Readiness** | **Travel** | **Job** | **Saving** | **Qualifications** | Separation | **Distractions** | Family | **Timing** | Maturity | **Money** | **Break Experience** | **Friendships** | **Direction** | **Clarity** | **Purpose** | Reasons | **Certainty**

This chapter

This chapter helps you to:

→ find out some of the reasons that people give for going to Uni straight from school – and also for waiting one or more years before doing so;

→ put some time aside to think about the pros and cons of progressing to Uni immediately from school or college – or of waiting to do so;

→ consider a range of factors that can help you to weigh up the advantages of either decision in your own case;

→ identify some questions that you need to reflect upon so that you do not rush the decision.

3.1 What students wish they had known ...

Five years ago, time seemed so pressurised for this busy four: the rest of their lives were knocking so loudly on the door.

 ◁ **Waheed** *I am going to Uni straight from school to do film. I don't want to wait – I'll already be 21 before I finish. If I took some years out as well, I would be, like, seriously ancient by the time I got my degree.*

 ◁ **Busola** *I am going to do a degree in creative technologies at the same Uni as my father. If I know what I want, why wait?*

 ◁ **Duncan** *This is a trick question, right? You have to go to Uni after school or you miss your chance.*

 ◁ **Amy** *My teacher says I could study for a degree but I am not sure. I feel too busy to think about all that now. I have a very busy life, you know! There is plenty of time to study later if I want.*

Five years later, they are all a little older and wiser. Hindsight is such a wonderful thing.

 ◁ **Waheed** *I didn't get into Uni, so I got a job for a while. Then I found what I really want to be is in logistics so I started a degree in that this year. It is perfect for who I am now.*

 ◁ **Busola** *I left that Uni after a few weeks. I wasn't really ready for being so far from home and my family. This year, I started back but to another Uni. I feel much better about Uni now. I love it.*

 ◁ **Duncan** *I found out you can study at any age – at 18, 28, even 88. Just as well my dad didn't know or he would probably have come with me and done a degree too! I will tell him now though!*

 ◁ **Amy** *I didn't go to Uni when I had the chance. Now, I am on a foundation course so I can do a degree at college next year. It would have been much easier for me, personally, if I had gone to Uni after school.*

What can you learn from them?

- Jot down a list of the things these students may wish they had considered before applying to Uni. What ideas does this give you about the choices available to you?

3.2 Should I go or should I stay?

When to go to Uni

It can sometimes feel as though there is a great deal of pressure to go to Uni straight from school. There are advantages to this but there are also advantages to taking a gap year or waiting a few years.

Straight from school

Some of the reasons people give for going straight to Uni are:

> I wanted to build on the skills and subject knowledge I had just been working on for A level.

> I think it is the best route to moving into a higher paid job as soon as possible.

> I need the qualification for the work I want to do.

> There will be lots of people of my age at Uni at that point, so it will be a great experience.

> I won't have other commitments to distract me from study and from having a good student life.

> I don't know what else to do.

Waiting one or more years

Some of the reasons people give for going to Uni after one or more years' break are:

> I took a gap year. I needed a break from study after school before going back to do more learning.

> When I was at school, I thought I wouldn't fit in at Uni. Now I am older, I feel freer to be my own person.

> It felt like decisions were being made for me. I wanted time to decide.

> I didn't go to Uni for nearly 15 years. It is great now because I have a clear idea about why I am doing this.

> I nearly went to Uni but then couldn't go. Now I am studying Architecture – the last subject I would have imagined. I am glad I waited until I knew what I wanted to do in life.

Also look at:
- Studying part-time (pages 51; 95–6)
- Taking a gap year (page 288)

3.3   Am I ready for Uni?

One key consideration is whether you think you will be ready for Uni when you leave school. Consider the following points to help formulate your thinking. Jot down any thoughts you have that would help your decision-making.

The right commitment?	Better qualifications?	Opportunities?
Do I have sufficient motivation and commitment to take on everything required to succeed at Uni – such as putting in that many years studying? Taking on the financial commitments?	Would I have better choices of Uni or programme if I strengthened my qualifications first, such as taking an additional subject to those I have started, or taking longer to get higher grades before applying?	Are there opportunities that I am keen to pursue at this point and that I want to focus on before going to Uni – such as in sports, the arts, work, travel, as a young parent?
Yes / No / Don't know?	Yes / No / Don't know?	Yes / No / Don't know?

Distractions?

Are there things going on in my life now or that are expected over the next few years that would distract me from getting the best from Uni if I went straight from school? These might be anything from managing an illness to moving to a different country.

Yes / No / Don't know?

Am I ready emotionally?

Do I feel that I will want to go away to study but won't yet be ready for living independently? Socialising? Peer pressures? Separating from family, boyfriend or girlfriend? Abrupt change?

Yes / No / Don't know?

Best time financially?

Would I be better to work first and save some money towards the costs of being a student? Or do I feel OK about the way that I will manage the costs of being a student?

Yes / No / Don't know?

Family commitments?

Are there people at home who are relying on me for care or support? Am I over-concerned about this? Who else could help? Are there ways of managing this whilst a student? Or should I wait?

Yes / No / Don't know?

Career/Professional focus?

Do I know what career I want? I will probably only get a student loan and student support once, so should I wait until I am clearer about a career route and the best degree for that?

Yes / No / Don't know?

Other benefits to me?

What would be the other benefits to me either of going straight to Uni or of doing something else first?

Yes / No / Don't know?

Jot down what you consider to be the potential pros and cons of going to Uni straight from school – or waiting a while.

When should I go to Uni?			
Straight from school		**Take a break of one or more years**	
Pros	**Cons**	**Pros**	**Cons**

Talk Discuss these with others in your group or with your family. Jot down any further thoughts in the appropriate columns above.

3.7 Make it happen

What will I do next?

It is a big decision to work out the best time for you to go to Uni. There are advantages and disadvantages both to rushing straight off to Uni and to waiting. Take time to consider the issue in a balanced way.

Decide which, if any, of the considerations listed below would be useful to pursue in more depth. Tick all that apply. Then identify your three priorities opposite.

1 ☐ Give more thought to going to Uni straight from school.

2 ☐ Give more thought to what I would do if I didn't, or couldn't, go straight to Uni.

3 ☐ Consider further my level of commitment for going to Uni from school.

4 ☐ Give more thought to doing something different before going on to Uni.

5 ☐ Find out about strengthening my qualifications before applying for Uni.

6 ☐ Consider more my emotional readiness for going to Uni straight from school.

7 ☐ Find out more about the best timing, financially, for me to go to Uni.

8 ☐ Consider whether family commitments would make it better for me to wait or to go to Uni.

9 ☐ Give more thought to how much I want to decide on a career before choosing my subject.

10 ☐ Think more about the pros and cons of when to go to Uni.

11 ☐ Find out more about gap years.

Prioritise

Choose between one and three of the strategies listed opposite to try out first. Enter the number given beside each strategy into the box below.

My first 3 priorities	
First choice	
Second choice	
Third choice	

Plan

Decide when you will give time and thought to your priorities.

- Jot those times into your planner or diary – or your timetable for planning towards Uni.
- In your planner, mark in a date within the next month to check that you are keeping to your plan.

> ### Give and take support
> Share findings with others in your group. Give serious thought to other people's emerging decisions, considering whether these might be helpful to you too.

4   Be fully informed

Summer schools | Open days | **UCAS website** | Unistats | **Prospectus** | **HEI websites** | **Brochures** | **Programme websites** | **Times Good University Guide** | **Guardian League Table** | HESA | **Videos** | Costs | **Government sites** | National Student Survey | **International** | **Teaching** | **Assessment** | **Student ratings** | **Case Studies** | **Key Information Sets** | Visit | Student Room | Discuss | **Investigate** | Share information | **Question** | **Differences** | **Share** | **Variety** | **Value for Money** | **Financial support packages** | Maps | **Comparison** | Rents | **Timetables** | Local jobs

This chapter

This chapter helps you to:

→ make your decisions on the basis of good information;

→ become aware of the *range* of information available to you, and also the *kind* of information included in some of the best sources;

→ make a preliminary investigation of the material available to you so that you can decide which you find the most interesting and useful for your purposes.

4.1 What students wish they had known …

Three years ago, this thoughtful four was amassing the information that would change their lives for ever …

◁ **Kyle** *I'm going to the same course as my teacher at school – he says he had a great time and the tutors were brilliant.*

◁ **Freya** *For me the most important thing is that the Uni has an all-weather sports pitch.*

◁ **Arabella** *I don't think I can afford to go to Uni for a few years.*

◁ **Kuljit** *I am not so bothered about the course – as long as the Uni is close enough for me to see every United home game.*

Three years later, here they are at Uni; they appear to be mulling thoughtfully over information about Uni that they had picked up at open days all those years ago …!

◁ **Kyle** *I wish I had read some of this a few years back, actually. I might then have taken into account that my teacher had been at his Uni in 1972. The programme was completely different then, and the tutors he had were long retired.*

◁ **Freya** *The sports pitch is great but maybe I put too much weight on the sports facilities. In retrospect, I should have looked more into what the course was like, especially as I found that the student ratings had been bad here for several years.*

◁ **Arabella** *I wish that someone had pointed me in the direction of all the part-time and vocational programmes I could have taken – and all the financial support available – I could have applied years ago.*

◁ **Kuljit** *I hardly ever have time to get to the game – and other things interest me now just as much. It might have been better to have chosen a Uni near a good cricket ground, come to think of it …*

What can you learn from them?
- Jot down a list of the things these students may wish they had known before going to Uni.
- What ideas does this give you about things you should find out?

4.2 Get fully informed

Making informed decisions

When making your decisions, you need to be sure you are doing so on the best information available. This is important for the following reasons.

- It is such a big decision, you want to make sure you get it right.
- Degree programmes last several years. Consider whether you are likely to enjoy your subject and the Uni's location for all that time.
- The programmes available for any subject can vary a great deal from one Uni to another – so you need to make sure that the programme is right as well as the subject.
- When you make your application, it will be apparent both through the kinds of choices you make, and what you say about yourself, whether you have made sensible decisions based on good use of the available information. This may influence the decision about whether you are offered a place or not.
- If you are offered an interview, you may be asked to account for your different decisions – you would want to come across as a serious candidate who makes decisions in a sensible and well-informed way.

Managing the range of information

You will find that there is a vast amount of information available. The following will help you to navigate the main sources.

Where to start?

When you are beginning your search for information about Uni, it can feel as though there are a 1001 places to start. There isn't one 'best place' for everyone to start looking – it really depends on what kind of background information you might have already and how far you have already started to make decisions about the kind of Uni you want.

No real ideas yet?

Begin with a broad overview to get a feel for the range of Unis, programmes and resources. (See 4.3.)

Know which Unis?

If you have a good idea already which Unis interest you, then you have a natural starting place. Look up those Unis first. Keep an open mind about whether they really are what you are looking for. Be prepared to consider others just in case they might be even better.

Know which subject?

Start by finding out:

- Which Unis offer the subject?
- Which are good for that subject?
- What courses are offered in that subject and sister subjects (see chapter 7)?
- What qualifications and grades are needed?

4.3   Gain an overview of the options

It makes sense to feel your way gradually into the range of materials available and to gain a sense of which you prefer for which purposes. The following order is recommended for working through the key resources.

1 www.UCAS.com

This is an essential, must-see site and an excellent place to start your search. See page 40 for more.

2 *The Times* Good University Guide

This is a comprehensive, easy-to-use resource that is updated annually. It provides a profile of each university with details of what it is like, where it is, the numbers of undergraduate, graduate, mature and international students, its costs, student accommodation and a range of other information. It also helps you to find out easily about:

- universities' league table rankings;
- the top universities by subject;
- the most popular subjects and where to study these.

3 www.Unistats.com

Unistats provides a quick, easy and free method of comparing different universities and colleges using official data. You can, for example, compare two or more HEIs for:

- student satisfaction in any given subject, or for aspects of their course, as given in the latest National Student Survey;
- the UCAS tariff required for different subjects at each HEI;
- the number of students in work 6 months after they finished their degree, and what kinds of jobs they were doing.

4 The Student Room

This website is set up and run by students, so it gives you a feeling for the kinds of issues of interest to them. It also has guides to choosing universities, colleges and subjects from the perspectives of current students.

5 Nat West Student Living Index

This provides information for 25 university locations. It is based on the average living costs (including accommodation) divided by students' average weekly income. This is very useful if you are planning to work whilst a student. If not, it is worth comparing student accommodation costs separately, especially for London.

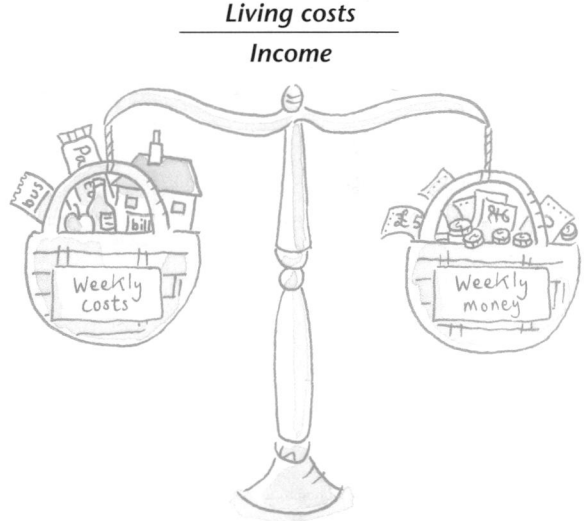

$$\frac{Living\ costs}{Income}$$

4.4   The UCAS website

The University and Colleges Application Service (UCAS) is one of the most important sources of information for applicants. Use this for:

- information about Unis;
- the UCAS Course Search;
- general information about applying to Uni;
- making your application to full-time programmes.

It pays to become familiar with this website as soon as you can. Use it to plan ahead for Uni. As a start:

- Browse the website to get a feel for what is available.
- Using the Course Search, type in a subject and see what kinds of programmes it brings up; be prepared for a lot of choice.
- Use the drop down menus for 'course type' and for 'region'.
- Jot down information you find helpful.

What kinds of information are available?	**Which is the most useful for you?**	**When do you think you will need to come back to this again?**
		Make a note of this in your planner or diary.

4.5   Check out your HEI favourites

Websites

Browse widely

At an early stage, just browse websites to gain a feel for at least 10–20 HEIs rather than closing your mind too early to the options.

Save favourites

Select as favourites the website addresses of HEIs that interest you, so that you can check details again easily.

Keep records

With so much information to cover, it is easy to forget the information you have gained about each HEI. Jot down notes about the features that interest you about each Uni or HEI – you can copy the checklist in 6b (page 63) to help do this.

Focus your search

As you become clearer about which Unis might be right for you, start to jot down a running list of questions to guide your more detailed searches. The detailed checklist provided at 4a can help you to identify questions that are important to you.

Prospectus and brochures

HEIs produce a prospectus each year. Although these are usually available online, applicants tend to like a paper copy. As these are quite weighty documents, it is best to send off for the prospectus only for those HEIs that interest you the most. These give you an impression of the Uni, although as they are marketing documents, they will, naturally, present the most positive perspective on the Uni.

An alternative prospectus?

Find out if there is an alternative prospectus written by students for the HEIs that interest you. These tend to be 'warts-and-all' accounts written by the students themselves.

Conventions

These free events bring together staff from many universities and colleges for you to meet in one place. You can book a place via the UCAS website or just turn up. To attend exhibitions at these conventions, you need to book in advance.

Things to look for

Subject: Does the HEI teach the subject you want to study?

Programme: When you read about the programmes it offers in that subject, do they sound right for you?

Entry requirements: What are these? Are there any alternative arrangements that might benefit you?

Costs: What is the fee? What costs would you have as a student?

Financial support: How much financial support is available and to whom?

The student union: Does the student life sound as if it would suit you?

Facilities: What is available on site?

Use 4a to help you identify other things you might want to check. Use 4b to jot down a list of things you want to find out at the open day.

© Stella Cottrell (2012) *You2Uni*, Palgrave Macmillan

4.6   Open days

Open days

There is no substitute for visiting the Uni. Each HEI is likely to offer several open days. Aim to attend these as early as possible, so that if you do not like the HEI once on site, you have plenty of time to visit others.

Prepare well for each visit. Avoid going to too many days as it will be harder to undertake the preparation you need for each and to remember one place from another. Your school may also limit the number of days you can be away for such visits.

Don't make up your mind about which HEI to choose without visiting it first.

What happens at open days?

The open day visit gives you a general feel of the Uni or college, its location, the local area and the amenities. The event varies from one HEI to another, but you can expect to see some or all of the following:

- the campus, through a tour;
- the student union – the union may put on information events for the open day;
- sports facilities, shops, libraries, etc.;
- student accommodation and refectory;
- the department where you would study;
- some teaching or administrative staff;
- students there to answer questions.

Find out the dates of open days

Go to www.opendays.com for the dates of open days at HEIs that interest you most. Make a note of these.

Plan out which open day you will attend at each Uni that interests you. Write these into your diary or planner.

It is a good idea to go with friends or family members as they can offer helpful insights about whether the Uni seems right for you.

Before each open day

- Find out all you can about the HEIs. Use resource 4a to look up things important to you.
- Check their websites to find out about the students' union at each.
- Use resource 4b to jot down a list of things you want to find out at the open day.

4.7　Make it happen

Which strategies will I use?

Decide which of the considerations listed below would be useful to pursue in more detail. Tick all that apply. Then identify your three priorities opposite.

1　☐ Become familiar with the UCAS website.

2　☐ Become familiar with Unistats.

3　☐ Browse information on a range of HEIs using resources listed on p 4.3.

4　☐ Jot down a list of initial things I want to find out about each Uni/college (Resource 4a).

5　☐ Check the websites of Unis and colleges that interest me.

6　☐ Send for the prospectus of Unis and colleges that I like the sound of.

7　☐ Check if there is an alternative prospectus or student views available, such as through the Student Room.

8　☐ Find out the timing of open days of Unis and colleges that interest me.

9　☐ Make plans to attend relevant open days.

10　☐ Prepare a list of things to find out at the open day (Resource 4b).

11　☐ Find out about the range of information available. See Appendix 4.

Prioritise

Choose between one and three of the strategies listed opposite to try out first. Enter the number given beside each strategy into the box below.

My first 3 priorities	
First choice	
Second choice	
Third choice	

Plan

Decide when you will give time and thought to your priorities.

- Jot those times into your planner or diary – or your timetable for planning towards Uni.
- In your planner, mark in a date within the next month to check that you are keeping to your plan.

> **Give and take support**
>
> Share findings with others in your group about sources of information that you find useful.
>
> Let them know what kinds of information you need, so that they can pass on relevant facts to you too.

Resource 4a:
List of things I want to know

If it helps, make a copy of this sheet for each Uni or college that you are going to look up. Go to their website or prospectus, and record your finding for each HEI separately.

University/HEI name:	
Things I want to know	**What I found out**
1	
2	
3	
4	
5	
6	
7	
8	
9	
10	

Resource 4b:
Things to ask at the open day

University/HEI name:	
Things to ask staff	**Things to ask students**
1	
2	
3	
4	
5	
6	
7	
8	
9	
10	

5 Employability and life chances

Careers | Health | **Professional** | Sandwich programmes | **Lifestyle** | **Values** | **Well-being** | **Employers** | **Placements** | **Skills** | Enterprise | Work experience | Co-curricular | **Employability** | Self-employment | **Unistats** | **Attributes** | **Evidence** | **Variety** | **Timetabling** | **Work culture** | Business acumen | **Entrepreneurship** | Specialism | **Work-based** | Foundation Degrees | **Time scales** | **Postgraduate** | **Spin-offs** | **Breadth** | **Vocational** | **Employer endorsements** | Internships | Sponsorships | Interest | **Research** | Masters | **PhD**

This chapter

This chapter helps you to:

→ gain a sense of what a degree is worth in terms of employment and life chances;

→ consider the potential impact of your choices now and the jobs and careers you will have later;

→ decide whether you want to take a vocational or professional degree or choose from the full range of degrees on offer;

→ investigate which Unis and programmes are more likely to support your life ambitions;

→ understand how universities and colleges contribute to developing your skills for employment.

5.1 What students wish they had known ...

Six years ago, these industrious students were making their UCAS choices with their futures firmly in mind ...

◁ **Aled** *I love art and music but my brother says I should study for a professional qualification as that is more likely to get me a job later.*

◁ **Abika** *I will do anything as long as I never have to do physics again.*

◁ **Sana** *I want to work with children but my parents want me to be a doctor. I can see that that would set me up for life – maybe I could be a paediatrician. I am so worried about making the wrong choice.*

◁ **John** *I want to be an engineer in the motor or air industry. I love engines but don't fancy spending four years in a library.*

Six years later and they are facing the reality of the choices they made ...

◁ **Aled** *I really wanted to study art history but chose law as I thought it would lead to a job. My current employer tells me she would have accepted any good degree.*

◁ **Abika** *I wish I had been in less of a rush to get to Uni and had taken a year to really get to grips with physics. I could have become an ophthalmic optician. I enjoyed my degree but it isn't what I need now.*

◁ **Sana** *I wasn't cut out to be a medic. In the first year, I switched to health technologies. I am on placement with a fantastic company. It researches solutions for injured children and I have been offered a job there after Uni.*

◁ **John** *A local employer let me do a foundation degree on day release. There was a lot of reading but at least I was at work most of the week. I am now taking a 'top-up' to get an honours degree and then I want to study for a Masters degree.*

What can you learn from them?

- Jot down a list of the things these students might wish they had known or done before finalising their choice of subject at Uni.
- What ideas does this give you about things to do before making your choice?

5.2   A degree? What is it worth?

Impact on salary

The Office of National Statistics (2011) reports that, over the course of the last decade, those with a degree earned an average of £12,000 per year more than those without a degree. For graduates, earnings increased faster than those for non-graduates for each year of age. They also continued to increase for longer.

This indicates that, if you use the opportunity well, you are more likely to be better off financially over the longer term if you have a degree. However, there are no guarantees and this doesn't mean that every graduate automatically gets a better salary once they graduate.

Even with a degree, you would still need to look for, and plan towards, good career opportunities over many years. Usually, to get a good job, you need to commit to personal development and training before, during and after Uni.

It is also important to remember that many graduates choose to study for higher degrees, travel, be artists, raise families and take other paths that are not associated with high incomes. These would lower the average income expected by graduates.

Impact on other life chances

Having a degree tends to have an impact on many other aspects of life. For example, graduates are:

- more likely to be in excellent health;
- less likely to suffer from depression;
- more likely to engage actively in their communities;
- more likely to lead a healthy lifestyle;
- more likely to be involved in their children's education – and their children do better at school;
- more likely to show positive attitudes towards diversity and equality.

(www.prospects.ac.uk; downloaded 11/12/2011)

What employers say

Employers see graduates as adding substantial value to their organisations. They are seen as bringing a mixture of subject-specific knowledge, as well as higher level generic skills such as critical thinking, planning and communication.

(Connor and Brown, 2009)

Reflection	What do you value?

Of the aspects mentioned above, what matters to you most about going to university or college?

What other routes could you take that might also give you what you wanted out of life?

5.3 Professional and vocational degrees

Have a career in mind?

Realistic understanding of the career?

Find out what the profession or job really involves. Don't be swayed by the glamour, reputation or potential income without weighing up what the day-to-day work would be like and the length and costs of the training.

Right qualifications and experience?

If your mind is made up on a particular career route, make sure you know exactly which qualifications and grades you need at each level, from GCSE through to postgraduate. What kinds of grades are expected for which subjects?

Courses in professional areas such as medicine, law and social work generally prefer you to have had paid or voluntary experience, such as through work undertaken in your vacations or a gap year in work relevant to the field.

Time scales?

- Would you be able to achieve the career you want through taking a shorter, one- or two-year, qualification such as an HNC, HND, BTEC or Foundation Degree?
- Do you need an honours degree to progress in the kinds of career that interest you?
- Would you need a Masters degree to progress in that career?
- Is there a certain number of years you would have to be employed in order to be accepted for higher professional qualifications?
- How many years in total would it take you to become fully qualified for the career you want?

Professional and vocational programmes

These are designed to lead to specific jobs and careers. Once you have your degree, you could still opt to use it to enter the wide range of jobs that are open to graduates, irrespective of the subject studied.

If you are certain that you want a particular career, then you need to take the qualifications that lead to it. However, you may not have to specialise in this way until you have a degree and are deciding on your postgraduate route. This is worth finding out if you would prefer to take your degree in a subject that you have an interest in but which is not linked directly to that career route. You may be able to choose a subject you love and still enter the career you want.

Not sure the obvious options are for you?

Many students are encouraged down medical, legal, accountancy and teaching routes as these are the ones that are better known. The range of job opportunities is much wider than this. If you want to take a professional/ vocational course because this makes you feel more secure about job prospects, this really means putting time in now to find out about your options. If you don't get your first choice of degree, you are then more likely to have a back-up career in mind.

5.4 Non-vocational courses

These still lead to graduate jobs

The overwhelming majority of graduates enter jobs considered to be 'graduate level'. Around two-thirds enter such jobs within 6 months of graduating (Prospects, 2011b, *What do graduates do?*). Nonetheless, most do not go into jobs related to their degrees.

In 2010, research by the Chartered Institute of Personnel Development (CIPD) found that as many as 59% of graduates were not currently working in a field or profession related to their degree.

Don't have a career in mind?

The two key routes open to you are these.

(1) Love the subject?
- Choose the subject that fires your imagination.
- Enter one of a wide range of graduate jobs when you graduate.

(2) Wait until you know what you want
Take a break of one or more years and try out a few jobs. Work out which career you want and the degrees that will take you there. Then apply to Uni, so that you use your loans and grants wisely.

Personal planning

If you take a non-vocational course, it really helps your chances of gaining a good job if you spend your time as a student in other activities alongside your course. This could be work experience; having a job; running a student society; student politics; starting your own business; arts, dance, drama, music; community volunteering; learning a new language or anything which makes you stand out from other job applicants.

Reflection	Personal planning

Although this may sound a long way off, it is worth planning, even before you go to Uni, how you will use your time there.
- What kinds of activities would you want to spend time in? How would you gain responsibilities and skills through these?
- What can you do now to develop a foundation in those areas?

Work placements

These are especially helpful if you study a non-vocational subject. They give you an advantage in gaining real work experience, especially if there is a substantial placement of 6–12 months. Students are often offered jobs by the companies where they undertake their placement. Check whether placements would fit with your course.

Overseas work placements

Overseas placements can look even better on your CV when you apply for work; these suggest you are more capable of taking on a challenge and working independently. Some employers will value your experience of other cultures or an additional language. Check whether your preferred university offers or supports such placements.

5.5 Will it help me find a job?

You will find that most HEIs state that they take graduate employment seriously. Examine claims about employability carefully. Check the statistics available. Look out for the following.

Personal planning within the curriculum

Is time planned into your course each year for such things as careers education, personal planning, guidance, guest speakers, visits to industry, and work-related projects? Or are you expected to undertake all or most of this yourself outside of the taught curriculum, such as through student volunteering activities?

Work

Being in work develops attributes that are hard to acquire in the classroom. Employers value graduates who have worked in jobs, paid or voluntary, where they learned to:

- develop business acumen;
- cope with day-to-day work culture;
- get on with colleagues over a longer term;
- contribute to workplace targets;
- comply with work regulations;
- deal with the public;
- multi-task in order to get the job done;
- take on responsible roles.

Short-term jobs don't generally offer such opportunities. Check:

- How feasible will it be for you to combine work and study?
- How does the HEI make this possible?

Timetabling that supports work

Consider whether the timetabling for your programme would enable you to:

- study part-time if you preferred;
- study full-time but attend on campus for only certain days or evenings in the week;
- undertake 'sandwich' provision (a year in work organised as part of the course);
- take a year out for an industrial placement, year abroad, or equivalent.

Enterprise and entrepreneurship

Check how well the HEI supports students in developing enterprise and entrepreneurship skills. In practice, how many students can be involved in this? Would it fit within the requirements of your course? Does the Uni offer any financial support for enterprise? Skills workshops? Specialised modules or units of study? Accommodation for student spin-off companies?

Sponsored places

Does the course have any placements sponsored by industry for which you could apply?

Internships

How many internships does the university organise for its graduates?

Employer endorsements

Look to see if the course has employer endorsements. If not, this doesn't tell you much, but if it does, that is a positive indicator of its value.

5.6   What I can do now

Unistats

Check how good Unis and colleges are at getting graduates into graduate level jobs.

You can find out the proportion of graduates in work after 6 months. Many graduates progress to a graduate job later on, so this is only a broad indicator of whether you would get a job, or a graduate level job. However, it is a useful way of seeing how well one Uni or programme compares with another at that point.

Understanding the jobs market

Many students have a limited sense of the jobs open to them. Browse graduate job websites to gain a feel for the range of jobs that may be open to you in a few years' time. Look for the more unusual options. See: www.prospects.ac.uk

Consider your preferences

If you don't have a clear career route mapped out, that is not unusual and isn't something to worry about. However, it pays to consider, even in very broad terms:

- the kind of work that would suit you;
- the qualifications that lead to good jobs in such areas.

For example, can you see yourself in any of the following roles?

- **Care:** Looking after children? The elderly? People with disabilities? Others' health, mental health, medical or social needs?
- **Creativity:** the arts, designing, performing?
- **Researching and experimenting** with chemicals, machinery, animals, plants?
- **Technologies:** computing, games, engineering, design, disabilities, communications?
- **Working with people:** teaching, advising, management, leadership, HR and personnel, sales?
- **Governance:** local and central government, civil service?
- **Finance:** banking, insurance, stock market, accountancies, actuarial?
- **Preserving and sustaining:** the environment, buildings, documents, arts, nature, heritage, coast lines?
- **Business:** development, sales, logistics, marketing, exports, enterprise, business aspects of an arts subject? Tourism?
- **Outdoors and active:** sports, agriculture, archaeology, geology, petrology, etc.?
- Other things?

Imagine yourself as the employer

The labour market is changing, with fewer graduate jobs provided by the really big employers. Many people are setting up their own businesses, especially in areas such as Creative and Digital enterprises. If you were to set up your own business, in what area would you choose to work?

5.7   Make it happen

Which strategies will I use?

Decide which of the strategies and activities outlined below will be useful to you in making your choice of course and Uni. Tick all that apply. Then identify three priorities.

1 ☐ Weigh up the pros and cons of taking a vocational programme.

2 ☐ Find out what kinds of graduate jobs I could get if I took a non-vocational degree.

3 ☐ Make a list of the kinds of work that might interest me. Which qualifications, if any, would these require?

4 ☐ Use Unistats to compare Unis and programmes for graduate employment.

5 ☐ Look at graduate job websites to see what kinds of jobs are available and for what rates of pay.

6 ☐ Compare university and college websites for the methods used to support employment.

7 ☐ Consider whether it would suit me to be my own employer?

8 ☐ Compare universities and colleges for their provision for enterprise and entrepreneurship.

9 ☐ Check whether I would be able to combine study with opportunities for employment and/or placements.

10 ☐ Start to think now about how I will use my time as a student, from the time I arrive there, so that I build a strong CV.

Prioritise

Choose between one and three of the strategies listed opposite to try out first. Enter the number given beside each strategy into the box below.

My first 3 priorities	
First choice	
Second choice	
Third choice	

Plan

Decide when you will give time and thought to your priorities.

- Jot those times into your planner or diary – or your timetable for planning towards Uni.
- In your planner, mark in a date within the next month to check that you are keeping to your plan.

Give and take support

Share findings with others in your group.

Look out for information that you know would be of use to others who have expressed an interest in a given profession or career – or for those who want to keep an open mind for now.

---

6   Choosing your Uni

Subject | Course | **Reputation** |
Scholarships | **Bursaries** | **Teaching**
| **Library** | **Academic Support**
| **Distance** | **Family** | City |
Campus | Employment | **Careers** |
Accommodation | **Resources** | **Friends**
| **Teachers** | **Information** | **Guides**
| **Guidance** | Visits | **Open days** |
Students | **Tutors** | Facilities | **Food**
| **Personal development** | **League**
Tables | **Ambience** | **Student**
Satisfaction | **Entertainment** |
Lifestyle | **Costs** | Assessment |
Curriculum | Entry Requirements
| **Jobs** | **Friendliness** | **Facilities** |
Timetabling | **Part-time** | **Location**
| Size | **Childcare** | Disability
arrangements | **Parking** | Transport
| **NIGHTLIFE** | **Fees** | **Architecture**

This chapter

This chapter helps you to:

→ identify the range of factors to take into consideration when choosing a Uni;

→ start to focus on what matters to you most about a Uni, so that you can make your search more manageable;

→ begin to identify Unis that best suit your preferences;

→ select things you can do now to make sure you are well informed when you make your ultimate choice of Uni.

6.1 What students wish they had known ...

Three years ago, this gifted four were designing their strategies for choosing their Uni ...

◁ **Caitlin** *When I'm a student, I am going to get a job to help keep a handle on student debt.*

◁ **Ilhom** *I am going to study at the Uni up the road. It's near home so that will be handy. I want to be near my family.*

◁ **Julie** *I want to have a ball as a student – for me it's all about the lifestyle.*

◁ **Gabriel** *One HEI will be pretty much like another. I am going to put all their names in a hat, pull one out, and go there. It will save me time in the end.*

Three years later and it appears our heroes have mixed feelings about their rather rushed choices.

◁ **Caitlin** *My student timetable made my job options quite limited. I never gave a thought to studying part-time, or what timetable I would need, or Unis in areas where I could easily find work.*

◁ **Ilhom** *I did get into the Uni but now I wish I was a bit less near to home. I can feel very divided between doing what my family want and living student life to the full.*

◁ **Julie** *I have had such a brilliant time. The only thing is, I could probably have had just as good a time at a Uni that better prepared me for a job.*

◁ **Gabriel** *I find this town really gloomy, I hate it. And the drains smell. How did I ever end up here?*

What can you learn from them?

- Jot down a list of the things these students may wish they had considered before finalising their choice of Uni.
- What ideas does this give you about things to do before making your own choices?

6.2   Finding the right Uni for you

It can feel a little overwhelming when you start to look at all the different universities offering degree programmes that could be open to you. It isn't likely that you will be able to cover all of the information available on every Uni. You will probably find it helpful to start narrowing your list from relatively early on in order to make the search manageable.

Are all Unis the same?

Every Uni has its own character and specialisms, areas where they excel and areas where they shine less well than others. They vary in size, location, facilities, the programmes they offer, the way they teach, the kinds of students they recruit, their missions and values, and the kind of student life you would experience. This means it is worth finding out about them and considering which would best help you achieve what you want.

Is there a Uni/HEI for me?

The variety of HEIs in the UK means that it is probable that there will be a Uni that will feel right for you. There is a lot of competition for Uni places and many people apply more than once before gaining a place. This should not put you off. If you don't find the right Uni first time around, there are other chances, either after school or in a few years' time.

However, as there is such a lot of competition, it is all the more important that when you come to complete your personal statement or attend an interview as part of your application, you sound well informed about the Unis you choose, and convincing about why you want to go to these.

How do I choose between them?

Ultimately, everybody chooses a Uni on the basis of a combination of factors that are very personal to them. Some select a Uni solely on the basis of its reputation, especially if the Uni is well known globally. For others, the most important factors might be such things as the reputation of the Uni for a particular subject, the distance from home, the financial support it offers, whether sandwich years or work placements are part of the course, or the availability of part-time work locally. For many, the determining factors are the look and the feel of the Uni when they visit.

How important will my grades be?

Students with the highest grades are generally able to choose from any Unis. However, there are Unis and programmes that accept students with lower grades. Unis take into account which programme you want to study and your personal statement. In order to be as fair as possible, they may take into consideration such factors as disability, where you live and family circumstances, the type of school you attend and its record for GCSE grades and for getting students into Uni, and whether you or a sibling are the first of your family to go from school straight to Uni. Even if you think you will not achieve very high grades, you may still be considered by even the most selective Unis if they decide that there are good reasons why your grades may not show your full potential.

6.3   What do I want from a Uni?

To help narrow your focus a little, have a go at completing the following table. If you rate an item highly with a 4 or 5, then look at that aspect in more detail early on.

Deciders	Does it matter to me ... a lot .... a little?						What next? See
1 The overall reputation of the Uni or HEI	5	4	3	2	1	0	Page 58
2 The reputation of the Uni for a particular subject	5	4	3	2	1	0	Pages 58
3 A programme that really interests me	5	4	3	2	1	0	Chapter 7
4 Student satisfaction rates	5	4	3	2	1	0	Page 58 and chapter 4
5 The financial support on offer	5	4	3	2	1	0	Chapter 9
6 Academic and pastoral support	5	4	3	2	1	0	Page 59
7 Its record on graduate employment	5	4	3	2	1	0	Chapter 5
8 Arrangements for career and personal development	5	4	3	2	1	0	Chapter 5 and page 59
9 The range and quality of facilities	5	4	3	2	1	0	Page 59
10 Particular facilities that matter to me	5	4	3	2	1	0	Page 59
11 Geographical location	5	4	3	2	1	0	Page 60; chapters 8 and 24
12 Whether it is, or isn't, campus-based	5	4	3	2	1	0	Chapters 6 and 24
13 Student living accommodation	5	4	3	2	1	0	Pages 60, 66, 105–6
14 The kind of student lifestyle likely at that Uni or location	5	4	3	2	1	0	Page 60 and chapter 9
15 The quality of teaching and the kinds of teaching and assessment methods used	5	4	3	2	1	0	Chapter 8
16 Option to study part-time or full-time, depending on preference	5	4	3	2	1	0	Chapter 5; pages 85, 95–6

Many students choose a Uni for its reputation – this might be for:

- its overall reputation and prestige;
- its reputation for a subject;
- its student satisfaction ratings;
- its record on graduate employment.

1 Its overall reputation and prestige

Some Unis are more prestigious than others, especially globally renowned universities such as Oxford and Cambridge in the UK, and Harvard, Yale and MIT in the USA. There are league tables that rate and rank Unis nationally and internationally (see Appendix 4). The prestige of world famous universities is built largely on their age and their research record, as well as factors such as the impact of their relative wealth and size, and the achievements of their most successful graduates.

In Britain, the leading research-intensive Unis with medical schools are known as 'Russell Group' Unis. There is usually more competition for places at these, so they can select the students they feel will do best. Generally, they require higher grades or UCAS tariffs, but they also look more broadly at students' potential.

2 Its reputation for a subject

There are some Unis that have a particularly strong reputation for certain subjects. For example, Imperial College London for sciences, Loughborough for sports sciences and Middlesex for work-based learning. Those Unis usually have a strong field of applicants in those subjects. *The Times* Good University Guide provides details of which Unis are most popular for which subjects.

3 Its student satisfaction ratings

There is excellent data easily available on student satisfaction at English universities. These data are collected annually from final year students via the National Student Survey (NSS) and can be seen on the websites of UCAS, the Unis themselves, Unistats and elsewhere.

You can use Unistats to look up student satisfaction for specific subjects and compare these from one Uni to another. You can also compare their teaching and assessment, support, personal development, facilities and programme organisation.

4 Its record on graduate employment

There are league tables on student employment. These should be used with some caution as they record those in employment 6 months or 18 months after graduation. Many students prefer to travel or take a year or two after graduation to do other things before searching for a graduate job in earnest. This is especially true for students in more creative subjects. From 2012, Unis in England will be required to provide details of student employability as part of their Key Information Sets (KIS). See also chapter 5.

Reflection	Reputation
Consider how important to you are the reputation and prestige of the Uni you attend.	

Consider which of the following factors are important to your choice of Uni. Tick all that apply, in order to focus your thinking on what matters most. Highlight any that are essential.

Financial considerations

- [ ] Its overall fees and financial support package
- [ ] The bursaries and scholarships for which I am likely to be eligible
- [ ] Financial guidance available
- [ ] Whether its timetabling of classes will make it easier for me to do part-time work
- [ ] Support and encouragement for finding part-time work whilst a student

Academic and pastoral support

- [ ] Having a named personal tutor or equivalent throughout my time at Uni
- [ ] The amount of contact time with teaching staff
- [ ] The teaching and assessment methods used
- [ ] Its support for developing academic skills
- [ ] The emphasis given by the HEI to developing students academically

- [ ] NSS scores for academic support
- [ ] The range of student services
- [ ] The location of student services
- [ ] Arrangements for religious practice

Careers and personal development

- [ ] The prestige of the Uni – as employers would recognise its reputation
- [ ] Its programmes being designed to support career development and employment
- [ ] Availability of sandwich years
- [ ] Practical support for work placements
- [ ] Emphasis on entrepreneurship and enterprise
- [ ] Its schemes for developing employability
- [ ] Its NSS scores for personal development
- [ ] Its ratings for graduate employment
- [ ] Its online resources for, and information about, employability

Facilities

- [ ] The overall quality of its resources, ambience and

maintenance
- [ ] The quality of the library
- [ ] The quality of sports facilities
- [ ] On-campus facilities such as refectory, shops, cash points, services
- [ ] Parking arrangements
- [ ] Arrangements for cyclists
- [ ] Transport arrangements such as a Uni bus
- [ ] Particular facilities essential for me (e.g., swimming pool, disability-related features, childcare)

Other

- [ ] Its research record
- [ ] Its league table rankings
- [ ] How 'Green' it is (that is, sustainability)

Reflection	Support and facilities
Draw together your thoughts on the relative importance of the support and facilities to your choice of Uni. Complete table 6a on page 62 to help you bring together your decisions about what you want from a Uni.	

6.6   Student lifestyle

The best student lifestyle for you is ultimately one of personal taste. Consider which of the following factors are important to your choice of Uni. Tick those that apply. Highlight any that are essential.

- [ ] city [ ] town [ ] country [ ] location
  - [ ] Good nightlife
  - [ ] Good clubs
  - [ ] Arts, theatres, cinemas
  - [ ] Range or quality of restaurants
  - [ ] Good shopping
  - [ ] Good music scene
  - [ ] Public transport

- [ ] **Campus-based Uni**
  - [ ] Attractive campus
  - [ ] Size of campus
  - [ ] Range of facilities on one site
  - [ ] Importance of living on-site
  - [ ] Location of the campus in relation to travel and amenities

- [ ] **Off-campus living**
  - [ ] Living at home
  - [ ] Living in private rental with other students
  - [ ] Living with a local family
  - [ ] Distance between campus and accommodation

- [ ] **Living accommodation**
  - [ ] The overall quality of the student accommodation provided
  - [ ] Having a choice in which facilities I use – and pay for
  - [ ] The option of sharing a room
  - [ ] Not having to share a room

- [ ] Having the choice of an en-suite
- [ ] Being able to live on campus in Year 1
- [ ] To live on campus any year I want
- [ ] To live off campus any years I want

- [ ] **Student-led activity and facilities**
  - [ ] The quality of the student union
  - [ ] The range of student-led activities and clubs
  - [ ] Students active in areas that interest me
  - [ ] Other students like me (e.g., background, parents, entrepreneurial, etc.)

- [ ] **Other**
  - [ ] Uni – or other kind of HEI
  - [ ] Size of Uni or HEI
  - [ ] International student body
  - [ ] Travel abroad as part of programme

Other factors that matter to me:

Reflection	Student lifestyle

Draw together your thoughts on the relative importance of the student lifestyle to your choice of Uni.

Complete table 6a on page 62 to help you bring together your decisions about what you want from a Uni.

6.7　Make it happen

Which strategies will I use?

Decide which of the considerations listed below would be useful to pursue in more detail. Tick all that apply. Then identify your three priorities opposite.

1　☐ Use the 'Finding out more about Unis' pages below to see where I can get the info I need.

2　☐ Consider what it means to go to a prestigious Uni. What would I need to do?

3　☐ Investigate the reputations of different Unis for particular subjects. See chapters 4 and 7.

4　☐ List Unis in the geographical range that suits me.

5　☐ Browse websites of HEIs to get a feel for the range of financial support packages on offer.

6　☐ Consider more what it would mean, in practice, to study on campus or off-site.

7　☐ Consider the realities of studying in a city or town centre, or at some distance from these.

8　☐ Consider further which facilities, if any, would be essential to me or that I could live without.

9　☐ Find out more about the student union and student organisations at Unis that interest me.

10　☐ Make a short list of the features that I want most from a Uni. See 6a.

11　☐ Record and rate things that I like about each HEI that I investigate and that I like the sound of (6b).

12　☐ Identify Unis that best fit my 'most wanted' list (6c) and rate best for those features which are top priority for me (6d).

Prioritise

Choose between one and three of the strategies listed opposite to try out first. Enter the number given beside each strategy into the box below.

My first 3 priorities	
First choice	
Second choice	
Third choice	

Plan

Decide when you will give time and thought to your priorities.

- Jot those times into your planner – or your timetable for planning towards Uni.
- In your planner, mark in a date within the next month to check that you are keeping to your plan.

Give and take support

Share findings with others in your group about the practicalities of applying to and living at particular kinds of Uni.

Give serious thought to other people's views, considering whether these might be helpful to you too.

Resource 6a:
My 'most wanted' list

Use your thinking about pages 58–60, and your discussions with students and others, to make a list of those features of a HEI, Uni or college that you consider to be the most important for you. Then number these in order of priority, giving 1 to the most essential feature for you.

My 'most wanted' features from a Uni	Order of priority	Details (Add any details or reasons that will help you check Unis for that feature)
a		
b		
c		
d		
e		
f		
g		
h		
i		
j		

Investigate which Unis match your top 7 priorities on the list above. Either look up these features for Unis that interest you already, or browse websites and Unistats (see page 39) to look for Unis that have these features. Jot down their names on the following chart (6b).

Resource 6b:
Things I like about this HEI

It is easy to lose track of which information applied to which Uni. If it helps, make a copy of this sheet. Use it to keep track of features you like about each HEI you research. Use the star rating column to add as many stars as you like to signal how much you liked any features of the HEI.

University/HEI name:		
Things I really like	**Star rating**	**Things I don't like**
1		
2		
3		
4		
5		
6		
7		
8		
9		
10		

Resource 6c:
Rating HEIs according to my 'most wanted' list

1 On your 'most wanted' list (6a), you identified those features of a Uni that you consider most important for you. Write these features into the 'My Features' column below.
2 Write the name of the first HEI that interests you at the top of column 'HEI 1'. Rate this HEI for each of your 10 features, using a scale of 0–5, where *0 = terrible*, *1 = not very good*, *2 = OK*, *3 = quite good*, *4 = very good* and *5 = brilliant*. Add up and write in the total score.
3 Repeat for each HEI that interests you. You can copy the page to consider more HEIs.

My Features	HEI 1 Name	HEI 2 Name	HEI 3 Name	HEI 4 Name
1				
2				
3				
4				
5				
6				
7				
8				
9				
10				
Total score				

Resource 6d:
HEIs that rate best against my priority features

For the top 7 features that you identified as priorities (6a), jot down the names of any HEIs you consider to be 'good enough' for each. Highlight any that you consider excellent for that feature.

My priorities for an HEI	Names of HEIs List as many HEIs as you wish for each of your priorities.
1	
2	
3	
4	
5	
6	
7	

Resource 6e:
Accommodation Checklists

If accommodation issues are important to you, copy and complete one of these for each HEI you consider. Before copying, tick the questions that matter to you, and focus on finding answers to those.

(1) Living in student halls		
Question	Matters to me? ✓	Details
1 Is accommodation provided in the first year? Every year if I want it?		
2 Are meal costs included? Even if I don't want to eat them?		
3 Where is the accommodation located? How safe is it?		
4 How far is accommodation from other facilities and from where my lectures would be located?		
5 What transport is provided (if located off campus)?		
6 What other transport is available? What does it cost?		
7 Are there different price rates, depending on facilities? If so, what are these?		
8 What would it cost me a year for the accommodation I would choose?		
9 Are there en-suite facilities? How much do these cost?		
10 How many people share each bathroom and kitchen?		
11 Are there common room facilities (such as a lounge, TV, dining room)?		
12 Is a hand-basin provided in the room?		
13 Would I need to share accommodation? If so, what would I be sharing?		
14 Is accommodation single sex or mixed?		
15 Is there free wi-fi or internet access in the rooms?		
16 How comfortable and pleasant are the rooms? What furniture is provided?		

(1) Living in student halls		
Question	**Matters to me? ✓**	**Details**
17 What are the security arrangements for the building?		
18 What are the arrangements for cleaning of the room and/ or building?		
19 Do you have to clear the room during vacations? If so, is storage provided?		
20 How noisy would the building be?		

(2) Living in private rented accommodation *This is not usually recommended for, or required of, first years*		
Question	**Matters to me? ✓**	**Details**
21 Does the HEI have an accommodation office to help?		
22 What is the typical cost of student rented accommodation?		
23 Typically, where is this located? What transport is available?		
24 How many months' rent a year would you be expected to pay as a student?		
25 Typically, what is the quality of student accommodation in the area?		
26 How easy is it to find suitable student accommodation in the area?		
27 Is most of this approved by ARLA, NALS, NAEA or RICS?		

Biotechnology | History | **Sports** | Nursing | **Nanotechnology** | **Food science** | **Geography** | **Computer science** | Archaeology | **Performing arts** | Physics | Environmental sciences | Genetics | **Travel and Tourism** | Medicine | **Fine Art** | **Business** | **Management** | **English** | **Earth sciences** | **Spanish** | Accounting | Psychology | Maths | **Early childhood studies** | Radiology | **Classics** | **Chemistry** | **Sociology** | **Film studies** | **Civil engineering** | **Criminology** | Petrology | Music | French | **Social work** | Textiles | **Media** | **Dentistry** | **Architecture** | **Middle Eastern Studies** | Community development | **Sustainability**

This chapter

This chapter helps you to:

→ think through what it means to study a particular subject at Uni;

→ give thought to which subject will be the best one for you to study;

→ recognise the importance of choosing the right subject and programme for your interests;

→ work through the process of considering the range of options open to you;

→ consider whether a single or joint honours degree would suit you better.

Three years ago, for this fabulous four, the world was their oyster.

◁ **Vishua** *I know which Uni I want to go to. I don't care what I study as long as I get a place there.*

◁ **Isobel** *My teacher says to consider engineering. Maths, drains and bridges? Boring! And not for girls!*

◁ **Susan** *My teacher says I'm really good at Art so I'll study that ...*

◁ **Jack** *My mum has put something down for me – botany, I think, or maybe biology.*

Three years later and, no doubt, they are happily curled up with their books.

◁ **Vishua** *I got turned down, probably because I didn't sound committed enough to any subject. I ended up with a place at a Uni I don't like. I find it really hard to study as I don't care about the subject much either.*

◁ **Isobel** *I chose product design. It's great but I could do more things that now interest me if I had chosen engineering. I thought it sounded too difficult and I lacked confidence in my maths but I could have managed it.*

◁ **Susan** *I wish I had put more thought into what I chose. My friends who combined Art with Business or Design have a much better sense of how they will work as artists once they leave Uni.*

◁ **Jack** *I had a bit of a shock – I thought I was going to be drawing plants but I spend all my time with snakes and creepy crawlies.*

What can you learn from them?

- Jot down a list of the things these students may wish they had considered before finalising their choice of subject at Uni.
- What ideas does this give you about things to do before making your choice?

7.2 Choosing your subject

Once you are at Uni, you study fewer subjects but in more depth. You will be studying the same subject(s) for around 3600 hours – and more for programmes that last over 3 years – so it is essential that you choose the right one. Consider carefully whether you would be happy studying the subject(s) you choose for so many hours.

What do you enjoy now?

Use the box below to make a list of subjects linked to activities and topics you enjoy already. You may not end up choosing any of these subjects for Uni but this is a good place to start. Consider such things as:

- a subject you like studying now;
- a subject you enjoy reading about or seeing programmes about;
- subjects at Uni that relate to a personal interest or leisure activity (this might be a sport, art, language, culture, or religion);
- subjects that relate to jobs or work experience that you enjoyed.

What I might enjoy

Talk to friends

Discuss with friends, either informally, on line or in a group arranged at school, the subjects that they think they would enjoy at Uni. You may gain inspiration from them – if so, jot this below.

Inspiration from friends

Type of subject

Consider which broad areas you are drawn to, such as: Arts and Humanities (History, Classics, English, Cultural studies, Philosophy, Politics)? Languages? Subjects where you make things (Art, Design, Architecture, Engineering)? Science and maths-based subjects? Caring professions? Business and entrepreneurship? Land-based or maritime subjects?

Broad subject areas that interest me

7.3 Choosing your subject (2)

More than 1000 subjects
Over 40,000 courses
Lots of interesting combinations
Degrees but also other qualifications to choose from …

Start with a broad search

Start your thinking and searching early so that you have time to be adventurous in considering a range of possibilities before narrowing down your shortlist. Don't just settle on the most obvious subjects, such as those you studied at school, or most obvious professional routes, such as medicine and law.

Know all your options

- Browse the UCAS website.
- Find out the subjects on offer.
- Look up any subjects that look unfamiliar so that you know what they are: they may be just what you are looking for.
- Investigate these further on university and college websites.
- Consider interesting combinations of joint or combined honours subjects, or look for interdisciplinary or 'liberal arts' degrees.

List sister subjects

If one subject attracts you, check for others similar to it. These may be even more interesting or useful for you. There may also be less competition for a related subject. So, for example, if you enjoy biology, look at related disciplines, such as microbiology, botany, ecology, zoology, biotechnology, biochemistry, genetics, etc. If you like history, consider subjects such as archaeology, anthropology, and medieval, cultural or heritage studies. You can copy resource 7a on page 76 to help record sister subject details.

Read for the subjects

Gain a feel for the subject by browsing the material you would have to read once at Uni. This could be a book, journal article, blogs by experts in that field, or information online. See if the subject still appeals. If you feel you can't be bothered to read into the subject now, it probably will not maintain your interest for 3 years or more.

Distinguish between sister subjects

Where subjects are closely related, each will still have its own distinctions. These differences are important within the subject discipline so it pays to become familiar with what they are.

Once you have narrowed your search down to two or three subjects, explore each in more detail. Look for such things as its focus, philosophy, source materials and its methods of working with these.

> **Investigating the subject**
> Use resource 7b on page 78 to help you investigate in more detail the main subjects that interest you.

7.4   Choosing your programme

As you start to clarify the subjects you are most likely to study, start to investigate the programmes associated with these.

Same name, different degree?

Be aware that degree programmes at two Unis may have names that look similar but be very different in practice. Check carefully to see which one is closest to your interest. In particular, note the following.

Theoretical or more practical?

This can be especially important for programmes in fine arts, media, performing arts, computing: some emphasise the creative side with more 'making' and 'doing', whilst others focus on theory, with more reading and writing.

Reflection	Theory or Practice
In general, would you prefer to study a programme that is more practical – where you make things, do things and apply knowledge? Or one that is more theoretical, where you explore ideas in the abstract?	

Science or social science?

Some programmes, such as those in psychology, business and sports sciences, can take a science-based or a number-based approach; others with similar names focus much more on the human and social science aspects.

Reflection	Science or social science?
Would your own preference be for a more science-based programme (with laboratory work and maths) or for human sciences (with more focus on human interaction and possibly contact with people or clients)?	

Attitude to employment

Some programmes require you to be in work already, or you may be interviewed for a job and university place at the same time. Some encourage, or even expect, you to undertake a work placement or sandwich course in Britain or overseas. This is especially true of programmes linked to professional areas.

Others, especially in arts, languages and humanities, may discourage you from working more than a few hours a week.

Foundation Degrees and HNDs are vocational programmes and so more focused on the workplace, as are specific professional routes in areas such as nursing, social work, and physiotherapy.

Reflection	Approach to employment
What combination of work and study would you want to be part of your student experience?	

7.5 Choosing your programme (2)

Be informed

There is a wealth of information available to help you choose your programme. Key sources to investigate are:

- the UCAS website;
- Unistats, to compare programmes from one HEI to another, using nationally recognised data;
- each HEI's website and prospectus;
- printed sources such as *The Times* Good University Guide.

See chapter 4 and Appendix 4 for more details.

Activity

Either on your own or with a group of friends or others planning to go to Uni:

- make a list of the resources that look most interesting and useful;
- share out items on the list, so that you each check out a few;
- compare your findings and decide which sources you want to use for which kinds of information.

Make a long list of programmes

- Jot down any programmes of study that interest you.
- Put time aside to browse your own list in more detail.
- Highlight the ones that sound most appealing after an initial search.

Refine your thinking about choices

As you look through the details of a number of programmes, you will start to notice which ones capture your attention and interest, and which ones feel less attractive. Start to jot down the aspects that you find appealing. These will be very personal to you but some points to consider are:

- Do you like the way your time would be spent in that subject, such as on field trips, in labs, as time abroad, on placement, working with certain kinds of material?
- Does finding out about the subject make you want to go and get a book on it at once or to look up more about it?
- What kinds of things are you finding off-putting? Take these seriously.

Choose a good personal fit

You may find it helpful to speak to a careers adviser to help identify which programme would best fit you. This is free via the UCAS website.

Account for your choices

Be clear why you would short-list or dismiss one programme rather than another. The reasons for your choice should be apparent:

- when you make your personal statement;
- if you were asked at interview.

Jot down your thoughts and reasons as they occur to you and decide whether these reasons are sensible and significant. Draw upon these when you come to narrow your choice of programme.

7.6   Choosing your programme (3)

Find out the competition

Some programmes are easier or more difficult to enter than others. Use the UCAS website or a text such as *The Times* Good University Guide to gain a feel for such things as the following.

- The UCAS tariff for the programme: in general, the higher the tariff, the higher the quality of candidates seeking a place.
- The subjects that have the highest and lowest numbers of places available. If there are fewer places, it is likely to be more competitive to gain one.
- Subjects taught at many HEIs or at only a few: depending on the level of demand, which may make it more difficult to find a place on a programme.

Check for a match to your 'A' levels

It will be important that your ultimate choice will be one for which you have the right qualifications.

- For the Unis that interest you, jot down which subjects, if any, you need to have studied at A level (or equivalent).
- Note the grades needed in which subjects for which programmes at which Unis.
- Balance your ambition with realism: make sure that your choices are of interest and are realistic for your projected grades.

Study more than one subject?

Consider whether you would prefer to combine two or more subjects. If so, it is worth checking:

- whether HEIs that interest you offer combined, joint honours or interdisciplinary degrees;
- the subjects that you can study in combination at those HEIs;
- which combinations would complement each other well. For example, business studies and a language go well together whereas history with engineering is not usually a good combination.

Narrow your programme search

As you develop a sense of which programmes interest you the most, look in more detail at these.

- Look for subtle differences in the programmes at each of the Unis that interest you, such as the options offered, styles of teaching, and any special features.
- Compare the Key Information Sets for those programmes on each Uni website or Unistats.

7.7   Make it happen

Which strategies will I use?

Decide which of the strategies and activities outlined below will be useful to you in making your choice of subject and programme. Tick all that apply. Then identify three priorities opposite.

1 ☐ Decide what subjects I would enjoy.
2 ☐ Speak to a careers adviser.
3 ☐ Talk to friends for inspiration.
4 ☐ Decide on a type of subject.
5 ☐ Conduct a broad initial search of subjects.
6 ☐ Find out all my options.
7 ☐ Find out and list sister subjects.
8 ☐ Read material from these subjects.
9 ☐ Distinguish between sister subjects.
10 ☐ Decide between theoretical and practical programme types.
11 ☐ Consider programmes' approaches to employment.
12 ☐ Make a programmes long list.
13 ☐ Refine my thinking.
14 ☐ Choose a good personal fit.
15 ☐ Account for my choices.
16 ☐ Find out the competition.
17 ☐ Check for match to my 'A' levels.
18 ☐ Consider combining subjects.
19 ☐ Narrow my programme search; use Unistats to compare programme ratings.

Prioritise

Choose between one and three of the strategies listed opposite to try out first. Enter the number given beside each strategy into the box below.

My first 3 priorities	
First choice	
Second choice	
Third choice	

Plan

Decide when you will give time and thought to your priorities.

- Jot those times into your planner or diary – or your timetable for planning towards Uni.
- In your planner, mark in a date within the next month to check that you are keeping to your plan.

> **Give and take support**
> Share findings with others in your group. Post comments about what you find helpful.

Main subject that interests me:	
Sister subjects or programmes of study at Uni related to this subject	**Uni site where I saw this programme listed**
1	
2	
3	
4	
5	
6	
7	
8	
From first browsing these, the subjects that most interest me out of these are:	

Main subject that interests me:	
Sister subjects or programmes of study at Uni related to this subject	Uni site where I saw this programme listed
1	
2	
3	
4	
5	
6	
7	
8	
From first browsing these, the subjects that most interest me out of these are:	

Resource 7b:
Investigating the subject

Subject name:	
1 Roots: what were the origins of the topic? How old is it? How did it emerge from other disciplines (if known)?	
2 What topics does it regard as most appropriate for its field of study? What kinds of issues does it address?	
3 Does it regard itself as an Art? A Social Science? A Science? Why does it think this? Or are there mixed opinions on this?	
4 What is its theoretical basis – what does it regard as the underlying explanation for problems in its field?	
5 What are the kinds of data or source materials that it uses (e.g. surveys, experimental data, case studies, interviews, historical, legal or policy documents, slides, artworks, etc.)?	
6 What kinds of methods does it use for researching the subject and working with source materials?	
7 What kinds of issues come up for researchers when using these sorts of source materials or data?	

8	What are the key ethical considerations for researchers in this subject?	
9	Who are the main names associated with the subject, historically and now? Why are these so important within the subject?	
10	What are the main journals associated with the subject?	
11	What are its sister subjects?	
12	How does it differ from its sister subjects?	
13	What are the careers that graduates of programmes in this subject tend to enter?	
14	What is it that really appeals to me about this subject?	
15	Which Unis that interest me at present offer programmes in this subject?	

Resource 7c:
Choosing a programme

Programme that interests me	Uni site where I saw it	What I like about the programme	What I am less keen on
1			
2			
3			
4			
5			
6			
7			
8			
9			
10			

Programme that interests me	Uni site where I saw it	What I like about the programme	What I am less keen on
11			
12			
13			
14			
15			
16			
17			
18			
19			
20			

Read through your notes above. Highlight the subjects that most appeal.

8   Teaching and assessment

Feedback | Experiments | **Discussion** | Independent study | **Distance learning** | **Essays** | **Exams** | **Coursework** | **Presentations** | **Posters** | Group work | Autonomy | Seminars | **Tutorials** | Blogs | **Lectures** | **Projects** | **Reports** | **Podcasts** | CASE STUDIES | **Personal tutor** | **Workshops** | **On-line** | Research | **Student support groups** | Clinical Practice | **Work placement** | **Workplace project** | **Resource-based** | **Peer-based** | **Practicals** | **Handouts** | Workbooks | Critical sessions | Social networking | **Work-based** | Lecture capture | **Guest speakers** | **WIKIS** | **Reading**

This chapter

This chapter helps you to:

→ find out more about teaching and assessment at Uni and the variety of approaches used;

→ identify which methods attract you most;

→ consider the relative importance, to you, of the teaching and assessment you would experience at Uni – and whether that would affect your choice of HEI;

→ look into the information available to you if you wanted to find out more about the methods used on particular programmes.

8.1 What students wish they had known ...

Three years ago, this studious four had got school-level study sorted; they were up for doing things differently ...

◁ **Freya** *I am so excited at the prospect of sitting all day listening to words of wisdom from world-leaders in their fields.*

◁ **Kwame** *I'll be paying back a lot for my degree – I want a course where you get to see the teachers every day.*

◁ **Arabella** *I want something practical – I don't want to be stuck on a campus all day.*

◁ **Kyle** *It'll be great at Uni – for the courses I like, you only have to turn up for, like, a few hours a week?*

Now they are at Uni, and they appear to be learning hard in ... is that a café, they are sitting in?

◁ **Freya** *We do have some great teachers but it was a shock coping with so many hours independent study every day. The amount of face-to-face teaching seemed so little at first.*

◁ **Kwame** *I ended up choosing a course with very little contact time but it is fantastic. The overall design of the programme is what is really important – the teaching, support, feedback and assessment.*

◁ **Arabella** *I spend 4 days a week at work in landscape design – and it counts towards my degree. I have classes two evenings a week.*

◁ **Kyle** *I ended up choosing a lab-based programme. I spend nearly 20 hours a week in laboratories and workshops, and I'm forever working online, but I don't even notice! Want to get back to it now – Bye!*

What can you learn from them?

- Jot down a list of the things these students may wish they had known about the methods used for teaching, learning and assessment before they arrived.
- What kinds of ideas does this give you about things to do, or find out, now?

8.2 How many hours must I study?

Hours per year

Each year of successful full-time study is assumed to be the equivalent of around 1200 hours. These may include relevant clinical or workplace activity.

Hours per week

Divided equally between 52 weeks in the year, 1200 hours would work out at around 23 hours a week. If you took holidays and breaks equivalent to 7 weeks over a year, then 1200 hours spread over 45 weeks would mean around 27 hours a week. The number of hours per week will vary depending how many weeks' break you take.

Nominal hours versus actual hours

The figures given above are a nominal requirement – that is, a general assumption of how long the study would take. The actual hours spent in study vary from student to student, and will depend on such factors as:

- how motivated you are to achieve high marks;
- how interested you are in finding out as much as you can about the subject;
- how quickly you complete the work;
- the care you take with your work;
- whether you find the subject easy;
- the number of work-based or clinical hours required on your programme.

Part-time study hours

For part-time study, the number of hours would be a pro-rata proportion of the amount of the degree you studied that year. If you take the equivalent of half your programme each year, that would mean 600 hours a year, or around 11–12 hours a week. If you study at 80% intensity, that would mean 960 hours a year, or 18 hours a week.

Where time goes

The 1200 hours translates differently depending on your programme. See page 85 for examples of how study patterns can vary.

Time in scheduled sessions

For science-based and work-based subjects, you may find that up to 20 hours a week or more are spent in labs or in the workplace. For arts, humanities and social sciences, this is usually much less.

Lectures usually take 50–60 minutes, but may last 2–3 hours. Typically, seminars and tutorials take 1–2 hours, 2–4 times a week. Sometimes, teaching is scheduled into blocks, with long days of up to 12 hours.

Time in independent study

There would be at least several hours of independent study a week. Where there are fewer hours expected for lab-work and lectures, you would normally make up that time in further independent study – reading, research, practical work, discussion and thinking.

Students also tend to put additional time into areas where their emotional and creative energies are engaged, such as for arts, performance, research projects, community projects and entrepreneurship.

8.3 Weekly study patterns

In higher education, the amount of time and patterns of study are likely to differ from those you have experienced so far. They also vary from one programme to another. The following are just some examples. Consider what it would be like to study on each of these.

Programme 1 (Full-time)

Hrs/ activity	Formal taught	Self-directed	Practical /other
24–28			
20–24			
13–16			
9–12			
5–8			
0–4			

Programme 2 (Part-time)

Hrs/ activity	Formal taught	Self-directed	online contact
13–16			
9–12			
5–8			
0–4			

Programme 3 (Full-time)

Hrs/ activity	Formal taught	Self-directed	Practical /other
24–28			
20–24			
13–16			
9–12			
5–8			
0–4			

Programme 4 (Full-time)

Hrs/ activity	Formal taught	Self-directed	Practical /other
24–28			
20–24			
13–16			
9–12			
5–8			
0–4			

Programme 5 (Part-time)

Hrs/ activity	Formal taught	Self-directed	Practical /other
13–16			
9–12			
5–8			
0–4			

Programme 6 (Full-time)

Hrs/ activity	Formal taught	Self-directed	Practical /other
24–28			
20–24			
13–16			
9–12			
5–8			
0–4			

Reflection	Your preferences

- What would be your own ideal study pattern?
- Is that pattern likely, or possible, to be found for the kind of programmes that interest you most?

The Key Information Sets on HEI websites provide details of teaching hours for each programme.

8.4　How will I be taught?

Independent study

For most programmes, the bulk of study is through directed independent learning. Taught sessions, resources and programmes are designed to develop your abilities to take on increasing levels of independence.

Lectures

Lectures are a key teaching method used at most universities. They generally consist of a lecturer providing an overview of the subject to large groups, sometimes of 200–500 students.

Seminars, lab groups, workshops

Students are then divided into smaller groups for seminars, lab groups or workshops, where there is more opportunity for contributing to discussions or making presentations. These vary in size from 3–6 students to 60 students or more. For part-time programmes or programmes with small intakes, workshops and seminars may take the place of lectures.

Reflection	Group size

Does it matter to you how big the groups are that you would study in?

If you prefer to work in a particular group size, ask about this before you apply or check for details on the web-pages for the relevant programmes on HEI websites.

Tutorial Groups

Tutorial groups tend to be the smallest group used for teaching, and are often offered on an individual basis, once or twice a term. At a small number of universities such as Oxford and Cambridge, tutorials are the main teaching method for some subjects.

Supplementary methods

A variety of other methods are used. These vary from one tutor to the next, and include some or all of the following:

- experiments, lab-work and practicals;
- problem-solving and enquiry-based learning;
- individual and group research projects;
- studio-based: performance and creative;
- group discussion, face-to-face or on-line;
- resources-based and distance learning, whether paper-based, on-line or virtual;
- using technologies such as blogs, wikis, podcasts and social networking;
- peer learning and peer support groups;
- clinical practice and work-based projects;
- guest speakers;
- field trips, placements overseas or a year abroad.

NSS Information for your use

NSS data include student ratings on different aspects of teaching such as:

- how well tutors explain things;
- whether they make the subject interesting and intellectually stimulating;
- whether good advice is available on study choices;
- how easy it is to contact staff.

8.5 Assessment and Feedback

The range of assessments

Consider how strongly you feel about how you will be assessed. Some programmes will rely almost exclusively either on exams or on coursework. You could choose a programme that uses the assessment method you prefer.

Some programmes use a wide range of assessment methods. This can provide more interest and help you to develop a range of skills, but can also be challenging, as you are less likely to excel in all kinds of assessment and there are fewer opportunities to practise each.

Professionally-focused programmes may include work-based knowledge and experience as part of the assessment process.

Allocation of marks

If you are much better at one kind of assessment than another, you may want to find out what proportion of your marks would be allocated to:

- exams of different kinds;
- coursework such as essays, reports, case studies and dissertations;
- practical work;
- clinical or work placements;
- other kinds of assessment (such as posters, presentations, portfolios).

Feedback

As there is a high proportion of independent study at Uni, the feedback you receive is especially important. This may be provided primarily on assignments that you hand in for assessment. However, there may be many other methods used, such as verbal feedback, group feedback in seminars or on-line, on-going feedback on clinical placements or structured peer feedback in organised sessions.

You may find it useful to find out about:

- the kind of feedback you would receive;
- how satisfied students are with feedback that they receive on that programme.

Information you can use

Key Information Sets

KIS data on Uni and programme websites: this should give you a general background on the breakdown of assessments for your programme.

Programme website

You can often burrow down on the Uni websites to see the assessment for each year, module or unit of study.

NSS student satisfaction data

These provide data on student ratings about assessment and feedback, such as:

- whether marking criteria are clear;
- if feedback on returned work is detailed, helpful and prompt;
- if assessment and marking are fair;
- if sufficient support was provided.

8.6 Personal preferences

Draw a (circle) around those aspects of teaching and assessment that are most important to you.
Highlight any aspects that are essential for you.

Lots of scheduled sessions | Lots of contact time with tutors | Oral work | Lots of independent study | Group assessment | Individual project work | Posters | Time abroad | Lectures and note-making | Lab-work | Experiments | 1:1 tutorials | Practical work | Guest speakers | On-line discussions | Peer learning | Group project work | Enquiry-based learning | Field trips | Work-based assessment | Studio work | Performance | Distance learning | Client work | FACE-TO-FACE GROUP DISCUSSION | Resources-based learning | Virtual Learning Environments | Creativity | Mainly coursework | Seminars | Use of new technologies such as blogs, wikis, podcasts, social networking | Portfolio | PEER SUPPORT GROUPS | Clinical practice | Work placements | Work-based projects | Assessment mainly by exams | Problem-solving | Absolutely no exams | Exams | Presentations | On-line assessment

Reflection	Personal preferences

- Reflect on the choices you made above.
- Draw together any themes that characterise the way you prefer to be taught.
- Which aspects of teaching and assessment are most important to you in choosing a programme?

8.7　Make it happen

Which strategies will I use?

Decide which of the strategies and activities listed below will be useful to you in making your choice of programme. Tick all that apply. Then identify three priorities opposite.

1 ☐ Look up the Key Information Sets (KIS) on teaching and assessment for programmes at different Unis for subjects that interest me.

2 ☐ Look up NSS results for programmes that interest me, to see how well current students rate the teaching and assessment.

3 ☐ Think through what my week would be like, depending on the balance of teaching or independent study on a programme.

4 ☐ Use HEIs' websites to investigate in detail the teaching and assessment that I would experience on their programmes.

5 ☐ Find out more about types of teaching that seem unfamiliar to me, by reading the websites of programmes that interest me.

6 ☐ Complete the teaching and assessment rating sheets for programmes that most interest me (8a).

7 ☐ Give more thought to my preferences for:
- as much contact time as possible, to keep me focused;
- little contact, and few taught sessions, so that I can use my time more flexibly.

8 ☐ Find out what kinds of subjects and programmes of study are likely to be taught and assessed in the ways I prefer.

Prioritise

Choose between one and three of the strategies listed opposite to try out first. Enter the number given beside each strategy into the box below.

My first 3 priorities	
First choice	
Second choice	
Third choice	

Plan

Decide when you will give time and thought to your priorities. Leave plenty of time to investigate your options in depth before making your final choices.

- Jot those times into your planner or diary – or your timetable for planning towards Uni.
- In your planner, mark in a date within the next month to check that you are keeping to your plan.

Give and take support

Share findings with others in your group. Post comments about what you find helpful.

Share ideas on the pros and cons of different teaching and assessment strategies. Consider how the skills these develop would help you in your career aims.

Resource 8a:
My teaching and assessment ratings

Use the table below to jot down your key likes and dislikes about the teaching and assessment methods used for those programmes that interest you the most. Use your ratings to help short-list your favourites (5 = 'like a lot'; 0 = 'dislike a lot'). You can copy this sheet for your personal use.

Name of the programme:	
University or college offering it:	
UCAS code:	

Key features / provision	Features I like a lot	Features I don't like much	My overall rating ☺ ☹
NSS ratings for teaching and assessment (include those ratings that interest you the most)			5 4 3 2 1 0
Where: the location, quality and ambience of teaching spaces?			5 4 3 2 1 0
Teaching methods used			5 4 3 2 1 0
The amount of time spent in independent study? In taught sessions? In other ways?			5 4 3 2 1 0
Group size; student to staff ratio			5 4 3 2 1 0

Resource 8a:
My teaching and assessment ratings (continued)

Key features / provision	Features I like a lot	Features I don't like much	My overall rating ☺ ☹
Attendance requirements? Any penalties?			5 4 3 2 1 0
Amount and kind of academic support (e.g., personal tutor; year tutor; support staff; additional workshops)?			5 4 3 2 1 0
Type and quality of learning resources (e.g., use made of the virtual learning environment; specialist equipment)?			5 4 3 2 1 0
The amount and type of assessment?			5 4 3 2 1 0
Assessment: opportunities for practice and feedback?			5 4 3 2 1 0
Other key features of teaching and assessment on the programme ...?			5 4 3 2 1 0
Total score			

9 Money decisions and choice of Uni

Scholarships | Bursaries | **Fees** | Fee Waivers | **Eligibility** | **Expenses** | **Financial Support** | **Course costs** | **Books** | **Equipment** | Distance | Travel | Fares | **Rent** | Accommodation costs | **Housing** | **Food** | **Required meals** | **Earnings** | **Part-time option** | **Timetabling** | Work placements | Childcare | Work restrictions | **Local work** | Business opportunities | **Field Trips** | **Living at Home** | **Enterprise** | **Facilities**

This chapter

This chapter helps you to:

→ look at what first year students wish they had known about the costs and the financial support available to them, before they made their choice of Uni;

→ consider how your choice of university or college could impact upon your finances whilst you are a student;

→ consider things that you could find out now, as part of your decision-making about Uni, that could help you financially as a student.

9.1 What students wish they had known ...

Three years ago, money meant treats for this financially carefree four.

◁ **William** *Too much information! Enough already! I can't be bothered to wade through all this!*

◁ **Lily** *I want to make the most of every aspect of student life. I am saving up now so I can take gap years, do volunteering overseas, any chance that comes my way.*

◁ **Siobhan** *I will get a job at Uni so I don't need to borrow too much to pay for living costs. It might help me pay off part of my student loans as I go along.*

◁ **Marco** *You don't have to pay back the fees for years, and they give you a huge loan, so what's the problem?*

Three years later, and our big spenders are feeling a little impecunious ...

◁ **William** *If I had gone to a different Uni, I would have got a bursary of £1000 a year. I thought the support would be the same at every Uni so I didn't check that, when I applied.*

◁ **Lily** *This campus is quite isolated so there are hardly any jobs round here and they don't pay well. My journey home is always long and expensive and my course has lots of hidden costs such as field trips and equipment.*

◁ **Siobhan** *I started my own business as part of a project at Uni. I kept it going after the project ended, and it helps me with living costs. Once I leave college, it will be my job. Will it make me a billionaire? Maybe!*

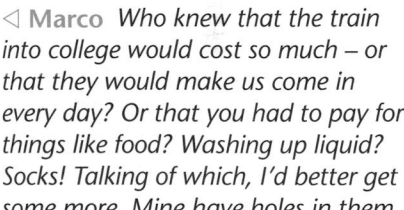

◁ **Marco** *Who knew that the train into college would cost so much – or that they would make us come in every day? Or that you had to pay for things like food? Washing up liquid? Socks! Talking of which, I'd better get some more. Mine have holes in them.*

What can you learn from them?
- Make a list of the financial matters these students may wish they had considered.
- What ideas does this give you about things to find out before choosing where to study?

9.2 Financial decisions: Choosing your Uni

When you arrive at university or college, you will already have made choices that impact upon the money you have at your disposal – that is, the amount of money you have to spend whilst you are a student.

When choosing your Uni or college

Your choice of HEI may have an impact upon your disposable income. Each differs in:

- how much financial support it offers to students in the form of bursaries and scholarships;
- its direct costs for accommodation and meals;
- additional costs such as field trips;
- whether teaching is timetabled in ways that help with taking on part-time work;
- the indirect costs that would arise, such as travel to campus combined with the required pattern for attending sessions across the week, term or semester.

How important is the difference in fees?

Although fees vary, looking at the cost of these is not the only, or the best, way of working out the best value for you. The fee level will not normally affect how much money you have at your disposal as a student. This is because you don't start to make repayments on the loans that cover your fees whilst you are still a full-time student, nor for the first three years of part-time study.

Some part-time students earning over £21,000 per year would start repayments towards the end of their degree.

What about repayments?

Once you earn enough to start repaying the loan (when you earn over £21,000 a year), the monthly repayments will be based on how much you earn, not the level of your fee. Your monthly repayment will be the same whatever the cost of your fee and loan.

Balance the costs and benefits

You need to balance what matters to you about the following.

1. How much you have to spend as a student (your disposable income).
2. The kind of student lifestyle you want.
3. Total costs and eventual repayments.
4. The university experience you want.
5. The impact that your degree is likely to have on your future income and life.

Your total repayment over 30 years could eventually be higher if you went to an HEI with higher fees. However, this would depend on whether you earned sufficient each year for this to be taken out of your salary. Also, after 30 years, any outstanding loans would be written off.

Reflection	Does money matter?

- How important are decisions about money in your choice of Uni?
- Do you think financial considerations will affect your choice of Uni?

9.3 Part-time study as a financial option

Part-time study as an option

For the first time, from 2012:

- part-time students will be eligible for loans to cover the fees;
- part-time fees are not paid up-front.

This means that part-time study is now a much more attractive option for school-leavers than it has been in the past. However, note that there are no loans to help with living costs for part-time study as it is assumed you would be working and earning to cover these.

The challenges of part-time study

Attendance requirements at Uni?

HEIs are not always flexible in the times they require you to attend on campus.

Fewer choices?

This means that you may have fewer programmes and Unis to choose from.

Commitment and motivation

It requires high levels of commitment and motivation to juggle work and study, and to maintain this over several years.

The benefits of part-time study

There are many benefits to studying part-time so it is an option worth considering.

Easier to work

You can work more easily than if you had a full-time study load.

More money

You may get a better paid part-time job – and you earn as you learn.

Reduced debts

You leave Uni with lower levels of debt.

Time to develop academically

As your study is spread over several years, you have a longer period to build your academic skills.

Employability

You develop the skills and qualities employers value the most. Employers prefer students who understand the world of work.

Less impact on grades

You spread your study over more years, so that your paid work can have less impact on your grades than if you studied full-time with a part-time job.

9.4 Part-time study as a financial option (2)

What employers think about part-time students

Employers find it hard to recruit graduates with skills that they really value, such as work-readiness, commercial awareness, and the kinds of confidence and people skills that come from working alongside other adults. Part-time students tend to compare very favourably with full-time students in the job market as they often have developed the skills to a higher level by the time they graduate.

Employers are aware of the challenges that part-time study involves, and value the personal qualities that this develops.

Employer attitudes

30% of respondents who employ people with qualifications gained via part-time study believe that part-time students are of a slightly better or much better standard than their full-time counterparts.

(London Higher, 2006, *Attitudes to part-time study*)

Employer-funded degrees

Some employers pay for their employees to take a degree as part of their job. The degree would usually be one relevant to the job so the choice of subject would be determined for you. This is a good option if you want a job with one of these employers: you could gain a degree without having to pay any fees and with excellent job prospects when you leave.

Employer-funded degrees are most common in the public sector, such as nursing, social work, teaching (which can also be studied full-time). For part-time students, you would generally take a job in a role such as a social work assistant and be trained up to a professional role, with a good chance of a job at the end.

In the private sector, there are fewer opportunities but employers have paid for their employees to take degrees part-time in areas such as business services, construction, manufacturing, accountancy, law, wholesale and retail. You would need to have a job with such employers first.

(BIS, 2011, 'Employer perspectives on part-time students in UK Higher education')

Things to consider

Which first?

If you haven't already got a job, you need to think about whether you look for a job or a Uni first – and where to locate yourself.

Job options?

You would need to check what the job options would be near the universities that you prefer.

Weigh benefits against challenges

- How important to you are the benefits of part-time study compared with the challenges?
- How would you manage the challenges?

9.5 Choices and costs: Accommodation

Financial decisions are not just about money ...

Financial decisions represent a balance of choices. This is especially true when you are making choices about where you will live as a student. A financial saving in one area such as the cost of accommodation may lead to different kinds of costs such as transport. You also have to take into account such things as:

- time spent in travel each day;
- how much independence you want;
- the cost of meals and other services.

Help with living costs

Full-time students can normally receive a loan to help with living costs and you may also be eligible for a grant that you do not need to pay back.

Accommodation: your biggest cost?

A high proportion of your loan and grant is likely to go on accommodation. Costs vary depending on such factors as:

- geographical location;
- the quality of the accommodation;
- which facilities are bundled in;
- any extras you choose to pay for.

As it is such a major cost, and as the quality of accommodation can vary, it is worth considering the student accommodation available to you, and for what costs, at the same time that you are choosing your subject and university or college.

Living in Uni accommodation

Uni accommodation varies in cost. Things to consider include the following.

- HEIs' accommodation may look more expensive but can work out similar in price to private rental if utilities and costs are included.
- You only pay during term or semester; for private rental you usually pay 11–12 months of the year.
- There may be high- and low-cost options available in HEIs' halls of residence.
- You may have to pay for a required number of meals in student halls.

Roger realised all too late that his cheap accommodation nevertheless came at a price ...

Private rental

Many HEIs require you to live outside of student halls of residence for one or more years; some will not allow this until the second year. If you have strong feelings about private rental, find out:

- what is permitted or required at HEIs you prefer;
- the cost and location of rentals in the vicinity of the HEI.

9.6 Choices and costs: Studying from home

Pros and cons of living at home

These will be personal to you and your family, as every household is different. Consider the following.

Impact on your finances?

You are likely to save money on the cost of accommodation, unless you have to pay a similar contribution at home. Depending on where you live, you may spend more on daily travel than living on campus.

Impact on your choices?

If you opted to study from home, you would have fewer Unis from which you could choose. There could still be a wide range of options. Consider:

- How far would you be prepared to travel to campus every day?
- Which of the HEIs that appeal to you are within that travel range?
- Is there transport available at the times you would need to travel?
- How much would the cost of travel amount to over the year?
- Do those Unis offer the subjects that interest you?
- Do these Unis offer the other things that you want from your time as a student?

Impact on your study?

- Will you be able to concentrate at home on your studies as you wish and need?
- Would you have more time to study as a result of staying at home, or less?
- If you live at home, will that mean that you are looked after by your family, so you have more time for study?
- Would you be expected to contribute to the household chores in a way that would give you less time for study?

Impact on your independence?

- Would you be able to take part in student activities as much if you lived at home?
- Would you feel you were fully part of the student community?
- Would you feel that you had missed out on the full experience of being a student if you lived at home?
- Would you feel more independent if you lived at home because of the responsibilities you have there?

You're home! Did you have a lovely day at the Uni, chicken?

Aw, Mum!

9.7 Make it happen

Which strategies will I use?

Decide which actions you can take now to help you to manage your finances once you arrive at Uni.

1. ☐ Complete the financial considerations chart (9a) to help me think through the financial issues.
2. ☐ Use the financial checklist (9b) when checking out HEIs that interest me.
3. ☐ Consider whether I want to live at home or go away to Uni.
4. ☐ Find out what kind of scholarships, bursaries and other financial support would be available to me.

If studying from home

5. ☐ Decide how far I am prepared to travel each day.
6. ☐ Find out which Unis are within that distance.
7. ☐ Find out if these offer the subjects I want.
8. ☐ Decide whether I am likely to get the required grades for these Unis.
9. ☐ Consider whether a distance learning course would suit me. If so, investigate the range of options available.

For going away to Uni

10. ☐ Find out about the different accommodation options open to me via the Uni.
11. ☐ Find out if I pay for meals in halls whether or not I eat them. (If so, am I OK about that?)
12. ☐ Check whether I have the option of an en-suite. If so, for me, is this worth the cost?
13. ☐ Find out how many weeks I would have to pay for if I lived in Uni accommodation.
14. ☐ Check if I am allowed to live in private rental in the first year. Would I prefer this?

Prioritise

Using the numbered list here, choose the three things that you need to consider or find out first. Insert those numbers in the priorities box. Use the resources listed on page 288 to help you find the answers to your questions.

My first 3 priorities	
First choice	
Second choice	
Third choice	

Plan

- Make a list of the other things that you need to find out in order to make the right financial decisions for you when choosing a Uni.
- Organise these in order of priority.

Give and take support

Share your ideas, thoughts and information about student financial and life choices with others in your group.

Post comments about resources you find helpful.

Resource 9a:
Financial considerations

Consideration	Your responses
1 Monthly repayments The monthly repayments on student loans (once you come to pay them) are the same whatever the annual fee, whether that is £6000 or £9000. Would that affect your choice of HEI?	
2 Total repayments Total repayments will be higher if the Uni charges a higher fee, even though the monthly repayment is the same. You might make repayments for longer – though after 30 years, student loans will be written off. Would that affect your choice of HEI?	
3 Financial support from the HEI Depending on your family's income, you may be eligible for financial support as scholarships, bursaries and fee waivers. Would that affect your choice of HEI?	
4 Earning as a student Would you feel more comfortable if you were able to work whilst you are a student in order to leave Uni with lower levels of debt? Would that affect your choice of HEI?	
5 Part-time study and work You can earn more if you study part-time and work either part-time or full-time. You may not get the £3000 loan for living expenses but you wouldn't have to pay it back. How does this affect your thinking about how to study?	
6 Hidden costs Be aware of the range of costs of being a student, such as accommodation, travel, field trips, books, and the social life. Would these costs affect your choice of HEI?	
7 A financial choice? How far will your choice of HEI be based on financial considerations? What other considerations would matter more to you?	

Resource 9b:
Financial checklist for choosing Unis

Name of the university or college:	

Consideration	Amount or details
1 **Fee:** Cost of the fees per year	
2 **Financial support:** Amount of financial support I am likely to get at this HEI in the form of bursaries, scholarships and fee waivers	
3 **Accommodation:** What would it cost me per year for the kind of accommodation and facilities that I want?	
4 **Daily travel:** How much would it cost me to get to class each day?	
5 **Weekly travel:** How much would it cost me in study-related travel costs?	
6 **Travel home:** How much would it cost a year to travel home to see my parents and friends?	
7 **Opportunities for a student job?** • Are there good opportunities for part-time work in the area? • Are the rates of pay reasonable compared with other areas and when compared with local costs?	
8 **Time to earn?** Would my study load allow me to study full-time and work part-time?	
9 **The HEI's attitude to part-time work?** Does the university/college put any restrictions on how much part-time work I can do as a student in term-time? Could I study part-time?	
10 **Timetabling:** Will the way classes are timetabled at this HEI help or hinder my chances of doing the jobs I want as a student?	
11 **Hidden costs?** What additional costs will I have to pay for trips, equipment, lab coats, books, etc.?	
12 **Value for money?** Overall, do I think it is worth the money? That means, ultimately, am I prepared to pay this?	

10 Making your decisions

What matters most – subject or Uni?
| Which Uni is best for my subject? |
Could I study a subject I don't love? |
When is it best to go? | Where would
I be happiest? | Should I study part-
time? | Does the financial support
package matter to me? | Would I feel
comfortable there? | Will it help me
get a job? | Do I want to study only
where there are people like me? |
Will I make friends there? | COULD
I STUDY AND WORK THERE? | How
much does the reputation of the Uni
matter to me? | Where would I enjoy
myself the most? | Would I be able to
get home easily at weekends from
there? | Where would I live? | Which
Uni gives me most of what I want?

This chapter

This chapter helps you to:

→ draw together your thinking about going to Uni;

→ bring together into one place the decisions that you need to make;

→ weigh up the various choices that face you, so that you are better placed to choose the right Uni for you.

10.1   What students wish they had known …

Three years ago, our four students were knee deep in prospectuses, brochures, and checklists.

◁ **Kwame** *I will be paying for this for a long time so I am reading everything to make sure I make the right choice.*

◁ **June** *I was overwhelmed by the amount of choice so I made a list, closed my eyes and pointed. Where my finger landed, that's where I applied.*

◁ **Soraya** *My teacher says I'm only really cut out for one of the top two, so that decides things for me.*

◁ **Jack** *It is all getting a bit complicated – I think I'll leave the big decisions to my mum.*

Three years later – and are our wild wayfarers on life's weaving paths where they expected to be at this point?

◁ **Kwame** *I did change my mind about 20 times before making my decision. In all that time, I didn't give a thought to whether I'd be really happy at any of them.*

◁ **June** *I was called for interview and they asked me why I made such an unusual selection of Unis. It was embarrassing. I got a place, but not at a Uni I really would have wanted …*

◁ **Soraya** *I didn't put too much thought into my full range of choices as I was sure I was going to Oxford. This meant I made some bad decisions. In the end, I went through clearing and got a place at a great Uni and I'm really happy.*

◁ **Jack** *I thought my mum would choose a Uni where I could live at home and be near to her. Strangely, she chose one at the other end of the country.*

What can you learn from them?

- Jot down a list of the things these students may wish they had considered before finalising their choice of Uni.
- What ideas does this give you about things to do before making your choice?

10.2 How students make their decisions

Case studies

Every applicant makes their choices in very personal ways. Several case studies are provided below to illustrate how, in practice, individuals work through the information and decision-making processes. These may help you when making your own decisions.

Ayeesha

I wanted to be a dentist. Well, my dad did. I kind of agreed because I found out that your chances of getting a good job are higher for dentistry than for almost any other degree. I told my own dentist and she offered me two weeks' work experience over the holidays. I was only there a day and realised it absolutely wasn't for me. It was back to the drawing board. I looked at other careers I might like but I couldn't really see myself in any of them. I felt a bit down.

Then I went to an open day at a Uni near home. One of the students I was chatting to said that he still didn't know what he wanted to do after Uni. I asked him if he was worried that he wouldn't get a job but he just laughed. He said that employers wanted to see you could think and help their business and weren't that bothered about the subject. He was studying music but was being interviewed to train with a top accountancy company.

I love geography and care about the planet so I decided to see what programmes there were in areas like environment and sustainable earth. There were lots, some with really interesting field work. I went to the open days at about six Unis but I felt most at home here – that may have been psychological because I knew I liked this course the best.

> **Learning from Ayeesha**
>
> What were the main considerations for Ayeesha in choosing a Uni and programme?
>
> How could her experiences help you when making decisions about Uni?

Liam

I found it hard to decide what to do. The programme I liked best was in Cornwall, about 300 miles from where we lived. The ones nearer home were OK but less likely to get me the job I wanted later. I didn't want to be separated from my girlfriend. She was two years younger so wouldn't be going to Uni at the same time. I decided to wait two years in case she went to the same Uni. Then she decided to study in the USA.

> **Learning from Liam**
> What advice would you have given Liam?

Malik

I didn't really think I would go to Uni at all. The school got invited to send people to a science festival at one of the Unis. It was a day out so I went along. I didn't know what to expect – I suppose I thought it would be just lots of stuffy lecture halls.

It was amazing, it was all so big. It was on a site in the countryside, and the students lived in halls in the middle of all this … grass! There was a supermarket, clothes shops, bars, cafes, restaurants, a theatre, art gallery, libraries, a bank, gym, a swimming pool,

sports fields … what else? A juice bar, book shop, places to pray, nice gardens, just everything. Like a little world on its own. Students were running a lot of the facilities and hanging out around the campus. There were posters up about bands that were coming, some I really like, and notices everywhere about things to get involved with. Parachuting, was one. Taking part in some student experiments for £5. A trip to Stratford. Loads of things.

I thought it would be brilliant to live like that for a few years, away from everything.

I told my parents and they were worried that I would miss living in a city. It's only an hour away from home so I thought that if I got stir crazy I could easily get home for a bit. I didn't want to move too far away.

I was ready to sign on the dotted line. I couldn't imagine that anywhere could be as good. Then, my maths teacher told me to look up other campus-based Unis, in the countryside and in the city.

She was right. I did find another Uni that was just as good for the campus life but had a better reputation for the subject that I wanted to study. I made that my first choice and I got in. It is a bit far both from the local town and I can't get home as often, but I like it because it is so different from everything I have experienced before.

Learning from Malik

What were the main considerations for Malik in choosing a Uni and programme? Would his choices suit you? If not, how would your preferences differ?

Gareth

I wanted a degree that I knew would lead to a job making games. I love games and there are loads of degrees in it but only a few do the computing programming that you need, to get the kind of job that I wanted. I spent ages finding out which degrees did contain the right computer programming and decided the one at a college in the next town was the best. I find the travel and the degree programme quite hard going, but it is worth it to me to get a job I really want.

Luke

I always loved reading and wanted to study English. The trouble was, when I looked up programmes at Unis that I knew most about, these all had things I knew I would find boring, like Norse and old English. I couldn't face that so I nearly chose a different subject.

Then, by accident, when I was browsing, I found a course where you could do English with a language. That gave me an idea, and I started to search for other joint degrees with English. Now, I am studying English with Spanish at a Uni I hadn't even heard of. I am very happy here. The main decider for me was that all the options look interesting and I get to study for a semester in Spain or a South American country.

Learning from Luke

How did Luke find the right programme for him?

How could you benefit from his experiences of selecting a Uni?

Sara

I have a little brother with a disability. My mum gets very tired looking after him and can't get out to work. After school, I wanted to help her out at home and get a job to bring us in more money. I didn't think about Uni at all.

Our careers teacher was really good and said I shouldn't feel pressurised either way. She got me information about programmes that I could study from home. I am now doing a part-time degree by distance learning. I work three days a week, and study in the evenings and weekends and just when I can. That means I can be home for two days a week and my mum can get out of the house. She got a job and now she is thinking of doing a degree by distance learning as well.

Learning from others' experiences

What were the main considerations for these students?

What further considerations, if any, does this raise for you when making your own decisions about going to Uni?

10.5 Decision-making flow-chart

Many students decide on a Uni mainly on the basis of the subject and programme. Look at the following flow-chart. Consider how far this process of decision-making would work for you. Then draw up your own flow-chart, adapting it to suit you.

5 Make checklists

Create checklists of other things you want from a university or college. Decide the features that matter most to you.

6 Investigate HEIs

Investigate HEIs on your 'long list' to see how they compare for the priorities on your checklists. Send for their prospectus or brochures.

7 Narrow your list

Make an initial short list of HEIs offering the best combination for you.

4 Investigate programmes

Look in detail at programmes that interest you most.

8 Entry requirements

Check UCAS tariffs and entry requirements. Compare these with what you expect to gain.

3 Long list

Create a long list of 10–20 programmes that look worth checking in more detail.

START

9 Entry schemes

Many HEIs have arrangements for those who have potential, but may not achieve the UCAS tariff. Check your eligibility for these.

1 Find out

Find out the programmes that are available in the subject that interests you. Consider joint options and sister subjects.

2 Browse

Browse details of these programmes on HEI websites.

10 Short list

Weigh up what you have found out and narrow your list to around 6–10 HEIs.

12 Decide

- Spend time on your checklists and ratings, weighing up the pros and cons of different HEIs and programmes.
- Talk through with family and friends.
- Keep narrowing your checklist.
- Decide the most important factor(s) for you, overall, in selecting your HEI and programme.
- Make your choices.

11 Visit

Visit the HEIs on your short list to get a feel for what they are like. Consider whether you would feel happy there for several years.

If possible, attend a summer school, open day or other event on campus.

10.6 Deciding by Uni? Career? Location?

Choosing a prestigious Uni?

Some people choose their Uni primarily on its reputation, especially for the following.

- Older, prestigious universities such as Oxford, Cambridge, Durham, Bristol and Exeter.
- Research-intensive universities (see page 58).
- HEIs that have a reputation for a specific subject, such as Loughborough for Sports Science, Surrey for Hospitality, Bath for Social Work, and Nottingham for Agriculture.
- Universities that have a reputation for a good student experience in their subject (see p. 25; quiz question 26).

Such HEIs tend to have high UCAS tariffs. It is advisable to put those with the highest tariff at the top of your list – otherwise, they will probably not consider your application.

Keep an open mind before settling on any Uni, even a very prestigious one. All HEIs have something different to offer. Make sure you visit the HEI, the area, and the student accommodation – and that you really like its programme – before rushing to make a decision.

Career first?

It is important to bear in mind that for a great many graduate jobs, employers are not concerned which subject you study. There are graduate routes from all kinds of degrees into areas such as law, business, education, insurance, government, accountancy, management and many more.

Employers vary in what they value: some will look at the reputation of the university, others will look for particular qualities and skills, and still others will want to see what else you did at Uni or college apart from study.

For certain professions, you will need a degree in a particular subject. For example, for careers in medicine, dentistry, nursing, social work, architecture, psychology, engineering and games technology, you would need qualifications recognised by the relevant professional bodies. If you know what career you want to pursue, talk to a careers adviser to find out exactly which qualifications you will need.

Locality?

Many students have personal reasons for wanting to live at home as a student, or to study relatively near home. If that is true for you:

Be selective

Don't just opt for the nearest university or college: find out the full range of HEIs in your area. Investigate these in detail. Consider the reputation and special characteristics of each, as HEIs even within a small area can vary a great deal.

Consider distance learning

If you need to study from home, it is worth considering the range of distance learning programmes on offer. The Open University is well known for such programmes, and some options can also be available through other HEIs. Check whether the HEIs that interest you have distance learning programmes you could take.

10.7   Make it happen

Which strategies will I use?

Decide which of the considerations listed below would be useful to pursue in more detail. Tick all that apply. Then identify your three priorities opposite.

1 ☐ Make an initial decision about what is likely to be the deciding factor for me in choosing an HEI. Use that to guide my initial long-listing of HEIs.

2 ☐ Go back over chapters earlier in this section to make sure I have covered all important angles that would help me make my decisions.

3 ☐ Find someone I trust, to talk through my thinking process for choosing a programme and HEI.

4 ☐ Use or adapt checklists in these chapters to help me keep track of the different things I find out about each HEI and make my final decisions.

5 ☐ Draw up my own decision-making flow-chart with steps that reflect my own priorities.

6 ☐ Check HEIs' entry requirements carefully.

7 ☐ Investigate my eligibility for any of the entry schemes or foundation programmes that are offered by Unis that have high UCAS tariffs.

8 ☐ Make sure my checklists and priorities are realistic. Amend my checklists if I find I am being unrealistic in what I am looking for.

9 ☐ Find out about summer schools offered by HEIs that interest me.

10 ☐ Find out about other opportunities to visit the HEI, such as for campus-based events.

11 ☐ Adapt and use the Decision-making checklist (10a).

Prioritise

Choose between one and three of the strategies listed opposite to try out first. Enter the number given beside each strategy into the box below.

My first 3 priorities	
First choice	
Second choice	
Third choice	

Plan

Decide when you will give time and thought to your priorities.

- Jot those times into your planner or diary – or your timetable for planning towards Uni.
- In your planner, mark in a date within the next month to check that you are keeping to your plan.

Give and take support

Share your decision-making processes with others in your group.

Give serious thought to other people's approaches, considering whether these might be helpful to you too.

10a Decision-making checklist

Use the checklist below to draw together all of your decisions on applying to Uni. Look back to the relevant chapters or pages of the book.

Aspect	Page	My decision
1 When should I go to Uni?		☐ Go to Uni straight from school? ☐ Take a gap year? ☐ Wait a few years to see what I want then? ☐ Wait until I am clearer about relationships and homesickness?
2 Want to go to one of the most prestigious universities?		☐ (a) Matters a lot to me ☐ (b) Is of some importance ☐ (c) Doesn't matter to me *If (a) or (b), then complete section 3.*
3 If you are aiming at a prestigious Uni, list opposite those you are considering.		(1) (2) (3) (4) (5) (6) (7) (8) *Highlight the ONE you prefer the most.*
4 Entry requirements		For which of the HEIs that most interest me am I likely to meet the entry requirements and UCAS Tariff? (1) (2) (3) (4) (5) (6) (7) (8) *Answer section 5 below if you think you may not achieve these for HEIs that interest you.*
5 Entry schemes		Which HEIs have special entry schemes and foundation years for which I would be eligible, especially if I am not expecting to achieve their UCAS tariff?

10a Decision-making checklist (continued)

Aspect	Page	My decision
6 Mode of study		☐ Full-time ☐ Part-time *Investigate whether that mode is available for the programmes at HEIs that interest you most.*
7 Home or away?		☐ Go away to Uni ☐ Live at home ☐ Live near home ☐ Don't mind
8 Maximum travel distance		I would consider travelling up to X _____ miles from home
9 HEIs within desired travel distance		☐ Lots of choice within that range: broadly how many? _____ ☐ Relatively little choice. List the options here.
10 Reputation of the HEI for programmes I want to study		☐ (a) Matters a lot to me ☐ (b) Is of some importance ☐ (c) Doesn't matter to me *If (a) or (b), then complete section 11.*
11 The HEIs that I prefer for the quality of programmes that I want to study (list opposite)		(1) (2) (3) (4) (5) (6) (7) (8) *Highlight up to 3 that you prefer the most.*
12 Joint (or combined) honours available?		☐ (a) Matters a lot to me ☐ (b) Is of some importance ☐ (c) Doesn't matter to me *If (a) or (b), then complete section 13.*
13 HEIs that offer the joint /combined options that interest me		(1) (2) (3) (4) (5) (6) (7) (8) *Highlight up to 3 HEIs that you prefer the most for their options.*

Aspect	Page	My decision
14 Student satisfaction ratings		☐ (a) Matters a lot to me ☐ (b) Is of some importance ☐ (c) Doesn't matter to me *If (a) or (b), then complete section 15.*
15 The HEIs I prefer in terms of student satisfaction		(1) (2) (3) (4) (5) (6) *Highlight up to 3 HEIs that you prefer the most for this factor.*
16 The amount of contact time		☐ (a) Matters a lot to me ☐ (b) Is of some importance ☐ (c) Doesn't matter to me *If (a) or (b), then complete section 17.*
17 The HEIs that I prefer in terms of contact time		(1) (2) (3) (4) (5) (6) *Highlight up to 3 HEIs that you prefer the most for this factor.*
18 The teaching and assessment methods used at the Uni		☐ (a) Matter a lot to me ☐ (b) Are of some importance ☐ (c) Don't matter to me *If (a) or (b), then complete section 19.*
19 HEIs I prefer for their methods of teaching and assessment		(1) (2) (3) (4) (5) (6) *Highlight up to 3 HEIs that you prefer the most for this factor.*
20 Size of Uni (number of students)		Tick any you would consider. Put a line through the rest. ☐ large ☐ medium ☐ small

10a Decision-making checklist (continued)

Aspect	Page	My decision
21 Type of campus /location?		Tick the types that you would consider. Put a line through the rest. ☐ City-based campus ☐ City-based non-campus ☐ Town-based campus ☐ Countryside campus ☐ Uni with a college structure ☐ Local college-based HEI ☐ Delivered in the workplace ☐ Distance learning (At home) ☐ Overseas ☐ Other: *Highlight your preference.*
22 Travel time to Uni: personal preferences		How many hours would you be willing to travel from where you would live to where you would study and spend your leisure time? **Weekly** ☐ up to 5 hours ☐ 5–10 hours ☐ 10–20 hours ☐ Over 20 hours **Daily** ☐ 10–15 minutes ☐ 15–30 minutes ☐ 30–45 minutes ☐ 45–60 minutes ☐ 60–80 minutes ☐ more than 80 minutes
23 Means of transport		Investigate the student accommodation you might have and local transport arrangements to work out how you would get to the HEI for taught sessions. (Walk? Bus? Coach? Bicycle? Car?) (1) HEI _____ Travel: _____ (2) HEI _____ Travel: _____ (3) HEI _____ Travel: _____ (4) HEI _____ Travel: _____ (5) HEI _____ Travel: _____ (6) HEI _____ Travel: _____ *Highlight your preferences.* Put a line through any HEI for which the travel requirements would be impracticable for you.

10a Decision-making checklist (continued)

Aspect	Page	My decision
24 Travel time to Uni/ college from short-listed HEIs		Of the HEIs that you are considering, how much travel time is likely to be involved each week from where you would be living to where you would study and spend your leisure time? (1) HEI _____ Travel a day/week _____ (2) HEI _____ Travel a day/week _____ (3) HEI _____ Travel a day/week _____ (4) HEI _____ Travel a day/week _____ (5) HEI _____ Travel a day/week _____ (6) HEI _____ Travel a day/week _____ *Highlight those where the travel demands would suit you best.*
25 Daily travel costs?		Of the HEIs that you are considering, how much would you spend on weekly travel from where you would be living to where you would study and spend your leisure time? (1) HEI _____ Weekly travel costs _____ (2) HEI _____ Weekly travel costs _____ (3) HEI _____ Weekly travel costs _____ (4) HEI _____ Weekly travel costs _____ (5) HEI _____ Weekly travel costs _____ (6) HEI _____ Weekly travel costs _____ *Highlight those where the travel costs would suit you best.*
26 The reputation of the HEI for the quality of its facilities		☐ (a) Matters a lot to me ☐ (b) Is of some importance ☐ (c) Doesn't matter to me *If (a) or (b), then complete section 27.*
27 The HEIs that I prefer for the quality of their facilities		(1) (2) (3) (4) (5) (6) *Highlight up to 3 HEIs whose facilities you prefer the most.*

10a Decision-making checklist (continued)

Aspect	Page	My decision
28 Fees and financial support packages		☐ (a) Matters a lot ☐ (b) Matters to some extent ☐ (c) Not very relevant to my choice *If (a) or (b), then complete section 29.*
29 Best overall financial support packages		(1) HEI _____ Fee _____ Total support: _____ (2) HEI _____ Fee _____ Total support: _____ (3) HEI _____ Fee _____ Total support: _____ (4) HEI _____ Fee _____ Total support: _____ (5) HEI _____ Fee _____ Total support: _____ (6) HEI _____ Fee _____ Total support: _____ *Highlight the best overall financial support package for you.*
30 Reputation of the HEI for graduate employment		☐ (a) Matters a lot to me ☐ (b) Is of some importance ☐ (c) Doesn't matter to me *If (a) or (b), then complete section 31.*
31 HEIs I prefer for their record of graduate employment		(1) (2) (3) (4) (5) (6) *Highlight up to 3 HEIs that you prefer the most for employability.*
32 Timetabling of classes enables me to work part-time		☐ (a) Matters a lot ☐ (b) Matters to some extent ☐ (c) Not very relevant to my choice *If (a) or (b), then complete section 33.*
33 Which HEIs' timetabling supports part-time work?		(1) (2) (3) (4) (5) (6)
34 Availability of suitable local part-time jobs		☐ (a) Matters a lot ☐ (b) Matters to some extent ☐ (c) Not very relevant to my choice *If (a) or (b), then complete section 35.*

Aspect	Page	My decision
35 HEIs where there are good chances of gaining suitable local part-time jobs		(1) (2) (3) (4) (5) (6) *Highlight up to 3 with the best local opportunities.*
36 Quality and cost of accommodation		☐ (a) Matters a lot ☐ (b) Matters to some extent ☐ (c) Not very relevant to my choice *If (a) or (b), then complete section 37.*
37 HEIs I prefer for their arrangements for student accommodation		(1) (2) (3) (4) (5) (6) *Highlight up to 3 HEIs that best match your requirements.*
38 Other key characteristics important to you (1):		Which HEIs best meet this requirement? (1) (2) (3) (4) (5) (6) *Highlight up to 3 that best match your requirements.*
39 Other key characteristics important to you (2):		Which HEIs best meet this requirement? (1) (2) (3) (4) (5) (6) *Highlight up to 3 HEIs that best match your requirements.*
40 Other key characteristics important to you (3):		Which HEIs best meet this requirement? (1) (2) (3) (4) (5) (6) *Highlight up to 3 HEIs that best match your requirements.*

10b Drawing your thoughts and findings together

Aspect	My thoughts and decisions
1 What kinds of Uni could I see myself at?	
2 What kinds of Uni definitely wouldn't suit me?	
3 Am I restricting my options too much by considering only subjects that I have heard about?	
4 Am I letting any other of my requirements restrict my options and/or my chance of gaining a place?	
5 Have I considered fully all issues that might be important for me once at Uni?	
6 What are emerging for me as the most important deciding factors in choosing an HEI?	
7 Which HEIs are emerging as the front-runners for me?	
8 What will I do if I don't get into my first choice?	

11 Making your application

UCAS | Tariff | **Informed** | Entry requirements | **Timely** | **Forms** | **Part-time** | **Full-time** | **Tests** | **Coherence** | Balance | Personal Statements | Interest | **Selection** | Reasons | **Values** | **Experience** | **Skills** | **Depth** | **Knowledge** | **References** | **Qualifications** | Interviews | Matriculation | **Personalised** | Qualities | **Potential** | **Individuality** | **Presentation** | **Personality** | **Convincing** | **Commitment** | Direct entry | Grade predictions | Foundation years | **Access schemes**

This chapter

This chapter helps you to:

→ find out how to apply for a place in higher education;

→ consider Access schemes and foundation years that may help you to gain a place at Uni;

→ appreciate the importance of making a good personal statement;

→ understand what contributes to a good personal statement;

→ recognise the value of preparing as early as possible towards making your application, developing your potential so that this can be recognised more easily by Admissions tutors.

11.1 What students wish they had known ...

Three years ago, this four thought they had the Uni application process covered.

◁ **Arun** *I have spent ages looking up all the facts about loads of Unis – I think I have found the perfect match for me.*

◁ **Barbara** *I have to get into this Uni. I really, really, really want it so they have to select me.*

◁ **Colm** *You can make a part-time application much later in the year so there is no rush.*

◁ **Pauli** *Who wouldn't want me as a student – I'm great.*

Three years later and our Uni wannabes have all found places at last.

◁ **Arun** *I put all my time into working out the best Uni for me. I didn't really think of how I would make the Uni see I was the best student for them. I didn't get into my first choices and I think that's because I undersold myself.*

◁ **Barbara** *I didn't get offered a place the first time round. My teacher says I didn't present good reasons about why I thought the Uni and the course were great or what I would bring to them myself. So 'wanting' isn't enough!*

◁ **Colm** *I left it too late. For the course I wanted, there was a lot of competition for places and they had all been filled when I applied. I had to wait a year.*

◁ **Pauli** *My friend got a scholarship to Uni. They told him they were impressed with his personal statement. He had told them all about how he helped out with his mum being ill and stuff like that. I am a carer too but I wanted to keep that private.*

What can you learn from them?
- Jot down a list of the things these students may wish they had known about applying to Uni before they made their application?
- What kinds of ideas does this give you about things to do now?

11.2 Meeting the entry requirements

For each HEI and programme that interests you, check carefully on their website and/or the UCAS website to find out the entry requirements.

Qualifications

Check that you have, or are working towards achieving:

- the required grades,
- in all the required subjects,
- at all levels, including GCSE,
- in accepted qualifications.

Don't assume that the requirements will be the same for similar programmes either at that HEI or at other HEIs.

Matriculation

Check the qualifications and grades you need to matriculate (join the Uni). These may be different from the requirements for the programme.

Programme requirements

These may be different from the matriculation requirement. For example, the HEI may ask for a minimum of 5 GCSEs at A–C, but the programme may require at least a grade B in maths or that you have a science subject.

Other entry requirements

Look out for other requirements, such as:

- entrance exams;
- work experience;
- portfolios of work;
- music exams.

Not likely to have the right qualifications or grades?

Many HEIs offer alternative pathways into higher education for students who do not have standard entry requirements. They may consider:

- personal and educational circumstances;
- access and special entry schemes (see below);
- certain overseas qualifications;
- the work and life experience of adult students returning to education.

Their admissions policies will provide the details, or you could speak to the Admissions tutors.

Access and other special entry schemes

HEIs often provide Access, foundation years or other entry schemes for applicants who demonstrate potential but who do not expect to achieve the entry requirements. Typically, these are offered to those who are:

- the first of their family to enter higher education from school (apart from siblings);
- from areas or schools where few people gain good GCSE results or go on to higher education;
- from families where the household income is below £25,000 per year.

> ### 'Go see' activity: Entry requirements
>
> For each HEI and programme that interests you, check carefully that you have, or are working towards achieving, the entrance requirements. If relevant to you, check carefully for details of Access and other entry schemes. The resource sheet on page 126 may help you to keep track of this information.

11.3   Making your application

Applying via UCAS for full-time study

Once you log on via your school or college, you can start to make your application. You can add to it, make changes and refine it before sending. Redraft it and proofread carefully. You provide:

- personal details;
- details of all exams and qualifications;
- your 5 choices of HEI;
- your personal statement.

There is an administrative charge of around £20.

Tutor reference and grade predictions

Your tutor or teacher will provide a reference about your academic record, character, extra-curricular activities, personal development and suitability for the programme. You do not usually get to see it.

The school predicts the grades that you are likely to receive. Use these as a guide when checking whether you are likely to meet entry requirements (unless you may be eligible for certain foundation year programmes and Access schemes).

Key dates

From September: You can apply for the following year's entry. Courses can fill before the deadline so it is worth applying early on.

15th October: For applications to Oxford, Cambridge, medicine, veterinary medicine and veterinary science, and dentistry. You may need to take entry tests for these subjects.

By 15th January: Applications must be in for equal consideration. Later applications may still be considered.

See Appendices 1 and 2 for a full list of key dates and a timeline to count down to Uni.

Tracking your application

You will receive a personal number. Use this to log on and track responses from the 5 HEIs you chose.

Applying directly for part-time study

Applications are made directly to the HEI. Contact them for an application form, or complete one on-line.

Understanding and commitment

Many programmes expect you to show your understanding of what the programme or career area will involve and your commitment to it. For example:

Medicine, veterinary, caring professions, law: these expect you to have worked in a relevant role or environment, such as through a part-time or holiday job, paid or voluntary, in the UK or abroad.

Fine art: looks at the strength and range of your portfolio, including art work undertaken outside of class.

Performing arts such as music, dance and drama: these look at how far you have engaged in performance, and your level of skill.

11.4 Personal statements

Along with your qualifications, the personal statement is one of the most important parts of your application and not one to rush. See chapter 25 on how to prepare early so that you have interesting things to include within your personal statement.

What do Admissions staff look for?

Page 120 looked at some of the things that Admissions staff at the HEI will look for in students' applications. Most will also put considerable weight on the personal statement. The value placed on this varies, depending on such factors as:

- the programme's admissions policies and entry requirements;
- the expectations and nature of the programme;
- what the HEIs or programmes want to see in their future graduates.

Who would you choose? (1)

Below are some examples of the kinds of things applicants include within their personal statements.

- Which TWO do you think the Uni is most likely to choose? Jot down your reasons why.
- Which ONE are they most likely to reject: jot down your reasons.
- Do your friends agree with your choices?

Compare your views with those on page 299.

Chelsea

I am very keen to study at this college because it has a reputation for fantastic sports facilities and I have also always wanted to live in London. I am an athlete and run the 400 and 800 metres at county level. I would like to take part in the next Olympics and my training routine will be an important part of my life at college. I would be proud to represent the college in track events and feel I would be a good ambassador for the college in the future.

I am currently studying modern history, French and English. I am applying for history as I find that easiest but I am flexible and would be happy to study French or Psychology too. They are all very interesting subjects.

Chelsea is expected to achieve ABB grades at A level, with an A in History.

Ben

I believe that a society needs to understand its past if it wants to understand the present. I have always valued our history lessons and have long wanted to read history at university. In recent years, I have derived great enjoyment finding out about the second world war as part of my A level studies. I would greatly welcome the opportunity to study history at a university with such an excellent research record in the subject. I would like to do a project or dissertation on this as part of my degree studies.

At present, I am also studying French and Geography. I have been fascinated by the work of Molière who we are studying for French. As well as the set text, Don Juan, I have also read several others of Molière's plays. I love reading and so it has been a pleasure to extend my reading into French.

Ben is expected to achieve ABD grades.

Arlene

I would be grateful if you would give serious consideration to my application as I really, really want to study History at this University more than anything in the world. I am probably the most enthusiastic student that you could wish for. I am dedicated to my A level study (History, French and English) and am expected to get high grades. I would work even harder at Uni and can guarantee that I would get a first class degree.

I am very committed to the study of history, which I believe is under-valued by society. I sincerely believe that we need to study our past if we are to make sense of our own times. We are all creatures in history and of history, so studying history is also a study of ourselves.

Arlene is expected to achieve BCD grades, with a B in History.

Marcus

Three years ago, my family took refuge from the rain inside the People's Museum in Edinburgh. I had never visited a museum that focused on the lives of ordinary people and, as the rain fell, I became hooked. After that visit, I hunted down everything I could find on social history. I especially loved the classic Ragged Trousered Philanthropist and The Making of the English Working Class.

I set up a history club at school. We talk about anything with a historical theme. We organised a visit to medieval buildings in Coventry, and then did research at the library to find out who lived in these in the nineteenth century. I would now like to study medieval history so as to get more of a feel for the social history of those times too and to understand how historians research that.

Marcus is expected to achieve BCC grades, with a B in History. His family's household income is less than £25,000 a year; he would be the first in his family to go to university.

Harjinder

My great grandmother assembled munitions during the second world war. She told us about this but I didn't really give it much thought as that kind of thing didn't come up when we did history at school. Then we went on a school trip to the Imperial War Museum and there was a display about this work. I was really shocked to find out how many women were not only involved in such work, but were injured and killed making grenades and other arms in that war.

This experience brought home to me that history isn't just about what is in history books and what we cover in class, but is all around us, in buildings and artefacts and people's stories. This is what prompted me to apply to study for a degree that offers options in contemporary history. I am hoping to specialise in areas that draw on oral history, film and photograph archives.

Harjinder is expected to achieve ABC grades at A level, with an A in History.

Who would you choose? (2)

Consider the same statements from the point of view of Admissions staff looking for students who meet the programme's entry requirements. The entry requirements for this programme are 3 A levels (or equivalent) with minimum grades of ACC, the grade A being in History.

See page 299 for feedback.

Who would you choose? (3)

Which two would you choose if you were an Admissions tutor looking for those who would make the greatest contribution to the HEI?

See page 299 for feedback.

Writing your personal statement

Prepare and polish

Word-process this off-line first. You have up to 4000 characters (including spaces) or 47 lines including lines left blank between paragraphs. The Apply system removes bold, italics and underlining. Edit, spell-check and proofread several times until it is polished. Then cut and paste into the Apply system. Consider ways of including information on most of the following.

Why this subject?

- What got you interested in the subject?
- Why do you want to study the subject?
- Which aspects interest you the most?
- What do you enjoy about it?

How interested are you in the subject?

- What have you done or read that demonstrates a genuine interest in the subject or programmes?

How will it help you?

- How will studying for this degree help you with your career ambitions?
- How would you make use of the knowledge, skills or experiences of the programme in the kinds of careers that interest you?

Range of experience

- What skills and qualities have you developed through experiences, work placements, part-time jobs or activities you have engaged in?
- How have you contributed to your community or to helping others?
- Include details of responsibilities that you have taken on. What made you do so?
- What other interests do you have?
- How have these all shaped you as a person or changed your view of the world?

Presentation

- Redraft your statement, fine-tuning the content and your writing style until you are happy with it.
- Proofread it carefully more than once. Look for any spelling or grammar errors.
- Admissions tutors may use the accuracy and style of your writing to help decide how well you will write for their programme – even if you have an A level in English.

11.7   Make it happen

Which strategies will I use?

Decide which of the considerations listed below would be useful to pursue in more detail. Tick all that apply. Then identify your three priorities opposite.

1 ☐ Go to the UCAS website and familiarise myself with the information about applying to Uni.

2 ☐ Identify the dates relevant to my application. Copy these and put them where I will see them.

3 ☐ Compare the entry qualifications for similar courses at several different Unis. Identify which HEIs would be realistic choices for me.

4 ☐ For HEIs that interest me, check exactly which qualifications I will need in order to matriculate.

5 ☐ Check that I am on track to achieve the qualifications and grades needed for HEIs I like.

6 ☐ Check whether I am eligible for Access schemes and foundation years.

7 ☐ Write a draft personal statement to see how strong this looks now.

8 ☐ Ask a careers adviser or other person I trust to give me feedback on my draft personal statement.

9 ☐ Consider any further work experience, activities, responsibilities or qualifications I could take on so as to strengthen my personal statement.

10 ☐ Look at the information on the relevant Uni websites to check for any details that will help me make my application.

11 ☐ If I am considering a part-time application, send off to the relevant Unis for application forms.

Prioritise

Choose between one and three of the strategies listed opposite to try out first. Enter the number given beside each strategy into the box below.

My first 3 priorities	
First choice	
Second choice	
Third choice	

Plan

Decide when you will give time and thought to your priorities.

- Use the timeline provided as Appendix 1.
- Mark into your planner or diary the key dates relevant to your own application.
- In your planner, mark in a date within the next month to check that you are on course to meet your deadlines.

Give and take support

Share findings with others in your group about the practicalities of applying to particular kinds of Uni.

Give serious thought to other people's views, considering whether these might be helpful to you too.

Resource 11a:
Which entry requirements?

Check the UCAS website or HEI websites for each programme that interests you. Take down the details exactly. You can copy this page for additional programmes.

Name of HEI	Name of Programme	GCSE requirements (or equivalents)	A level requirements (or equivalents)	Other entry requirements (e.g. work experience)	Access/ Entry schemes
1					
2					
3					
4					
5					
6					

A picture of Uni

The following pages include photos to help give you
a feel for life in higher education.

Key to photos featured on pages 128–31:

1 University of Sheffield | 2 Royal Holloway, University of London |
3 Durham University | 4 University of St Andrews | 5 Manchester
Metropolitan University | 6 Anglian Ruskin University |
7 University of Chichester | 8 University of Leicester |
9 University of Gloucestershire | 10 University of Ulster
| 11 The Courtauld Institute of Art | 12 University of Sussex
| 13 Leeds Metropolitan University | 14 University of Exeter |
15 University of Bolton | 16 SOAS, University of London | 17 Oxford
Brookes University | 18 University of Derby | 19 University
of Sunderland | 20 King's College London | 21 Loughborough
University | 22 Teesside University | 23 Swansea University

A picture of Uni

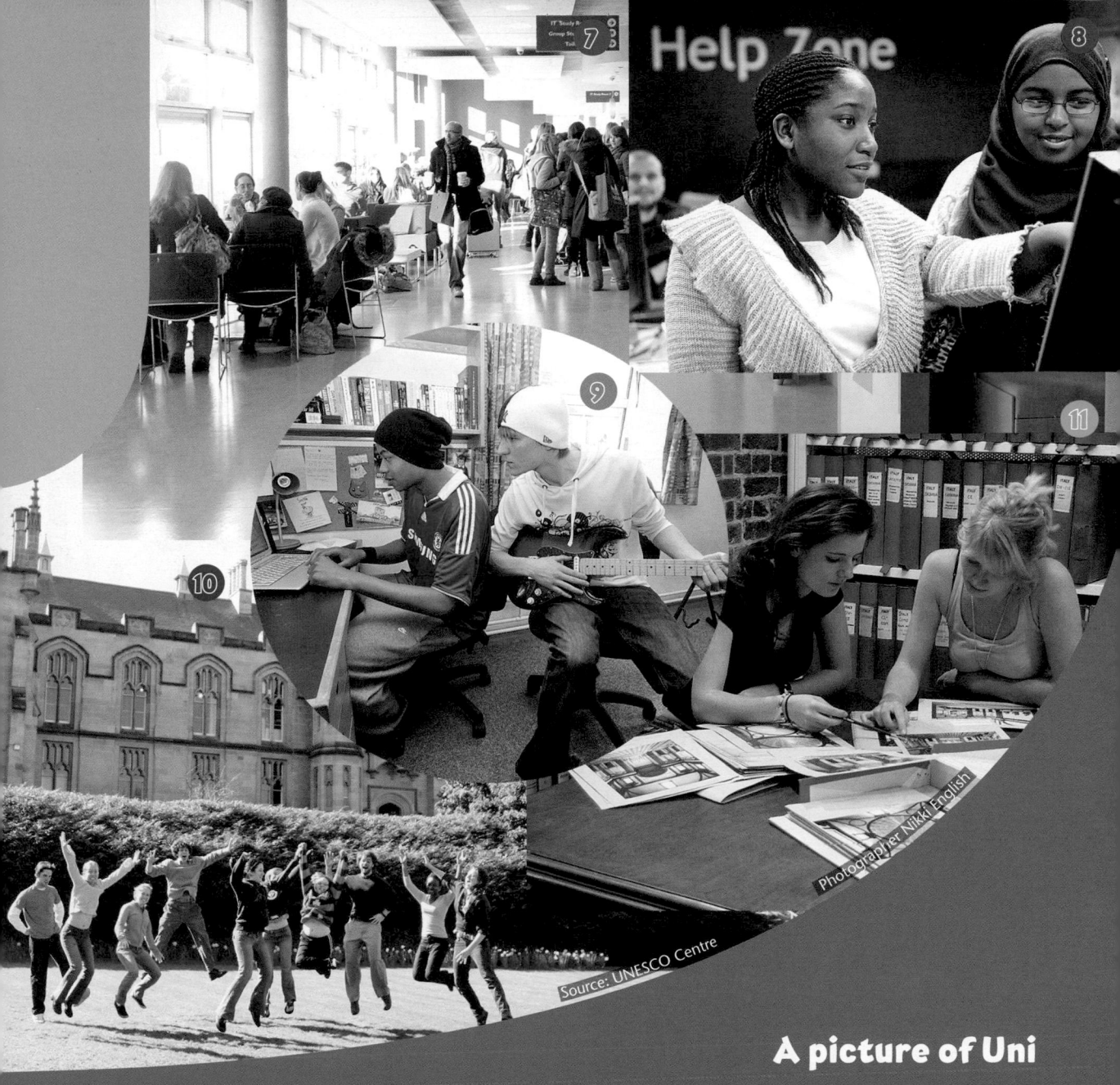

Help Zone

Source: UNESCO Centre

Photographer Nikki English

A picture of Uni

129

A picture of Uni

Photographer: Alfredo Falvo

A picture of Uni

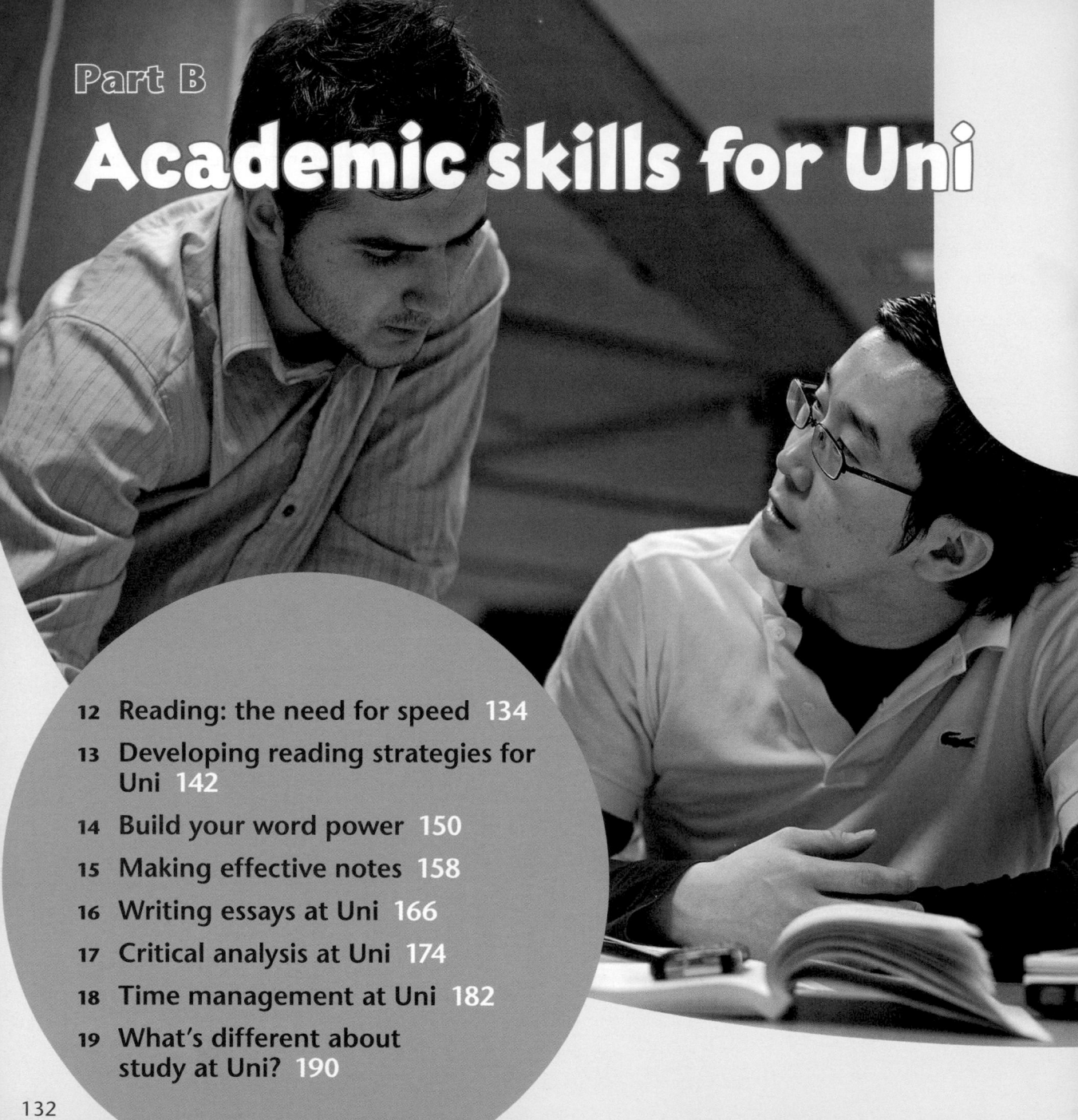

Part B

Academic skills for Uni

Introduction to Academic skills for Uni

Not a complete break ...

Once you enter higher education, it is probable that you will be able to draw very helpfully on the expertise that you are developing now as you study for your current qualifications.

More at every level ...

Nonetheless, the academic skills required at every level of study are greater than those at the previous level. This means that, when you go to Uni, you will notice increased demands being made on your academic skills. You may also note that these are greater for every year, or level, that you study. This will be reflected in higher levels of difficulty and complexity in the assignments that you are set and the marking criteria used.

It comes as a surprise ...

The majority of students surveyed (see page 2) feel under-prepared for academic work required at Uni. It can often feel like a great leap to the new level required.

This can make the first few months less enjoyable than they could be. It can be stressful to develop skills at speed in order to complete early assignments on time. Those who excel at school can find it disappointing if they don't automatically do so at Uni.

Most students do fine ...

Be reassured that, despite their initial reactions to the new levels of academic requirements, most students come through this and raise their game.

Make it easier on yourself

Put in place solid foundations for higher education

You can make it easier to settle into higher education, academically, through doing some groundwork now.

This section is not the equivalent of a study skills book that you would use once at Uni. Instead, it looks at underlying skills and habits, such as:

- building your familiarity with reading and writing at speed;
- developing your word power;
- taking charge of your own learning capacity;
- sharpening the way that you think.

These make it easier to develop study skills effectively once at Uni.

And it may help your current study

Building your academic skills in this way in preparation for higher education can also help you to do better in your current studies.

12 Reading: the need for speed

Amount | Frequency | **Fluency** | Books | **Word Recognition** | Sense | **Deadlines** | **Lists** | **Accuracy** | **Complexity** | Vocabulary | Meaning | Understanding | **Purpose** | Significance | **Journals** | **Range** | **Background** | **Articles** | **Interest** | **Selection** | Enjoyment | Comprehension | Discussion | **Digital** | Jargon | **Scanning** | **Anticipating** | **Barriers** | **Variety** | **Specialist** | **SKILLS** | Browsing | **Time scales** | Information | **Find** | Choices | **Breadth** | **Thought** | **Efficiency**

This chapter

This chapter helps you to:

→ look at what first year students wish they had known about the reading demands at Uni – before they got there;

→ gain a sense of the reading required at Uni;

→ find out why 'reading speed' is important at Uni;

→ understand what affects reading speed;

→ consider what may be slowing down your own reading;

→ identify things you could do now to start improving your reading speed.

12.1 What students wish they had known …

Three years ago, reading for Uni was but a distant dream for this smiling four.

◁ **William** *I'll have to read at Uni but I have other things to do right now.*

◁ **Kian** *I don't mind reading. I do a bit every now and again.*

◁ **Siobhan** *I read at least two books a week – and ten once on holiday. Murder mysteries, romances, vampires – I devour them.*

◁ **Lim** *I read every word in our course books. I don't want to miss anything.*

Three years later, and we discover them racing through texts.

◁ **William** *I knew there would be loads of reading to do, but I hadn't realised just how much. It was daunting at first. The up side is that when you read a lot, you do get faster.*

◁ **Kian** *You have to cover the reading list pretty quickly. If not, you can't finish your next assignments and they don't extend the deadlines. You need to get really smart at finding the best information across lots of books and journals.*

◁ **Siobhan** *When I started at Uni, I found I was reading really slowly because I didn't know all the academic jargon. It was pretty hard going but I got used to the way they write in my subject and then it was much easier.*

◁ **Lim** *I worked out that I used over a 100 books and 20 articles last year. I say 'used', rather than 'read', as I only read the introduction of one book, a chapter in another, that sort of thing. You have to get good at browsing and spotting the bits you need. You can't read it all.*

What can you learn from them?

- Jot down a list of the things these students may wish they had known about the reading demands at Uni before they arrived.
- What kinds of ideas does this give you about things to do to change your approach to reading before going to Uni?

12.2 The need for speedy reading at Uni

Reading speed matters because of:
1 The amount of reading
2 The kind of reading
3 The time scale for reading
4 Reading around the subject

1 The amount of reading

Typically, at Uni, for every piece of marked work you do, you are given a reading list that consists of the following items.

Overviews: One or more books that provide a broad overview of the topic. You would need to read some or parts of these.

Specialist books: Between 2 and 10 specialist books that look at aspects of the topic. You would usually skim these and select parts to read in depth.

Journal articles: Several articles, each focusing on a key development in the research, theory or practice in your subject. Each would contribute a small piece to the jigsaw of what you need to know for that assignment.

Websites, papers and documents: Depending on your subject, you might read web-based material, historical or legal documents; media sources or conference papers.

Although there may be some areas of overlap, it is likely that each assignment will focus on a distinct topic. The sheer amount means that you need to work quickly and smartly or you won't have time for anything else.

You will also have to read many other things, from on-line catalogues and course administration documents, to learning materials provided by the tutor, and interactive materials used for group work.

2 The kind of reading

At least some of your weekly reading will call upon the work of experts within the field. The level of specialist vocabulary and content will probably mean that this reading is time-intensive. You would need to read selectively in order to work through it within a reasonable time-frame.

3 The time scales for reading

The deadlines for handing in assignments cannot usually be extended just because you haven't finished the necessary reading.

4 Reading around the subject

You are expected to read generally around the subject, making your own selection from what you find available in the library, bookshops and on-line. This gives your work an individual stamp that can help you gain higher marks. You need to be able to read quickly to do justice to this aspect of your studies.

12.3   What slows reading speed?

There are many reasons why your reading may be slower than it needs to be. Some of the main ones are listed below.

1 Reading rarely

The less you read, the longer it takes to recognise words and the fewer words you may recognise at speed. If you have not read a great deal up until now, then reading may feel more of a chore until you start to develop a reading habit.

> **Is this true of me?**
> If so, how does it affect my reading?

2 Not recognising words

If you can't recognise a word quickly, it creates work for the brain to match the look of the word with the sound of the letters and to come up with a possible option. If your brain chooses the wrong match, the text may become nonsense.

> **Is this true of me?**
> If so, how does it affect my reading?

3 Stop-and-start

If you keep re-reading individual words and phrases, this takes up more time. Such re-reading also creates a stop-and-start effect that makes it harder for your brain to put the words together in a way that makes sense – as the text here shows.

The square on the, on the, hypotenuse, the hypotenuse is equal ... equal to the, the square, equal the square, square on the other two, the other two, two sides.

> **Is this true of me?**
> If so, how does it affect my reading?

4 No clear purpose

If you are reading without a clear sense of what you are looking for, everything you read can appear to be of equal relevance. This creates more work for your brain as it may try to hold onto everything it reads in case something becomes relevant later.

Conversely, if you are not reading to find out anything in particular, your brain may decide that nothing is relevant and fail to take in anything at all. If so, you may find that you remember nothing when you finish reading, even if you read the same piece several times.

> **Is this true of me?**
> If so, how does it affect my reading?

5 Boredom

Reading without a purpose or for too long can make it hard to find enjoyment in what you are reading. Your brain will be fighting the activity if it doesn't find it interesting.

Finished! No idea what it was all about though

> **Is this true of me?**
> If so, how does it affect my reading?

6 Other reasons

Other typical reasons for slow reading are:

- weak vocabulary;
- taking too many notes;
- reading every word;
- not enjoying solitary study activities;
- eyes getting tired easily.

> **Are any of these true of me?**
> If so, how do they affect my reading?

12.5 Build reading speed: Things I can do now

You can start to build your reading speed from now by adopting some or all of the strategies suggested in this and the next chapter.

1 Read rarely?

Build your reading stamina

- Increase the number of times you read each week.
- Every week, set yourself longer reading sessions than the week before.
- Set yourself a higher number of pages to read each time.

Find things you enjoy reading

You need to read a lot to build your reading speed, so you may as well enjoy it.

2 Not recognising words quickly?

Combine audio and text

Look for material that is available to you both as an audio-file and as text. Listen to the audio-file, then read the same material. This can help build word recognition.

'the aesthetic ramification of such architectural deceits …'

Read every day

- Your brain gets used to seeing familiar words, and processes them faster.
- The more you read, the more words become familiar.

3 Stop-and-start

'deceits'? It must mean things aren't what they appear, so …

Read bigger chunks

Read more before pausing, even if you don't understand all the words. Use the context to help you second guess what is written, then check back to see if you were right.

Browse the words

Check that you know what all the words are. Work out what these are and what they mean before reading.

Record and listen

Separate out the two processes of reading text and drawing out the meaning. Record yourself reading. Play this back to pick out the message and key points.

4 No clear purpose

Setting the focus

Each time you sit down to read, clarify for yourself what you want to achieve. Give yourself a purpose. For example:

- to check which parts of a chapter are useful for this week's homework;
- to browse a chapter quickly to see what it is about;
- to find out the best sections of the book to read for topics you will cover this term – jot down details of these;
- to re-read a difficult section to understand better what it means;
- to find a particular piece of information;
- to work out what motivates a character in the book;
- to answer a list of questions you have drawn up;
- to see how a chapter ends.

5 Boredom

Boredom is usually the result of reading in a passive way – your brain doesn't feel sufficiently engaged.

Little but often

Decide how much time you will spend reading in the day. Divide this into several bursts. Set a time to start each – and keep to it.

Reading quests

Set yourself quests to provide more interest to your reading. Jot down a list of three or more pieces of information to find out each time you sit down to read.

Set yourself challenges

Get used to setting your own challenges for reading – such as reading a certain number of pages in 20 minutes.

Read with others

Discussing your views about what you read can add to the interest.

6 Other reasons for slow reading

Weak vocabulary

Building your vocabulary can increase your reading speed and make you feel more confident. See chapter 14.

Taking too many notes

If you write many notes as you read, this can slow you down for a number of reasons. See chapter 15 for effective strategies for making notes when reading.

Reading every word

You don't always have to read every word – there are short cuts. See chapter 13 for reading strategies for Uni.

Not enjoying solitary study activities

Reading activities with other people can add focus and enjoyment.

Eyes getting tired easily

This may be eye strain – it is worth seeing an optician to have this checked out.

12.7   Make it happen

Which strategies will I use?

Decide which of the strategies suggested in the chapter above could help you to build your reading speed. Tick all that apply.

1 ☐ Build my reading stamina.
2 ☐ Find things I enjoy reading.
3 ☐ Combine audio and text.
4 ☐ Read every day.
5 ☐ Read bigger chunks.
6 ☐ Browse the words first.
7 ☐ Record and listen.
8 ☐ Set myself a focus.
9 ☐ 'Little but often'.
10 ☐ Set reading quests.
11 ☐ Set myself challenges.
12 ☐ Build my vocabulary.
13 ☐ Take notes in a different way.
14 ☐ Not reading word by word.
15 ☐ Set reading activities with other people.
16 ☐ Visit an optician to check my eyes are OK.

Prioritise

Choose between one and three of the strategies listed opposite to try out first. Enter the number given beside each strategy into the box below.

My first 3 priorities	
First choice	
Second choice	
Third choice	

Plan

Decide when you will give time and thought to your priorities.
- Jot those times into your planner or diary – or your timetable for planning towards Uni.
- In your planner, mark in a date within the next month to check what is working.

Experiment

Once you have used your first set of strategies, have a go with a new set. See which ones suit you best.

Give and take support

Share your ideas with others in your group.
Post comments about strategies you find helpful.

---

13 Developing reading strategies for Uni

Enjoyment | Focus | **Interpretation** | Selection | **Style** | **Meaning** | **Effectiveness** | **Choosing** | **Management** | **Application** | Need | Deciding | Relevance | **Making Sense** | Similarities | **Evaluation** | **Quality** | **Independent** | **Charting** | Noting | **Juggle** | Quality | Purpose | Analysis | **Critique** | Reasoning | **Texts**

This chapter

In this chapter you can:

→ find out more about the reading demands made at Uni;

→ gain a sense of why it is a good idea to start developing reading skills early, so as to build these over time;

→ look at things you can do now to start building your reading speed ready for Uni;

→ choose strategies that you think are most relevant to you.

Three years ago, this studious four were so blissfully oblivious of what reading would mean for them in the future …

◁ **Kyle** *Everything you need is on Wikipedia – what's the grief?!*

◁ **Freya** *I already read what the teachers tell us to – no problem.*

◁ **Waheed** *I read texts and tweets all the time – reading one thing is pretty much like reading another.*

◁ **Soraya** *I've been reading since I was 6. I think I know my way round a book by now!*

Now they are at Uni, and those grim faces don't suggest happy readers …

◁ **Kyle** *I used a brilliant book – but they marked my first essay down as you have to refer to lots of sources for every piece of work – not just one!*

◁ **Freya** *We had to choose a topic for our reports and create our own reading lists. I read loads but I just used the first things I found. Then the tutor told me these weren't good quality sources.*

◁ **Waheed** *I am sure I read the same thing ten times in ten different books. Not sure I get the point of this … !*

◁ **Soraya** *I have read so much! It all sounds good to me. I can't use it all! How do I decide what to include? My head hurts!*

What can you learn from them?

- Jot down a list of the things these students may wish they had known about the reading demands at Uni before they arrived.
- What kinds of ideas does this give you about things to do now?

13.2 Effective reading skills for Uni

Effective reading at Uni isn't mainly about how fast you read – although that is part of it. It is more about being able to juggle the following aspects of reading quickly and accurately.

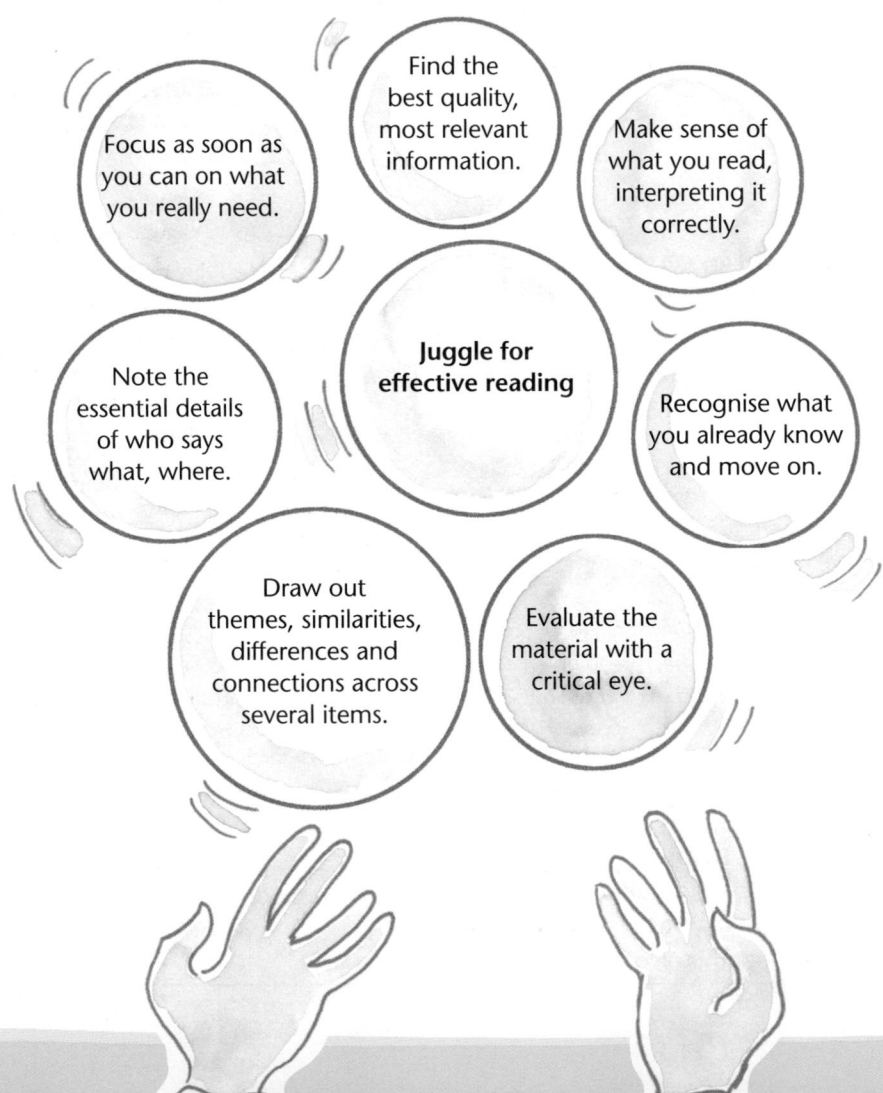

Focus as soon as you can on what you really need.

Find the best quality, most relevant information.

Make sense of what you read, interpreting it correctly.

Note the essential details of who says what, where.

Juggle for effective reading

Recognise what you already know and move on.

Draw out themes, similarities, differences and connections across several items.

Evaluate the material with a critical eye.

13.3 Effective reading skills for Uni (2)

Best quality, most relevant information

HEIs pride themselves on training students to study independently at the cutting edge of knowledge. This means that, usually, it won't be enough to read just the first thing you come across or a general source such as Wikipedia or thoughts in someone's blog. For Uni, you need to be good at finding and selecting reading material that is:

- up to date;
- written by experts who are acknowledged as such by other leading experts in the field;
- the most applicable to the question you are trying to answer;
- found by you through your own searches in the library and on-line – not just what is on the reading list.

Make sense of what you read

In practice, this means getting the basics right:

- learning specialist vocabulary;
- reading many specialist texts so that you get used to that style of writing;
- taking care to check exactly what is written and intended;
- making sure that your reading and notes are accurate – and going back to check if something doesn't seem to make sense.

At Uni, this really means thinking through what you are reading, making sure that you understand what it means in terms of what you know about the subject already and what other people have written. You need to understand the implications of what you read as well as the exact words on the page.

Recognise what you know – and move on

Many of the sources you use will cover similar ground although from different perspectives or with different emphases. You may find that all the books on your reading list summarise the same background research before focusing on their specific specialism or angle.

It can be helpful to see the same issues written in different ways – this can make the subject more understandable or bring out different points of view. However, it will save you a lot of time if you do the following.

- Read in ways that help you recognise what you have already read – making your own notes helps you to do this.
- Have the confidence to skip the material that you recognise without worrying about doing so.
- Remain focused on the task and don't become absorbed in searches and material that are not strictly relevant to the task in hand.

13.4 Effective reading skills for Uni (3)

Focus early on what you really need

When you start to search for material, you may find hundreds of items that look relevant. Some may look very dense and off-putting, at least at first. You will need to develop good skills in:

- browsing for what is available;
- finding a manageable number of items to look at;
- selecting the right sections to read;
- picking out what is really essential.

Draw out themes, similarities, differences, connections ...

It would be unusual for you to be able to rely on a single course-book or item for any assignment. It is assumed that you will:

- read parts of many items on your reading list, using these as a starting point;
- use the bibliographies and references in these and other books, and look up at least one or two that interest you;
- watch out for themes and trends that emerge across several books and journals;
- identify when and why there are strong differences in points of view.

In other words, you have to read in an active and joined up way, comparing and contrasting material as you go.

Evaluate the material with a critical eye

It can be easy to assume that if something has been published, or presents plausible tables of data, it must be right. However, knowledge is advanced, in part, by people:

- not taking anything at face value;
- checking things for themselves;
- asking searching questions about whether there could be a different story to explain what seems apparent at first view.

This is the approach to reading that you are expected to take at Uni. You do not need to create endless useless questions or assume that everything you read is wrong, but you do need to bring a questioning approach. You will need to balance skills in reading quickly with time spent reflecting on what you are finding out as you read.

Note 'who' says 'what', 'where'

Keep clear and full details of:

- the author;
- the title of the publication;
- when it was published;
- the name of the publisher and where it was published;
- the page numbers of points you note.

You will need this information:

- to help you find things again easily as needed;
- and to write references in ways that are required at Uni (see page 170).

13.5　Things I can do now ...

Find the best quality, most relevant information

Soraya has all the books out again!

Develop the habit of looking for more

When you are given reading to do, go to your school or college library and browse the range of materials that refer to that subject. Read parts of at least one book that hasn't been recommended by your tutors or teachers.

Get used to judging a source quickly

Use the bibliography or references

These tell you the sources that the author has drawn upon to write the book. Has the author read much about the subject? Have they written anything else on the subject themselves? Do they refer to journals?

Check out the author

Use the internet to see if there is anything there that indicates that the author is an expert, and if other people value their work on that subject.

Focus quickly on what you really need

Create a focus list

Jot down a list of questions to which you want answers. Use these to guide what you read and what you skip.

- *How many kinds of volcano?*
- *A good example of each kind?*
- *What makes one volcano different from another?*

 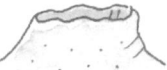 

Recognise what you already know and move on

Pause to register the points

Pause frequently as you read, to make a mental note of the key points so as to help future recall.

Summarise and note

Summarise and note what you read, to help you check back on what you have covered already.

Use good note-taking strategies

This will help you check quickly (see chapter 15).

Make sense of what you read, interpreting it correctly

Put down the book and summarise

Get used to putting down the book from time to time so that you can check that you are really making sense of what you are reading. Speak aloud, or jot down, what you have read. If you can't do that, this suggests you haven't yet grasped the material sufficiently. Go back over it in smaller chunks, making sense of each. Then summarise the whole.

Talk it through aloud

Tell someone else what is interesting about what you have been reading. By saying it aloud, you may soon find that there are points that you haven't fully grasped. If your audience is puzzled and you can't clarify the point, this can also indicate that you need to go back over the material so that your own thinking is clear.

Draw out similarities, differences, connections ...

More than one open

- Get used to having more than one book or source open at a time.
- Choose three items (books, articles) and open them all to the pages that cover the topic you are looking at for homework.
- See how one book covers an aspect of the topic, then read about that aspect in the other two sources before moving on to read about a new aspect.

Chart the links

Design a simple outline chart or table to help keep track of similarities and differences between two or more sources. See page 163.

Evaluate with a critical eye

Consider plausible alternative explanations

For each book or source you use, jot down at least three ways that it *might* be giving only part of the story. See chapter 17.

Get used to looking for alternative sources

When you finish one source, look in the library or on-line to see if you can find a different angle on the issue. Jot down why one convinces you more than the other.

13.7 Make it happen

Which strategies will I use?

Decide which of the strategies outlined in the chapter above could help you to build skills that support your reading. Tick all that apply.

1 ☐ Develop the habit of looking for more.
2 ☐ Use the bibliography and references.
3 ☐ Check out the author.
4 ☐ Create a focus list.
5 ☐ Pause to register the points.
6 ☐ Summarise and note.
7 ☐ Use good note-taking strategies.
8 ☐ Put down the book and summarise.
9 ☐ Say it as it is.
10 ☐ More than one open.
11 ☐ Chart it.
12 ☐ Consider plausible alternative explanations.
13 ☐ Get used to looking for alternative sources.

Prioritise

Choose between one and three of the strategies listed opposite to try out first. Enter the number given beside each strategy into the box below.

My first 3 priorities	
First choice	
Second choice	
Third choice	

Plan

Decide when you will give time and thought to your priorities.

- Jot those times into your planner or diary – or your timetable for planning towards Uni.
- In your planner, mark in a date within the next month to check what is working.

Experiment

Once you have used your first set of strategies, have a go with a new set. See which ones suit you best.

> **Give and take support**
>
> Share your ideas with others in your group. Post comments about strategies you find helpful.
>
> Combine your reading with chat. Get used to discussing material that you read. Talk through the concepts that you find difficult or confusing in what you read.

14 Build your word power

Eloquence | Create | **Ease** | Fluency | **Thesaurus** | **Adjective** | **Express** | **Dictionary** | **Articulate** | **Academic** | Comprehension | Influence | Understand | **Correctness** | Language | **Persuade** | **Negotiate** | **Clarity** | **Synonym** | Verbalise | **Discussion** | Write | Succinct | Pithy | **Lucidity** | Communicate | **Exactitude** | **Confidence** | **Enunciate** | **Scholarly** | **Intellectual** | **Convince** | Argue | **Dissuade** | Precision | **Convey** | Prose | **Reason** | **Impress** | **Debate** | **Authority** | Effect | **Speak** | Inspiration | Impact | Style

This chapter

In this chapter you can:

→ test your own word power;

→ gain a sense of why it is a good idea to start building your vocabulary ready for Uni;

→ look at things you can do now to build your vocabulary;

→ choose strategies that you think are most relevant to you.

14.1 What students wish they had known ...

Three years ago, our eloquent and loquacious four thought they had all the vocabulary they would ever need.

◁ **Julie** *I can ask for fish and chips in 8 languages.*

◁ **Arun** *If I don't know a word, it ain't worth knowing.*

◁ **Soraya** *I was reading Charles Dickens when I was still in my pram. My vocabulary is probably off the hook.*

◁ **Jack** *What does vocabulary mean?*

Now they are at Uni and ... are those dictionaries open on their screens ...?

◁ **Julie** *The lecturer just whizzes through the material. Every word seems to end in '-ism' or '-ological'. It drones over my head.*

◁ **Arun** *I almost understood ten words in a row that my lecturer said today. My lecture notes are as clear as a plate of spaghetti ...*

◁ **Soraya** *I know what most words mean when I read them but I am not always sure how to use them in my own writing.*

◁ **Jack** *For our last assignment, we had to lead a discussion on-line. I thought the international students were using foreign phrases but it turned out they were using English words I didn't know. I was well embarrassed.*

What can you learn from them?
- Jot down a list of the things these students may wish they had known about developing their word power before they arrived.
- What kinds of ideas does this give you about things to do now?

Making sense of lectures

Lectures tend to move at a rapid pace. Lecturers will explain some technical words, but not all. They will expect you to develop an understanding of words you don't know.

These doctors' questions alienated their patients.

These doctors … questioned … the aliens …? Amazing!

Making notes in lectures

Your own notes of what you hear in lectures are an essential tool for helping to recall the material later. If your vocabulary is weak, your brain will have to work harder to piece together the probable sense of what is being said. When it is doing this, it can't focus on the next thing that the lecturer is saying. If this happens, you may well find that your notes are incomplete, confusing and unhelpful when you come to use them later.

Making sense of what you read

If your vocabulary is good, you are more likely to understand what you read. Reading with a smooth flow can help you to absorb larger chunks, so your brain makes sense of more information at once.

If you have to keep stopping to look up words, your reading can become disjointed and frustrating. It also eats into your total reading time.

Writing style

Almost all university programmes require excellent writing skills. A good vocabulary will be an important part of your toolkit for success at Uni. The better your vocabulary, the better you will be able to:

- select just the word you need;
- generate the words that you need at speed;
- write clearly;
- write easily, manipulating language at your ease;
- devote your study time to areas that bring you higher marks, rather than spending it making sense of your writing and notes.

Speaking

It is likely that, for some of your assignments at Uni, you will be marked for the quality of your verbal presentations. A good vocabulary will help you to:

- prepare presentations more quickly;
- understand questions you are asked;
- feel more confident about how you express yourself on the day;
- make a good impression with lecturers and employers.

14.3   How good is my vocabulary?

Read each of the following sets of sentences. In each case, decide which sentences use the target word correctly and tick the box if you think the usage is correct. For each set, all, some or none of the sentences may be correct.

1   Target word – 'elucidate'

- ☐ (a) The criminal was asked why he robbed the house but would not elucidate further.
- ☐ (b) This study will elucidate my hypothesis.
- ☐ (c) The elucidate politician would not comment on the rumours about his party.

2   Target word – 'paradigm'

- ☐ (a) The best example of medieval building is the paradigm.
- ☐ (b) The discovery of penicillin resulted in a paradigm shift in medicine.
- ☐ (c) They travelled to the island on a paradigm.

3   Target word – 'pastiche'

- ☐ (a) He was feeling hungry so bought a pastiche to eat.
- ☐ (b) The pastiche filled her perfectly and showed off her small waist to great effect.
- ☐ (c) The quickest way to reach the village was via the pastiche.

4   Target word – 'tacit'

- ☐ (a) Her lack of response suggested a tacit acceptance of his plan.
- ☐ (b) In the face of an argument, he decided his best response was to remain tacit.
- ☐ (c) Mr Evans had a tacit knowledge of his subject but found it hard to share this with his students.

5   Target word – 'aggravated'

- ☐ (a) Joe found that Ben's approach to study really aggravated him.
- ☐ (b) Lifting up the baby aggravated Massa's back injury.
- ☐ (c) His use of a gun led to his being charged with aggravated assault.

6   Target word – 'infer'

- ☐ (a) The chocolate marks around Robbina's mouth infer that it was she who stole the cookies.
- ☐ (b) When Joyce's husband died she decided to infer him in a local cemetery.
- ☐ (c) From your red face and loud voice, I infer that you are angry with me.

14.4   How good is my vocabulary? (2)

7   Target word – 'deferential'

- ☐ (a) The deferential diagnosis was bronchitis or pneumonia.
- ☐ (b) Alex solved the maths problem using a deferential equation.
- ☐ (c) The worker was deferential to her manager on company decisions.

8   Target word – 'salient'

- ☐ (a) The diagram provided the salient points of the argument.
- ☐ (b) The food had been over-seasoned and tasted too salient.
- ☐ (c) The boat had been repaired and was now completely salient.

9   Target word – 'anodyne'

- ☐ (a) Marie did not think Pierre's designs captured the spirit of the brand – they were too anodyne.
- ☐ (b) The song played at the funeral acted as an anodyne for Lewis's grief.
- ☐ (c) The electrical circuit was completed by connecting the cathode to the anodyne.

10   Target word – 'synchronous'

- ☐ (a) The thunder and lightning were almost synchronous, meaning the storm was directly overhead.
- ☐ (b) The two divers' completion of the somersault was completely synchronous, earning them top marks.
- ☐ (c) The increase in inflation was synchronous with the increase in unemployment numbers.

11   Target word – 'obviate'

- ☐ (a) The horse refused to move forwards; whatever the jockey did, it remained obviate.
- ☐ (b) The availability of internet resources does not obviate the need for students to read books.
- ☐ (c) Mira remained completely obviate to what was going on around her.

12   Target word – 'serendipity'

- ☐ (a) He wasn't considered very bright; people had always thought he was a bit serendipity.
- ☐ (b) She played the cello piece with expert serendipity and the audience was mesmerised.
- ☐ (c) No sounds of traffic or people could be heard in the serendipity of the forest.

See pages 300–1 for the answers.

14.5 Things I can do now

Take the right attitude

Welcome the opportunity to learn new words

- Aim to enjoy using new words.
- Don't be 'word-shy' or put off by new 'long' words. You probably use long words such as establishment and international with ease, yet may be less comfortable using some short words such as ion, wan, or ire.

I hate big words! They're execrable!

And me! They're inevitably incredibly bourgeois!

Read to build your own word power

Vary your reading material

When you do this ...

- You will encounter more new words.
- Your brain gets used to processing new words and will cope better with the specialised language used at Uni.
- You will build your general vocabulary. This helps you to understand what you are reading more quickly and easily.

Read more

- It builds your speed for recognising relatively new words.
- You will see how new words are used in different contexts, so that they make more sense.
- You will gain a better sense of how to use them in your own writing.

Keep a vocabulary log

Look them up and write them down

- Use a light notebook – or set up a file to record new words.
- Break the word down into segments, so that you can see clearly how it is structured – this will also help with spelling.
- Be on the look-out for good words to learn.
- Look them up in the dictionary and write their meaning in your log.
- Use the thesaurus function on your computer to check for alternatives; note interesting examples in your book.

Spot good sentences

It is easier to make use of words that you learn in the context of a new sentence.

- Google the word to see how it is used in whole sentences.
- Watch out for examples of the word being used effectively in other people's writing.
- Note these sentences in your log to help you gain a feel for their use.

14.6 Things I can do now (2)

Make words your own

Write new words in whole sentences

Invent sentences of your own that include the new words you have selected.

Create opportunities for speaking formally

We tend to speak differently in settings which are more formal or where we hold positions of responsibility.

Look for opportunities to:
- take part in school or college debates;
- be a student representative;
- take part in a play at school or for a local society;
- read to other people, such as the elderly.

Use audio-files

If you prefer to listen rather than read, then listening to good audio-files can help to develop your vocabulary. This can help you to understand academic texts more easily.

Listen for meaning

You can play back the audio-file to take notes to build up your understanding of how unfamiliar words are used, and to capture new words to look up and learn.

Listen for pronunciation

You can re-listen to audio-files several times to build your confidence with the pronunciation of unfamiliar words.

Choose:
- podcasts of TV news programmes;
- audio-books of classic texts;
- university lectures available as open sources.

Create your own recordings to build vocabulary

Once you have found or written suitable sentences to help you use new words, you can record yourself reading these. You could even sing the sentences if it helps you remember them! Play back your recordings a week later to remind yourself of the words you chose to learn.

Test your use

- Cover up the meaning of the word and see if you can recall it.
- Check whether you can recall any alternative words for it.
- Construct a sentence that uses the word. Write this down. Check whether your usage was correct. If you are not sure, ask your teacher or tutor.

spe-ci-fic cor-oll-ar-y

14.7 Make it happen

Which strategies will I use?

Decide which of the strategies outlined in the chapter above could help you to build your word power. Tick all that apply.

1 ☐ Welcome the opportunity to learn new words.
2 ☐ Vary my reading material.
3 ☐ Read more.
4 ☐ Keep a vocabulary/spelling log.
5 ☐ Use the thesaurus to identify useful alternatives.
6 ☐ Spot good sentences.
7 ☐ Write new words in whole sentences.
8 ☐ Create opportunities for speaking formally.
9 ☐ Use audio-files to understand new words.
10 ☐ Use audio-files to help pronunciation.
11 ☐ Create my own recordings to build vocabulary.
12 ☐ Test my use.

Prioritise

Choose between one and three of the strategies listed opposite to try out first. Enter the number given beside each strategy into the box below.

My first 3 priorities	
First choice	
Second choice	
Third choice	

Plan

Decide when you will give time and thought to your priorities.

- Jot those times into your planner or diary – or your timetable for planning towards Uni.
- In your planner, mark in a date within the next month to check what is working.

Experiment

Once you have used your first set of strategies, have a go with a new set. See which ones suit you best.

Give and take support

Share your ideas with others in your group. Post comments about strategies you find helpful.

Share words that you find especially curious, interesting or challenging. See who comes up with the best words – or ones that nobody else could guess!

---

15 Making effective notes

Ideas | Summary | **Personal** | Interpretation | **Notebook** | **Remember** | **Style** | **Structure** | **Handouts** | **Abbreviations** | Lectures | Reading | Brevity | **Succinct** | Individualised | **Details** | **Quotations** | **Speed** | **Recall** | **Information** | **Facts** | Listening | Engage | Understanding | **Essentials** | Balance | **Type** | Time | **Colour** | **Similarities** | **Differences** | **Permanent** | Map | Draw | Trends | **Connections** | Key | **Recall** | CONNECT | **Network** | **Pattern** | **Efficient** | **Record** | Memory

This chapter

In this chapter you can:

→ find out why it is important to be able to make your own notes;

→ gain a sense of where note-taking can help you and how it can go wrong;

→ consider different ways of making notes that work for you;

→ look at things you can do now to start developing your skills and speed at note-making.

15.1 What students wish they had known ...

Three years ago, our magnificent four had just the right amount of notes for their needs.

 ◁ **Duncan** *I don't have a problem with taking notes as long as the teacher slows down their talking or dictation when we ask.*

 ◁ **Emily** *I don't think I'll need notes – I keep it all up here, in my head!*

 ◁ **Freya** *I just note down everything in case it is useful later.*

 ◁ **Arun** *Everything I need is in the set texts – I just underline the main points. No need for notes!*

Now they are at Uni. Apparently, they really are here, somewhere, beneath those piles of notes.

 ◁ **Duncan** *The lecturers and authors say things better than I can so I just noted down exactly what they said, and then copied it into my essay. My bad. Apparently, this is a big deal and they might chuck me off my course.*

 ◁ **Emily** *When I am doing the reading, I think 'That's great! That's what I need for my essay.' Then, a few days later when I come to write it up, I can't find half the things I wanted to use.*

 ◁ **Freya** *I have ten, twenty times more notes than I need – so now I have to go through them again and make a new shorter set I can actually use.*

 ◁ **Arun** *I can't afford all the books and some you can't take out of the library. My killer strategy of highlighting the text isn't enough!*

What can you learn from them?
- Jot down a list of the things these students may wish they had known about making useful notes before they arrived at Uni.
- What kinds of ideas does this give you about things to do now?

15.2   Why note-making skills matter at Uni

Good note-making skills can be your life-saver at Uni. They can be the difference between you feeling that you are on top of your studies – or you making mistakes that mean you are not allowed to continue with your studies.

Staying on top of your studies

At Uni, you will be required to manage:

- lots of information,
- on many different matters,
- all at once,
- by yourself,
- across periods of weeks, months or sometimes years of study.

Good note-making skills can help you organise this information so you know what you need to be using, in the right ways, for the right purposes and at the right times.

Poor note-making skills mean that you can make errors in your studies, miss essential deadlines, and generally fail to remember the things that you need to do in the ways that are required.

In lectures

At Uni, you may be in lectures with hundreds of people. It will be up to you to keep up and to find out any information that you miss.

At school and college, some teachers dictate notes, or talk through their own notes, at a reasonable speed so that you can then write down your own. This can work well for your studies now but not for Uni.

- The lecturers at Uni will go at their own speeds. They tend to move through the material quickly as there is so much to cover in the time available.
- You can't generally ask lecturers to slow down or repeat a point just because you missed it.
- You are expected to listen and just jot down the key points, following these up outside of class.
- If you miss too many points, your notes won't make sense and you won't be able to follow up the material that you need after class.

For handouts

Increasingly, lecturers make a set of notes available on the departmental website or virtual learning environment. These are to ensure that you have been provided with the basic information required. They are not a substitute for making notes of your own.

For reading

You will need to develop skills in making different kinds of notes, in order to make effective use of all the material that you read as well as that covered in class. It is a skill to get the right balance.

Too many notes: eats into your time and can be boring.

Too few notes: less useful for developing understanding and recall.

15.3   How good note-making skills help at Uni

Testing your understanding

Sometimes, it can feel as though we understand the material perfectly well until we try to put it into our own words. One of the most important uses of making our own notes, rather than working from teachers' handouts, is that this tests out whether we understand the subject well enough to be able to summarise it in our own words.

It will become apparent quickly that your understanding is incomplete when you:

- copy from the book or write out long quotations from it rather than making notes in your own words;
- make too few notes on a topic because you don't know what to write.

Recalling information

Your recall of what you have read can be greatly improved by:

- the physical act of writing your notes, combined with
- the thought processes that go into deciding what to note, and how.

Tracking

At Uni, you have to prepare assignments for several tutors simultaneously, reading many books for each. This can make it hard to keep track of:

- what you have read;
- what you thought important;
- where the best material was for each assignment.

Making the right notes can help you to keep track of each book or source you use and what you wanted to remember from each.

Storing your ideas

If you jot down your thoughts as they occur to you, these will be at your fingertips when needed for assignments or class discussion.

Making the material your own

To make good notes, you need to work with the material to select the points that interest you and to summarise it in your own words. This activity helps to make the material your own. This usually helps understanding, which shines through in your assignments.

Writing speed

Writing notes on a frequent basis will develop writing speed, which will help with written exams.

Tips for making notes

☺ Keep notes brief.
☺ Date and label all notes clearly.
☺ Avoid copying from the book.
☺ Take notes that work for you – not because other people are taking notes.
☺ Look for the general gist or most important points – and note just these.
☺ Avoid taking down material word for word either in class or from audio-visual material.
☺ Highlight the most important points so that they stand out.
☺ Note exact details of 'who, what, where' for references (see pages 146 and 170).

15.4   Things I can do now

Develop the note-making habit

Put time aside at least once a week to make notes from a book relevant to one of your subjects, but which is not set reading.

- Select a section to note.
- After the first week, read through the previous weeks' notes to see how far they make sense after a week's gap.
- If they are hard to read or understand, decide how you can make this week's notes better.

Find your own style

There isn't a right way to make notes. It is up to you to decide whether you take:

- concise or lengthy notes;
- bullet points or sentences;
- diagrams, lists, charts, colours, highlights, abbreviations, or any other method that works for you;
- neat notes, messy notes or notes covered in doodles and drawings.

You will get a feel for the method that suits you. Your notes are fine as long as you:

- follow the 'golden rule' on page 163;
- can read them;
- have what you need;
- can make use of your notes when you come back to them.

Experiment with styles

Note in sentences

Write 5–10 sentences to summarise the material covered in one class you attended today or recently.

Note points/Add headers

- Write a list of the key points covered in that class.
- If there are more than 5, divide these up into groups so that no group contains more than 3–4 points.
- Give each a heading that sums it up.

List headings/Add details

- Jot down 3–6 headings that sum up the main areas covered in one class.
- Jot down around 2–5 bullet points under each, so that you add more detail about what you learnt.

Ethical consids.
a) Do no harm
b) Provide approp. Info
c) Seek consent/permiss.
d) Confidentiality/data protect
e) Debrief

Abbreviated notes

Jot down about half a page of rough notes to sum up the main things you learned on one topic you covered this term.

- Write quickly without spending too much time looking up the detail.
- Make sure you can read what you write – but don't waste time keeping these neat.
- Don't write every word in full. As long as you can remember what it means, it is fine to use abbreviations.

15.5 Things I can do now (2)

The golden rule of note-making

The golden rule of note-making is to keep your own summaries and ideas separate from any words that are taken directly from a text.

Following this rule is a must at Uni. When you hand in your work, if you made any error in presenting as your own words something taken from a book, this would be seen as cheating and could lead to expulsion from the university. The following strategies can help you to keep the golden rule.

Pen down

- Put your pen down whilst you are reading.
- Cover up the pages you were reading.
- Think carefully about what you will note, then write this down before looking again at the book.
- Before reading on, check that the way you have phrased your notes is not identical, or near-identical, to the phrasing used in the text.

Coloured inks

- Use a different colour ink or font whenever you copy text for use as a quotation.
- Keep such quotations very short – usually a phrase rather than a full sentence.
- Enclose the copied words within inverted commas: "quotation ... ".
- Write down exactly where you copied the quotation from; see page 146.

Interpret text more skilfully

Pause to interpret

- Choose a passage that you find difficult in one of your textbooks.
- Pause to think through the best way to phrase that passage in your own words.
- If necessary, look up information that helps you to make better sense of the passage.
- If you don't understand, don't write it down.

Similarity and difference

When reading several books or sources on a topic, your note-making can help you to draw out the similarities, differences and connections; see page 148.

Make a rough chart to list these easily.

BOOK	SIMILAR	DIFFER	CONNEC.
1	Chinese data	1985s data	
2		2003 data French data	BK2 develops the social theory of bK1
3	Chinese data	2011 data	

15.6 Things I can do now (3)

Keep an ideas book

Keep a small notebook on you at all times, to jot down the ideas that occur to you. You can start to do this now. Use it to jot down thoughts on:

- things you want to find out about Uni;
- skills to develop before Uni;
- things you could include in your application to Uni;
- how you can make your next piece of homework or class assignment stand out from everyone else's.

Note it just once

Choose 3 books on the same topic.

- Take brief notes on each book, using the method that you prefer.
- Before taking notes from the 2nd and 3rd books, check back over your notes to remind yourself of information you have already noted.
- Don't take down the same information twice. Once you recognise material covered in your notes, move on.
- Read back over your notes to check for repetition.

Use audio-visual material

Watch and note

Develop your skills in making notes when listening and taking in visual material by making use of TV programmes viewable on-line. You could use:

- BBC iplayer
- ITVplayer
- 4ondemand
- iTunes U

- Watch the first 10 minutes. Jot down the key points as you watch.
- Watch the same 10 minutes again to see whether you captured the main points. If not, consider why you may have missed some. For example, was it harder when two people were speaking? Or when your attention waned? Or if you tried to note down too much information?

Summarise podcasts

- Select a podcast. Listen to it all the way through.
- Mark three bullets on a page of paper.
- Jot down, next to the bullets, the 3 most important points made in the podcast.

Group consensus

- Summarise a podcast as above.
- Compare your three points with others in your group.
- How far did you agree on all, or some, of the points?
- If you came up with different points, decide between you what were the most important three.

15.7 Make it happen

Which strategies will I use?

Decide which of the strategies outlined in the chapter above could help you to make effective notes. Tick all that apply.

1 ☐ Develop the note-making habit.
2 ☐ Experiment with styles.
3 ☐ Find my own style.
4 ☐ Note points; add headers.
5 ☐ List headings; add details.
6 ☐ Note in sentences.
7 ☐ Abbreviated noting.
8 ☐ Pen down.
9 ☐ Coloured inks.
10 ☐ Pause to interpret.
11 ☐ Similarity and difference.
12 ☐ Keep an ideas book.
13 ☐ Note it just once.
14 ☐ Watch and note.
15 ☐ Summarise podcasts.
16 ☐ Group consensus.

Prioritise

Choose between one and three of the strategies listed opposite to try out first. Enter the number given beside each strategy into the box below.

My first 3 priorities	
First choice	
Second choice	
Third choice	

Plan

Decide when you will give time and thought to your priorities.

- Jot those times into your planner or diary – or your timetable for planning towards Uni.
- In your planner, mark in a date within the next month to check what is working.

Experiment

Once you have used your first set of strategies, have a go with a new set. See which ones suit you best.

> ### Give and take support
>
> Share your ideas with others in your group. Post comments about strategies you find helpful.
>
> Compare the notes you have made on a difficult passage of a book you are required to read. How different are the notes that each of you has made?

16 Writing Essays at Uni

Argument | Understanding | Ideas |
Structure | Reading | Introduction |
Drafting | Editing | Thinking | Ideas
| Depth | Critical analysis | Clarity |
Summarise | Word limits | Precision |
Conclusion | Style | Concise | Debate
| Academic | Engagement | Integrity
| Complexity | Relevance | Significance
| Selection | Brevity | Redrafting
| Audience | Proofreading
| Feedback | Paragraphs |
Inspiration | Focus | References

This chapter

In this chapter you can:

→ find out more about writing at Uni;

→ gain a sense of how writing essays at Uni is different from writing these at school;

→ consider things you can do now to build underlying skills that will help with essay writing once at Uni;

→ choose strategies that you think are most relevant for you to develop now.

16.1 What students wish they had known ...

Three years ago, this furious-fingered four were all authors in the making.

 ◁ **Julie** *I've got the formula down for essay writing: introduction, middle, end. Voila! An essay!*

 ◁ **Arun** *Just make sure you know a lot and describe it in detail. That's my trick.*

 ◁ **Duncan** *I get good marks for essays. I get the facts right and include lots of them. Stick to the facts, I say.*

 ◁ **Soraya** *My aunt says my essays are of publishable standard already. I can write easily, almost without thinking about it. I am looking forward to writing more essays at Uni.*

Here they are at Uni and their first novel seems just a little further away – for now.

 ◁ **Julie** *I do still use my formula but I have had to become a bit more sophisticated in the way I write – to convey more complex ideas, and there's so much more information to condense down and include.*

 ◁ **Arun** *All of my work comes back with 'less description please. More analysis needed'. They do mean critical analysis, not that I need to see a shrink – I think.*

 ◁ **Duncan** *At Uni, they seem to care less about how many facts you include compared with what use you make of them – and that you know how to write references.*

 ◁ **Soraya** *My first essay – I read more than anyone. I wrote masses as I had loads of ideas about it all. They took marks off me because they said I wrote nearly 5000 words and the word limit was 2000.*

What can you learn from them?
- Jot down a list of the things these students may wish they had known about writing essays before they arrived at Uni.
- What kinds of ideas does this give you about things to do now?

16.2   Essay writing at Uni

How essay writing is different at Uni

You may be used to writing essays already. However, at Uni, more is expected. You would need to build on the skills that you had developed at school in order to gain reasonable marks at Uni. If you build those skills before Uni, these can help you to gain higher marks for your current studies too.

The prevalence of essays at Uni

Apart from exams, essays are the main method used for assessment on most programmes of study. This is because essays do not simply test for facts – a multiple choice question exam could do that.

Essays enable you to demonstrate your understanding. They help the tutors to check such things as whether you:

- grasped what is important about the issues;
- can present the arguments effectively to others.

Word limits more exact

At Uni, you will normally be given a word limit for each essay or other written assignment. Typically, this would be 1000–1500 words in your first year of full-time study, rising each year.

Your answers should always be on, or very near, the word limit, typically within 5% of the limit. Otherwise, you would lose marks.

Concise, condensed writing style

As the word limit is restricted, students need to develop skills in making the word limit work for them. They need to write succinctly, conveying as much as possible in few words. This skill can make all the difference between lower and higher marks, as the example below demonstrates.

> **Abi's writing style**
>
> ☹ *There was a scientist who wrote about children's development in the 1950s. He was called Piaget. He claimed that children always develop through four set stages and that they do so in a particular order and at the same ages (Piaget, 1958).* (42 words)

> **Noah's writing style**
>
> ☺ *According to Piaget (1958), children pass through four developmental stages in a given order at set ages.* (17 words)

Noah can cover the same points as Abi in fewer than half the words. Within the same word limit, this frees up words for him to use for other purposes, such as:

- referring to additional sources;
- providing more about what he feels are the strengths or weaknesses of Piaget's position;
- a combination of these, using words saved across the essay.

This use of the word limit can help him achieve much higher marks.

16.3 Essay writing at Uni (2)

Engaging with the subject

At school, you are generally given more guidance about how to make judgements about what you read. This guidance may be invisible at times, because it is built into the way that your textbooks or lessons are structured.

At Uni, such guidance is greatly reduced. You will be provided with options, through lectures, through materials provided by your tutors, and from your reading. You may receive a strong steer from your tutors on how the evidence should be interpreted. However, it is then up to you to show that you have really engaged with the debates, thought about the issues for yourself, and can select from the range of evidence available to argue the case yourself.

More depth and complexity

At school, you cover subjects more as a broad overview of the issues with some examples to illustrate the points. As you move through each year at Uni, you study topics in increasing depth. This means:

- reading more about the key research undertaken on each topic;
- reading the original articles and papers rather than synopses of these;
- undertaking your own projects to collect materials and data to compare with those in published research;
- finding out about the complexities in the theories and data and the diverse ways that these can be interpreted.

Understanding of significance

You will need to understand the debates and issues that are considered to be significant in your subject area. This means finding out:

- What the points of contention are and why these arise.
- What evidence or theory leads different writers to come to the conclusions that they do.
- Which pieces of research are the most important to the debates on each issue.

Selection on the basis of significance

To include, or not to include, that is the question....

You will need to make wise choices about what you select for inclusion within your essay. This becomes an ever more important skill when you work with:

- greater amounts of information,
- on more complex issues,
- within restricted word limits,
- and with less guidance on what to include.

16.4   Essay writing at Uni (3)

Academic integrity and referencing

At Uni, you are part of a learning community that values academic integrity. As a student, this means:

- Never pass other people's ideas or words off as your own work: that is seen as cheating.
- Always make it clear in your essay whose work influenced your own; give their name and the publication date of the source you used (e.g. Smith, 2012).
- Put their words into quotation marks: "Cite your source".
- Write full details of the source of those words or ideas in a list at the end of your work (e.g. Smith, P.E. (2012) *Global warming*. London: Climate Publishers). Record this information when reading and making notes (see pages 146 and 163).

You shouldn't use the work of other students or, as a rule, unpublished sources, so you wouldn't include references to the opinions of friends and family.

Argue your point

Your essays at Uni need to present a convincing argument for your point of view on the issue set. This has to be more than just your own opinion and more than describing what you have read. You will need to do the following.

- Present different perspectives on the issue, with your critique of the evidence for each.
- Indicate which is the strongest case.
- Substantiate your points with good examples.
- Structure essays so that points follow each other in the best order, leading logically to conclusions.

Writing style

You will be expected to convey complex ideas in a succinct, precise, accurate and clear manner. This means, in practice:

- knowing what you are talking about – through solid background reading and giving thought to what you read;
- careful use of language, including specialist terms, so that you convey exactly what you mean to say;
- careful proofreading, to make sure that your arguments come across well and that errors and typos are removed.

Drafting and redrafting

It is not likely that you will produce a high-scoring essay in a first draft. You will need to:

- go back over your writing, editing, rephrasing, summarising, and generally fine-tuning it;
- manage your time so that you can rework your writing until it reads well.

My brother Kevin said, in 2012, that he thought the whole idea of global warming was a load of rubbish ... And Aunty Elsie agrees so that must be right.

16.5   Things I can do now

The following activities develop underlying skills for writing at Uni. Read through these, then decide which you will use.

Understand word limits

Guess the word count (on screen)

- Cut and paste a piece of electronic text into a word document.
- Guess how many words there are in the extract.
- Use the word counting tool to see how close you were.

Guess the word count (printed)

- Take a piece of printed text.
- Guess how many words are written.
- Count them to see how close you were.

Estimate your word count

Take a piece of your own writing that is typical of your style and layout.

- Guess how many words you write to a page.
- Count out the words to find out the actual number.
- Work out how many pages of your writing would be needed for a 1000-word essay.

Write to different word limits

Become skilled at summarising information with different levels of brevity.

- Choose one of your course-books.
- Sum up what the whole book is about in around 500 words.
- Then sum it up in exactly 200 words.
- Then sum it up in exactly 50 words.

Develop the writing habit

Writing on a regular basis, especially for an audience, helps you to develop your writing fluency and speed.

Keep a diary

Write a diary entry at least once a week.

Write a blog

Since thinking a bit more about global warming and reading a book by Pat Smith, I realise my brother Kevin may not be the last word on the issue.

Write a blog, restricting this to a closed audience such as your classmates or those who participate in a similar activity.

- Use it to develop a writing habit: set yourself a target of writing it every day or on set days of the week.
- Use it to develop audience awareness: select things to write about that will interest your reader rather than yourself.
- Use it to manage a word limit. Be disciplined: set yourself a target number of words to write each day.
- Encourage friends to post their thoughts about what you write.

Use opportunities to write

Find ways of writing for an audience. For example:

- Write articles for the school or local paper.
- Write reviews of books or music on commercial websites.
- Post more thoughtful comments on other people's blogs.
- Contribute to Wikipedia.
- Write a story for a child you know.
- Start your memoirs!

Nurture your own ideas

Develop the habit of thinking about what you read and learn, and coming up with your own observations, questions and thoughts. This habit will be invaluable when you get to Uni.

Keep an ideas book

As ideas occur to you, jot these down so that you catch the spark of your original thought straight away (see page 164).

- Return to this as soon as you can, preferably within a few hours.
- Develop the thought in writing – even if only in note form.
- Elaborate on your idea, adding details.
- Question your own idea: how could it be challenged or criticised? Who might object to it?
- Consider how you could improve on your idea so as to respond to potential challenges.

Ideas exchange

Arrange to meet a friend for a coffee or during a free period once a fortnight to talk through the ideas you have noted down. Take it in turns to present your best ideas, with the other person asking questions. Use their feedback to develop your ideas. This will help you to develop a range of skills that will be useful at Uni, such as:

- valuing and developing your ideas;
- getting used to giving and receiving feedback;
- developing your confidence in discussing your ideas.

Multiple redrafting

Start one piece of homework earlier than you would normally; complete it in the usual way.

- Leave the work for a few hours.
- During that time, find some new but relevant information on the topic, either on-line or in your textbook. Look for something that no-one else in your class might use.
- Re-write a section of your homework so that you include this.
- Re-read your work with a critical eye: rephrase any sections to be more concise or precise.
- Read it again to see whether it flows as well as it could. If not, be prepared to restructure it all, or to add sentences to add to the flow.
- Re-write any sentences that are not absolutely clear.

16.7 Make it happen

Which strategies will I use?

Decide which of the strategies outlined in the chapter above you will use to develop your own writing. Tick all that apply.

1 ☐ Guess the word count (screen).
2 ☐ Guess the word count (print).
3 ☐ Estimate my word count.
4 ☐ Write to different word limits.
5 ☐ Keep a diary.
6 ☐ Write a blog.
7 ☐ Write articles for a paper.
8 ☐ Write reviews on websites.
9 ☐ Contribute to Wikipedia.
10 ☐ Write a story.
11 ☐ Post better comments.
12 ☐ Start my autobiography.
13 ☐ Keep an ideas book.
14 ☐ Ideas exchange.
15 ☐ Multiple redrafting.

Prioritise

Choose between one and three of the strategies listed opposite to try out first. Enter the number given beside each strategy into the box below.

My first 3 priorities	
First choice	
Second choice	
Third choice	

Plan

Decide when you will give time and thought to your priorities.

- Jot those times into your planner or diary – or your timetable for planning towards Uni.
- In your planner, mark in a date within the next month to check what is working.

Experiment

Once you have used your first set of strategies, have a go with a new set. See which ones suit you best.

Give and take support

Share your ideas with others in your group. Post comments about strategies you find helpful.

---

17 Critical analysis at Uni

Argument | Relevance | **Critique** | Selection | **Validity** | **Evidence** | **Significance** | **Ideas** | **Evaluation** | **Thinking** | Decision | Reasoning | Analysis | **Criticality** | Judgement | **Balance** | **Theory** | **Reliability** | **Research** | **Conclusions** | **Reasons** | Position | Background | Alternatives | **Perspectives** | Expert | **Precision** | **Testing** | **Clarity** | **Discussion** | **Debate** | **Hypothesis** | Current | Convincing | Evaluate | **Engagement** | Skill | **Agreement** | **Journals** | **Rigour** | **Questioning** | **Credibility** | **Sources** | References | Demonstrate | Present | **Salience** | Specious | **Flawed** | **Irrelevant** | **Invalid** | **Unsupported** | Outdated | **Assumptions**

This chapter

In this chapter you can:

→ find out more about why critical analysis is important at Uni;

→ find out the different ways that you can benefit, as a student, from good skills in critical analysis;

→ understand more about what critical analysis means for the way you approach study at Uni;

→ identify ways of developing some of the underlying skills and habits that help you to apply critical analysis once at Uni;

→ select things to work on now that can help you when you get to Uni.

17.1 What students wish they had known ...

Three years ago, this trusting four had perfect faith in the Universe ...

◁ **William** *I like to trust people. You can't expect people to provide evidence for everything.*

◁ **Arun** *If I am reading it in a book, I assume it's by an expert. Why would I question them? What do I know about it?*

◁ **Ayeesha** *I don't like to argue or be critical – I'm a people person really.*

◁ **Jack** *If I'm not sure, I ask my mum.*

Three years later, and our heroic students now subject every detail to scrutiny in their endless quest for truth.

◁ **William** *You have to argue your case and back it up with good reasons – you can't just say, 'Well, I think I am right.'*

◁ **Arun** *It was weird realising that even the experts don't know everything – they know part of the story, but they can miss things, or some other expert may have better evidence . . .*

◁ **Ayeesha** *I like to focus on the positives in what we learn from every experiment. I was pleased to find out that there is a place for that, but I also see the value of finding out what doesn't work. Then you can do something about it.*

◁ **Jack** *I say now, 'Get real, mum! That's not good enough! There are flaws in your argument. Your reasons don't add up. What are your sources?'*

What can you learn from them?

- Jot down a list of the things these students may wish they had known about critical analysis power before they arrived at Uni.
- What kinds of ideas does this give you about things to do now?

17.2 Why critical analysis matters at Uni

The most important skill

Critical analysis is probably the most important of all the skills that you will need at Uni. Good skills in critical analysis will help you in the following areas.

Gain higher marks

Assignments at Uni tend to allocate the most marks to the critical analysis that is demonstrated in your work. Without this, you are unlikely to gain more than a bare pass mark.

For identifying significance

In the chapter on essay writing, we saw how important it is to engage with the subject so that you can identify what is significant in the debates in the subject and make sure that these are what you include in your own work.

Strong skills in critical analysis are essential for helping you to work out these aspects:

- why something is significant in the context of what has gone before;
- which features, debates, reasons, evidence or details are the most significant to a particular argument or line of reasoning.

Time management

Good skills of critical analysis help you to save time at each stage of the study process.

For example, they help you to:

- spot the most relevant texts to read quickly – and the most relevant parts of each;
- recognise the most salient arguments quickly, so that you can focus in on them at an early stage;
- identify quickly when an argument is based on sound reasoning and when it is specious, so that you identify, early on, what is likely to be useful content to include in your own work;
- identify what is worth noting, so that you don't waste time taking notes that you won't use;
- identify the best information to call upon for your own work, so that you spend less time selecting the right information and editing your work to fit the word limit.

Personal satisfaction

Critical analysis helps you to get under the skin of your subject so that you:

- understand it better;
- gain a sense of expertise;
- feel more confident that you know what you are talking about.

17.3 Critical analysis at Uni

Academic rigour

Unis place a high value on checking that information is sound. They do so by analysing information in different ways to make sure that the arguments and evidence stack up. This means thinking clearly and precisely about the details of what you read, and following things up to check for yourself rather than always relying on the work of others. You will be expected to apply increasingly high levels of academic rigour as you progress through your programme.

Weighing up different perspectives

At Uni, you will find that there almost always seem to be different viewpoints and debates that have to be taken into consideration. For each assignment, you will need to:

- identify the issues;
- identify the key perspectives on these issues.

It won't be enough to list or describe the different perspectives once you have found them. You will need to:

- evaluate them;
- make judgements about which you find the most convincing;
- provide reasons for your answer.

Evaluating the arguments

As a student, you won't always be able to tell which argument is the best, and your lecturers won't expect the impossible. However, you will need to demonstrate that you can apply the right kinds of thinking to evaluating different points of view. That includes asking such questions as:

- Does the author make a good case?
- What reasons do they give to support their case?
- Do they provide good evidence?
- Could that evidence lead to a different conclusion from the one presented?
- What do other experts think about this perspective?

Testing the evidence

To evaluate different perspectives and arguments, you will need to consider the quality of the evidence on all sides. You would be looking at such things as whether the evidence was up to date (current), trustworthy (reliable), and relevant to the point being made.

For example, you would need to consider why the different approaches arose. It might be because the authors took different theoretical viewpoints, wrote at different times or drew upon different evidence.

Questioning approach

Critical analysis of this kind means developing a questioning approach as a reflex. Whenever you are reading, you need to be asking such things as:

- Are there other perspectives on this?
- Why do they think this?
- When was this written?
- What is the evidence?
- Is there any research on this?

17.4   Things I can do now

You can develop your skills in critical analysis much as you develop muscles through exercise. Even if you feel critical analysis is not yet your strong point, it will develop through practice.

Express your own point of view

Take a chance on expressing your own perspective on an issue: you will have to do this when you get to Uni. Don't just express an opinion – find out about the issue first.

- Read about it in a source other than a class textbook.
- Based on your reading and thinking, jot down two or three reasons for the perspective you are going to take.
- Use at least one of these to make your point.

Criticise the TV

Watch a factual programme on the television, using a questioning approach. This will be especially helpful if you can record the programme and check back over anything that you might have missed.

Either during the programme or at the end, ask yourself if you are convinced by the arguments being presented. If you are, work out what it is that convinces you. For example, is it the amount or quality of the evidence? Or is it that the arguments are made in a particularly persuasive way?

If you are not convinced, work out why that is the case. Is there a lack of evidence? Do you already know something about this topic that suggests there is more to the debate than is being presented in the programme?

Make a list of the questions that you feel the programme does not fully address, or alternative perspectives that could be explored. Look these up to see how that affects your view of the programme.

Develop the habit of taking such an approach to everything you watch and read.

Look at the list of references

At Uni, you will need to gain a sense of what makes a good source, especially when using books and internet sources. One way of doing this is to check the references for that material. You can start now to develop the habit of checking the references.

To do this, choose a handful of your textbooks. Turn to the list of references or, alternatively, the bibliography. Browse these to gain a sense of:

- how many sources they use;
- how recently the sources were published;
- the kinds of sources they used.

17.5 Things I can do now (2)

Check a reference

Select one of the references listed in one of your current textbooks or in another academic source of your choosing. Follow up that reference by sending for the book or article. You will find this easier to do if you choose a reference to a journal or source you can find on-line or in your library. Otherwise, ask a librarian for help.

Once you have the article or other source:

- Browse it to see what it is like, in general. Could it be useful to your current studies?
- Look to see whether you can spot how the textbook made use of the reference.
- If possible, check how the wording differs between the textbook and the source used as a reference.
- Consider whether you feel the textbook makes accurate use of the reference.

Reflection	Where errors can slip in

- Give thought to the ways in which errors can creep in when an author quotes from another source.
- List these.

Discuss your list with others in your group.

Gain a feel for 'quality' sources

At Uni, you will need to make judgements for yourself about what is a good source of information. You will gain guidance to help you make such decisions. However, it helps if you can develop the ability to spot a good source yourself. The best way of doing this is to use journal articles.

Identify relevant journals

Find out the main journals relevant to one of the subjects that you are studying now, or that you intend to study at Uni. To help you do this:

- use a search engine such as Ingenta or Google Scholar;
- ask your teacher for suggestions;
- Google 'articles in … (subject name), and investigate the websites that come up.

Look for signs of academic quality

- Select 3–5 journals that you found through your search.
- Investigate these to see whether there is
  (a) an abstract;
  (b) a summary of the literature they have covered;
  (c) for sciences, a section on methods or approach; and
  (d) a list of references.
- Check whether the list of references includes other journal articles.
- Check whether the journal has an editorial board made up of professors or doctors from universities or institutes.
- If the articles do not contain these features, move on to other journals.

17.6   Things I can do now (3)

Investigate journal contents

- Choose 2–3 journals relevant to your current studies or to a subject that you may want to study at Uni.
- Browse the Contents list of several volumes of each journal to see what that journal covers.
- Make a list of the topics that are the focus of these three journals.

Use journal abstracts

Choose one topic that interests you in your current studies. Use a search engine such as Ingenta or Google Scholar to call up abstracts of journal articles written on that topic in the last 5–7 years.

From these, choose 3–5 abstracts, each from a different journal. Consider the following:

- Who were the authors of the articles you looked at? What aspects did each cover in their articles?
- What can you find out from the abstracts of each journal?
- From these abstracts, which journal appealed to you the most?

Identify a 'hot topic'

Choose one aspect of your current studies that interests you. Use an academic search engine such as Google Scholar or the abstracts of recent journal articles to help you to hunt out one key debate or hot topic on that subject.

- Jot down notes on the different points of view that you uncover.
- Note which names are associated with each.

Reflection	Use your insights
How could you make use of this knowledge: • In your current studies? • In your application to Uni?	

Spot the experts

It can help to build your confidence in recognising quality sources at Uni if you already recognise the names of experts associated with your subject and what they are best known for.

When you have browsed many journals and books on your subject, you will start to see the same names recurring.

- Make a note of these names.
- Note the main one or two major pieces of work, or research areas, associated with each one and the dates of these.
- Look up the authors to see what is considered to be the significance of their contribution to the subject.

Reflection	Spot the experts
Consider how the information you gained in completing the above activity could help you in your current study or your application to Uni.	

17.7 Make it happen

Which strategies will I use?

Decide which of the strategies outlined in the chapter above could help you to build your skills of critical analysis. Tick all that apply.

1 ☐ Express my own point of view.
2 ☐ Criticise the TV.
3 ☐ Look at the list of references.
4 ☐ Check a reference.
5 ☐ Check where errors can slip in – complete the reflective activity.
6 ☐ Identify relevant journals.
7 ☐ Look for signs of academic quality.
8 ☐ Investigate journal articles.
9 ☐ Use journal abstracts.
10 ☐ Identify a 'hot topic'.
11 ☐ 'Use your insights' – complete the reflective activity.
12 ☐ Spot the experts.

Prioritise

Choose between one and three of the strategies listed opposite to try out first. List these below.

First 3 choices	
First choice	
Second choice	
Third choice	

Plan

Decide exactly when you will make use of each strategy. Set times that help you to build up a routine and that won't clash with other things you want to do.

- Jot the times into your planner or diary.
- Jot down a date within the next month to check what is working.

Experiment

Once you have used your first set of strategies, have a go with a new set. See which ones suit you best.

> **Give and take support**
>
> Share your ideas with others in your group. Post comments about strategies you find helpful.
>
> Set up a group to debate issues so as to develop your critical skills. Take it in turn to present the evidence on a given issue.

18   Time management at Uni

Timetabling | Clothes | **DEADLINES** | Phoning home | **Browsing the internet** | **COOKING** | **Writing essays** | **Travel** | **Proofreading** | **Group Project** | Social networking | Redrafting the essay | Exercise | **Referencing** | Talk | **Checking details** | **Printing** | **Sleeping** | **Attendance** | **READING** | **Work placement** | Thinking | Shopping | Drafting my essay | **Meeting friends** | Eating | **Earning** | **Money** | **Lectures** | **Food** | **Clubbing** | **Planning** | Seminars | **Coffee** | Tutorials

This chapter

This chapter helps you to:

→ gain an appreciation of why time management is so important at Uni;

→ find out what students wished they had known about time management;

→ consider things that you can do now to develop the right approaches to time management, so as to be more effective once you go to Uni.

18.1 What students wish they had known …

Three years ago, time and space seemed like such easily managed entities to these timeless heroes …

◁ **Vishua** *I like to go with the flow – let time take care of itself.*

◁ **Diane** *I'm fed up with people telling me what to do! I can't wait to get to Uni and get away from them all!*

◁ **Soraya** *I am a very organised person. I always make a very neat timetable at the start of term so I know which class I am in.*

◁ **Jack** *If it's really important, mum can remind me.*

Now they are at Uni and I was expecting to interview them here today, but they all seem to be late …

◁ **Vishua** *I was a bit casual about turning up for lectures – well, I didn't make many. I passed my exams with flying colours but they are making me retake the year for failing the attendance requirements.*

◁ **Diane** *At school, it's all organised for you – where you're supposed to be and what you've got to do. Nobody does that here. I have to put time aside just to plan my time.*

◁ **Soraya** *It was a shock to find out how many more things I had to plan. Juggling all the different aspects of several assignments at once! Timing these around my social life and activities. Planning the small details for meals – like cooking oil! Salt! Then when to pick up library books, get bicycle oil, conditioner …*

◁ **Jack** *I asked my mum to phone me to wake me up in time for my labs. I was shocked at her response. People her age shouldn't use words like that.*

What can you learn from them?

Jot down a list of things that these students may wish they had known before they went to Uni. What thoughts does it give you about challenges you might face at Uni?

18.2 Time management at Uni

You will be in charge of your time

When you get to Uni, there will be no-one to:

- make sure you are up and out to class in the morning;
- tell you which pages to read today;
- tell you what to do first when you sit down to study;
- tell you to write a shopping list, shop, cook, eat, wash, clean, study, etc.

For taught sessions

There are usually attendance requirements and you are expected to be there at the start of the session. It will be up to you to:

- find out when and where you should be;
- make sure you remember;
- plan your time and travel and everything else to make sure you are there, clothed and fed, with what you need.

Unis often use a smart card system or a register to check you are present. If you miss the first few minutes, you may be counted as absent. After a certain number of absences, you may automatically fail the module and have to retake it. That may mean studying for an additional year, with extra costs.

For independent study

For most subjects, the majority of your study time is spent in untaught sessions as independent study. Whilst you may get away with wasting 'free periods' at school, this would not work at Uni because independent study is so central to how you are expected to learn. You need to be able to manage this time effectively. You will have an advantage if you have the right skills and attitudes to manage this study time well, right from the start of your course.

For effective study

Your success as a student will be strongly affected by the combination of two time-related factors:

- how much time you spend in study;
- how well you use that time.

If you both spend more time in study AND manage that time effectively, you are much more likely to achieve well.

For coordinating your life

At Uni, you will have to think about a very long list of things to do. If you coordinate these well, the results are positive.

- You have more time for fun.
- You have more time to choose what you want to do with your time.
- You'll be less exhausted. If you don't manage the small details, this often means having to take a long way round to get things done, or racing back to the shops time after time, or finding people to borrow things from once the libraries or shops are closed.
- You'll be less stressed.

18.3   Time management at Uni (2)

Demands on your time at Uni

The demands on your time at Uni will vary depending on a host of factors such as these.

- How long travel takes you each day.
- Whether you choose to live on campus, at home, or in a student house or halls.
- Whether you are on a programme with a high number of scheduled hours for compulsory attendance such as for clinical courses, some lab-based courses, or performance-based courses.
- Whether you are on a programme where almost all study is on-line, at a distance or by independent study.
- Whether you eat in student halls and refectories, cook for yourself, or share cooking with others.
- The kinds of activities that you engage in – such as joining many societies, taking part in sports, keep-fit, drama, music, and general socialising.
- The amount and kind of work you do in paid employment.
- Any other commitments you have – such as a sports scholarship or community volunteering.

Things you'll need to manage

For each of the following items, tick any that you organise completely for yourself at present.

Study

- ☐ Reading time
- ☐ Searching for material to use
- ☐ Thinking time and problem-solving
- ☐ Drafting and re-writing assignments
- ☐ Coordinating group assignments
- ☐ On-line study tasks
- ☐ Getting to taught sessions on time
- ☐ Seeing your tutors or teachers
- ☐ Seeing course and Uni admin staff
- ☐ Preparing for exams
- ☐ Organising your assignments so that you meet competing deadlines
- ☐ Sorting out IT and stationery.

Life

- ☐ Making friends and socialising
- ☐ Shopping, cooking, eating
- ☐ Organising life basics such as personal hygiene, laundry, sleep, travel, appointments
- ☐ Time and transport for daily travel to lessons, library, shops, activities, etc.
- ☐ Keeping things organised – or looking for things you can't find
- ☐ Keeping fit and healthy
- ☐ Taking care of documents, files, security
- ☐ Personal safety, especially at night
- ☐ Earning money and looking after finances

Who saves you time now?

All of these activities take time. Jot down a quick list of the ways anyone else helps you to plan or coordinate any of the above now – such as organising your timetable, travel, shopping or getting you organised.

18.4   Managing time effectively

Managing your time

At Uni, you continue to work on an assignment until it is ready. You cannot easily set a clock to say when you will finish. Much will depend on such factors as:

- how quickly you can find the material you need for it;
- how long it takes you to make sense of the material;
- how long it takes you to come up with your own ideas;
- how quickly you can organise your material to use for the assignment;
- how many times you need to draft your work so that it reads well and meets the assignment criteria.

Key steps in time management

Time management starts with four basic stages.

1 Finding out the time requirements.
2 Identifying your priorities.
3 Observing your own current use of time.
4 Planning your future time.

1 Find out the time requirements

This means 'knowing how long it will take'. To find out:
(a) Compile a list of everything you need to do.
(b) Work out how long each of these will take you.
(c) Identify where there could be delays which add to the time needed.
(d) Work out where you could save time, such as by combining two tasks or sharing tasks with others.

2 Identify your priorities

If there isn't time for everything that you have to do and want to do, you have to decide what the priorities are – the things that have to be done.
(a) List the things you have to do.
(b) Organise these in order of importance, with the most important at the top.
(c) Write down beside each how much time it will take you.

3 Observe your current use of time

(a) Keep an accurate record, for a few days or weeks, of what you do and how long it takes.
(b) Add up how much time you spend on each kind of activity.
(c) Compare this with your priorities list.

4 Plan your future time

This means making sure that you organise yourself so that you complete your priorities by the right date and time.
(a) For each priority, write the deadline onto a planner or chart.
(b) List all the things you need to do to complete that priority – and by when, at the latest.
(c) Write all of these details into your planner or onto your chart.
(d) If there are conflicting demands on your time, work out the best way of resolving these so that everything gets done on time.

18.5   Things you can do now

Find out about time requirements

(1) Find out about time at Uni

Browse the sites of several universities or colleges – look up any that catch your eye. If you are looking up a Uni in England, check their Key Information Sets (KIS) for some of this information. Look for such things as the following.

- How many hours of study are expected in a year?
- How many hours are students at each Uni expected to spend in independent study?
- How many modules or units of study will you take each term (or semester)?
- How many assignments do you have to hand in for each module or unit?
- How many pieces of work do you have to hand in altogether each year?

(2) Guess the timings

- Jot down a list of activities that someone else does for you now, or helps you with.
- Make a guess at how long each one takes – jot down your guesses next to each activity.
- Find out how long that activity actually takes. Either ask the person, or do it yourself and time how long it takes.
- Compare the actual time with the times you guessed. How accurate were your guesses?
- If the activity took much more or much less time than you expected, find out why. What kinds of things did you overlook?

(3) Take charge of your own time

Start to assume responsibility for things that, at present, your parents or others do for you.

- List all the things you have to do in order to complete each responsibility that you take on.
- List how long each one will take you in the week.

It looks like our Timothy but it can't be ... Not with an iron?

18.6 Things you can do now (2)

Identify your priorities

(4) Make decisions about priorities

As you assume new responsibilities, you may not be able to fit in everything you do now.

- List everything you would like to do.
- Put these in order of importance.
- Decide on the order in which you will do these – and which you will not do if there is not enough time.

Observe your current use of time

(5) Find out what eats your time

- For one evening, jot down everything you do – everything – and your start and end times. Do this even for things that take only a minute or two – such as checking your phone or posting a message.
- At the end of the evening, add up the total time spent on each kind of activity.

(6) Identify your time traps

Find out where your time gets trapped now – that means, where it is wasted. Ask someone who knows you where you waste time, or use the activity above (5) to see where your time disappears unexpectedly. Consider such possibilities as:

- taking a long time to settle down to study or other tasks;
- browsing on the internet;
- texting and posting;
- watching TV/DVDs;
- playing games;
- inefficient study strategies;
- being a perfectionist, so you don't get things finished.

Plan your time

(7) Get used to keeping a planner

- If you don't have one already, find a diary or planner that works for you.
- Develop the habit of writing everything in it.
- Develop the habit of checking it several times a day – so you actually use it.

(8) Get used to planning a task in detail

Develop the habit of planning out academic tasks, such as completing longer homework assignments, in terms of their component parts.

- Choose a task. Decide what you think are the different steps that you have to take in order to complete it.
- Decide on the best order for completing these steps.
- Calculate how long you will need for each step.
- Write into your diary or planner when you will start and finish each step.
- Check to see how accurate your time calculations were.

18.7   Make it happen

Which strategies will I use?

Decide which of the strategies outlined in the chapter above could help you to develop your time management skills. Tick all that apply.

1 ☐ Guess the timings.

2 ☐ Find out about time at Uni.

3 ☐ Take charge of my own time.

4 ☐ Make decisions about priorities.

5 ☐ Find out what eats into my time.

6 ☐ Identify my personal time traps.

7 ☐ Get used to keeping a planner.

8 ☐ Get used to planning an academic task in detail.

Prioritise

Choose between one and three of the strategies listed opposite to try out first. List these below.

First 3 choices	
First choice	
Second choice	
Third choice	

Plan

Decide exactly when you will make use of each strategy. Set times that help you to build up a routine and that won't clash with other things you want to do.

- Jot the times into your planner or diary.
- Jot down a date within the next month to check what is working.

Experiment

Once you have used your first set of strategies, have a go with a new set. See which ones suit you best.

> **Give and take support**
> Share your ideas with others in your group. Post comments about strategies you find helpful.

19   What's different about study at Uni?

Creating knowledge | Theory | Intellectual Curiosity | Enjoyment | Research | Amount | Diverse Perspectives | Criticality | Self-reliance | Learning Community | Ambiguity | Expectations | Innovation | Conventions | Responsibility | Cutting Edge | Innovation | Personal engagement | Time | Objectivity | Academic integrity | Applying knowledge | Challenge | Getting involved | Currency | Knowing the subject | Independence | Searching | Process | Methodology | Variety | Change | Depth | Questioning | Thinking

This chapter

This chapter helps you to:

→ understand the purpose of higher education, and how this influences the kinds of academic skills and personal qualities that you will need as a student;

→ gain a sense of how your tutors will think and, as a result, what they look for in their students – and in applicants;

→ understand the kind of motivation and intellectual curiosity expected of you as a student;

→ draw together your understanding of the academic skills you will need in order to succeed in such an environment.

Three years ago, our brilliant four were at the peak of their social and academic powers.

◁ **Kian** *I expect Uni will be pretty much like school only with more drinking.*

◁ **Diane** *I wish people wouldn't keep telling me about what Uni is like – I think I can work it out for myself.*

◁ **Soraya** *I am so ready for Uni – I wish I could go there today.*

◁ **Jack** *I should do well in my exams. I have a good memory and have learnt all the answers off by heart.*

Now they are at Uni and they are soaring to greater heights than they had ever imagined …

◁ **Kian** *It is a different world here – you are mostly left to your own devices. My time is packed with my part-time job, all the things I do outside of study, as well as reading up for assignments.*

◁ **Diane** *We have to work closely with other students on our group project – I have had to learn how to take other people's ideas on board.*

◁ **Soraya** *It is really exciting working with ideas that are still new in the field but I get frustrated that there aren't always clear answers.*

◁ **Jack** *I wish my tutors would just tell me the answers so I can learn them!*

What can you learn from them?
- Jot down a list of the things these students may wish they had known about Uni before they arrived.
- What kinds of ideas does this give you about things to do now?

19.2　How will it be different at Uni?

Creating knowledge

Unis are places where new knowledge is created. This can make them exciting places to study. It also affects the way you are expected to think and behave as a student.

The role of your tutors

For your lecturers, teaching will be only part of their work. Typically, they must also undertake research so as to contribute to creating knowledge. This means that they will not have as much time to help you as your teachers at school or your tutors at college.

At the cutting edge of knowledge

The purpose of research is to find out things that are not yet known, or to which we don't have all the answers yet. Academic staff, and students too, work in areas where:

- the results or answers may be ambiguous or inconclusive;
- there are not clear 'right' or 'wrong' answers;
- there are conflicting points of view.

It can feel quite challenging and strange when the answers are not known now and may not be known in your lifetime or, conversely, seem to change rapidly.

Keeping up to date

When you study issues at the 'cutting edge', you may find that your reading list has become outdated: you need to keep an eye on new publications and developments in the subject.

Any further and we'll be the first people to sail over the edge.

No, we're all right. There's a message here that they now think the world is round.

Being part of a learning community

As a student, you will be part of the learning community described above. You will be expected to study and think more independently than at school or college. Part of your study will be about engaging with areas of new knowledge. This may mean:

- much more theory than you would cover for vocational programmes outside of higher education, or at your current level of study;
- much greater emphasis on you thinking things through for yourself – rather than the answers, or the route to the answers, being given to you;
- presenting your own thoughts, based upon your own research into the issues.

19.3   How will it be different at Uni? (2)

Amount, depth and meaning

For many students, the greatest challenges of study at Uni are managing the sheer amount of information, making decisions about it – and making sense of it – in a short time. This is why academic skills in reading, note-making and time management are so important.

As a student, you would:

- cover many topics, considering different theories and approaches to each;
- read many items for every assignment;
- work with the material over and over, making sense of it and sifting it down to essentials that you will use;
- look for information or perspectives that set your work aside from everyone else's.

You will do this to some extent in the Sixth Form or at college, but it helps to be prepared for this change in scale.

Level of criticality

In order to extend knowledge, researchers have to challenge what has been accepted up until now. This means that they bring a questioning, or critical, approach to their work, reading and observations.

At Uni, you are being trained to think in this way too. This does not mean questioning everything all the time, nor wasting time challenging the obvious just for the sake of it. If you did this, you would never be able to manage day-to-day life.

It does mean, though, bringing a high level of questioning to new material that you cover, and being prepared to defend your position, based on your study. Chapter 17 helps you to develop this criticality.

Level of objectivity

For academic work, you will need to treat evidence as objectively as possible. This means examining it in an even-handed way, even if it contradicts your own views. You will need to be comfortable in having your assumptions challenged and not taking this as personal criticism.

Applying knowledge rather than describing what you know

For work prior to Uni, the emphasis is often on describing what you know about the subject. At Uni, it is taken for granted that you can find out information, learn it and describe it. The emphasis there is on what you *do* with the material once you know it.

Recognising significance

Your tutors look for such things as:

- whether you can recognise what is significant – in what you choose to read and to include in your work;
- whether you can see strengths and flaws in other people's research and arguments;
- whether you could apply research findings to develop your own ideas, or in projects that you design yourself or on work placement.

The thinking process

The emphasis at Uni is less about whether you are right and more about how you demonstrate your thinking. It is part of the business

of academic life to think through issues afresh and create new ways of looking at things. Fresh thinking is valued, as long as it is sensible, clear and relevant.

If you show that you can use information in intelligent ways to arrive at different conclusions, this will generally count for more than simply summarising the known findings and theories of key writers in the subject. This is something that Unis also look for when choosing applicants.

Taking charge of your studies

You will be provided with a great deal of information about your programme and assignments. Although there will be guidance, you are left more or less to your own devices to:

- find out what you need to know and do – and get it done;
- complete your work as well as you wish – or not, and take the consequences.

Intellectual curiosity

It is assumed that students as well as tutors have intellectual curiosity, and are strongly motivated to find out things for themselves.

It is also assumed that your intellectual curiosity will drive you to want to discover new things – and that you won't be counting the hours spent in study.

Develop your curiosity in the subject

If you already know what you want to study at Uni, you can start to find out now as much as you can about the nature of the subject you want to study. If not, find out more about those subjects that interest you the most – which may help you to decide on the right subject, and academic community, for you.

Questions to consider

- What interests academics in your subject? How do they think or work?
- What evidence or source materials do they value?
- What issues do they feel are worthy of research and debate?
- Who are the main theorists that they call upon?
- What makes them feel their subject is so important?
- How do they feel their subject differs from all others?
- What are its ethical considerations?

How is it different?

Many university subjects are close relations of each other, but that does not mean that they work in the same way. Each will have its own, much valued, distinctions. Gain a feel for how your preferred subject differs from others. Choose at least one other subject as the focus for your investigations. Compare it, using the questions listed above.

19.6   Things I can do now (2)

Engage with the subject

Read something new

- Find a book that covers a specialist aspect of the subject in more detail than you would normally use for your current studies.
- Browse this to see what it covers.
- Read the introduction to see why it was thought important to write the book.
- Read at least the conclusion or final chapter.

Draw out insights

- Read one or more chapters of the book.
- Jot down three or more insights into the subject that you gain from reading this book.
- Does reading this make you more, or less, interested in studying the subject at Uni?

Identify the writing style

Each subject discipline has its own styles of writing and of presenting its findings.

- Look up articles from three journals you have identified for the subject (see page 180).
- Browse these to gain a sense of how academics write in this subject, looking for aspects that are common to all three articles.
- Jot down a list of things you notice.

Know the field

Find out the burning issues

From browsing articles and websites, identify at least three issues that are hot topics in your subject at present.

Jot down answers to these questions.

- What are the issues?
- What are the different perspectives?
- Who has written articles on the subject in recent journals? Can you tell whether their work was well received?
- Are any of the authors based at HEIs that you are considering?

Take a position

- If you were asked at interview about your own perspective on the issues, what would you say?
- Which of the perspectives that you read about would you most identify with – and why?

My position on the issue? You mean, there could be more than one? Who knew?

19.7   Make it happen

Which strategies will I use?

Decide which of the strategies outlined above could help you to build your understanding of Uni and studying your subject in higher education, so that you are well prepared for:

- writing your personal statement when you apply to Uni;
- studying once you arrive at Uni.

Tick all that apply.

1 ☐ Develop my curiosity in the subject.
2 ☐ How is it different?
3 ☐ Read something new.
4 ☐ Draw out insights.
5 ☐ Identify the writing style.
6 ☐ Find out the burning issues.
7 ☐ Take a position.

Prioritise

Choose between one and three of the strategies listed opposite to try out first. List these below.

First 3 choices	
First choice	
Second choice	
Third choice	

Plan

Decide exactly when you will make use of each strategy. Set times that help you to build up a routine and that won't clash with other things you want to do.

- Jot the times into your planner or diary.
- Jot down a date within the next month to check what is working.

Experiment

Once you have used your first set of strategies, have a go with a new set. See which ones suit you best.

Give and take support

Share your ideas with others in your group. Post comments about strategies you find helpful.

Uni-facts

In August 2010, there were 165 Higher Education Institutions in the UK, of which 115 were universities.
(UUK website, August 2010)

The oldest university in the world is believed to be the University of Bologna in Italy, founded in 1088.
(University of Bologna website, Oct. 2011)

The oldest university in the UK is Oxford. Teaching is believed to have existed there since 1096.
(Oxford University website, Oct. 2011)

The largest university in the world is the Indira Gandhi National Open University in New Delhi in India, which has 3.5 million students. This is a state-funded university.
(Indira Gandhi University website, Oct. 2011)

The second largest university is in Pakistan – the Allama Iqbal Open University – which has 1.8 million students. This is a state-funded university.
(The Allama Iqbal Open University, Oct. 2011)

The third largest university is the Islamic Azad University in Tehran, Iran. This has 1.5 million students and is a private university.
(Islamic Azad University website, Oct. 2011)

The largest HEI in the UK is the Open University, with 253,000 students.
(Facts and figures 2009–10, OU website, June 2011)

The second largest HEI in the UK is the University of London, with 120,000 students. The University has 19 self-governing colleges and 10 small research institutes.
(University of London website, June 2011)

The total number of students enrolled in UK HEIs in 2009–10 was 2,493,420 students.
(BIS, Jan. 2011)

Of the total enrolments at UK HEIs, 861,260 were part-time.
(BIS, Jan. 2011)

56% of first degree graduates in England in 2009–10 were women.
(BIS, Jan. 2011)

Uni-facts

198

More students come from China to the UK than from any other country outside Britain: 57,000 in 2009–10.

(UKCISA, accessed Oct. 2011)

The University in the UK with the largest proportion of international students in 2009–10 was the London School of Economics and Political Sciences (LSE), with 65%.

(UKCISA, accessed Oct. 2011)

The University of Manchester was the HEI in the UK with the largest number of international students in 2009–10, with 9,900 students.

(UCKISA, accessed Oct. 2011)

Ohio University in Athens, Ohio, USA, claims to be the most haunted college campus in the world.

(Forgotten Ohio website, Oct. 2011)

The Queen's University, Belfast, offers a module called Feel the Force: How to Train in the Jedi Way.

(The *Independent* newspaper's website, 9 Sept. 2010)

The University of Baltimore offers a course in Zombie Studies.

(The *Independent* newspaper's website, 9 Sept. 2010)

University College London was the first university to admit women, in 1878.

(UCL website, Oct. 2011)

Kermit the Frog was awarded an honorary degree by Southampton College, New York, in 1996.

(The *Telegraph* website, 28 Oct. 2011)

David Attenborough has more honorary degrees from UK universities than any other person. He has at least 29.

(The *Telegraph* website, 1 Aug. 2010)

The University of Durham offers a module called Harry Potter and the Age of Illusion.

(The *Independent* newspaper's website, 9 Sept. 2010)

Uni-facts

Part C
Uni-Life

Introduction to Uni-Life

Life at Uni is about much more than study.

This section focuses on the non-academic side of student life in higher education. It provides insights into the 24-hour experience and some of the issues that are likely to arise for you as a student.

Students commence higher education with different levels of life skills. You may already be a very independent person, taking primary care of yourself and helping out with the running of the household. If so, you may be well equipped already with the skills you will need for coping with life as a student.

However, it is not unusual for students to arrive at Uni having never even made a piece of toast. Whilst the basics are not hard to learn, the lack of such skills can make the first few months at Uni unnecessarily stressful, expensive and sometimes embarrassing.

The activities in the chapters will help you to develop some of the thinking and habits that will help you to take care of yourself at Uni.

Shop, cook, eat healthily, and keep yourself safe – and enjoy yourself in the process.

Create and use well the opportunities open to you, so that you can present yourself well in your application to Uni, make the most of life at Uni, and be more employable as a graduate.

Manage your money so that you can pay your bills as a student as well as having a good time.

Uni-Life: Wall of words

Each chapter of this book opens with a 'wall of words' related to its content.

- Which words do you associate most with student life? On your own or with a group, compile your own word wall to demonstrate what Uni-life means to you.
- If you can, compare your word wall with that of a friend, or that of another group. How do your wall words compare or contrast? Is that because you hold different views about life at Uni?

New Friends | Freedom | **Tutorials** |
Lectures | **Food** | **Clubbing** | **Planning**
| **Seminars** | **Coffee** | **Books** |
Attendance | Reading | Work
placement | **Thinking** | Shopping |
Time | **Drafting my essay** | **Meeting
people** | **Eating** | **Getting a job** |
Earning my own money | Phoning
home | Browsing the internet |
Cooking | **Writing essays** | Travel |
Proofreading | **Group Project** | **Social
networking** | **Redrafting the essay**
| **Exercise** | **Referencing** | Talk |
Checking details | Printing | **Sleeping**

This chapter

In this chapter you can:

→ check your own assumptions and fantasies about what higher education will be like;

→ identify what these assumptions and fantasies are based upon;

→ take a reality check: consider how likely it is that your fantasies and assumptions would match reality;

→ give thought to which aspects of your positive fantasies about Uni or college you could turn into a reality.

20.1 The fantasy

Managing money

Cool! One Nice Big Loan! I'll never spend all that!

Managing time

There's hardly anything in my timetable – wow! All that time to do what I want!

Managing your lifestyle

So that would be … Eating? Getting from A to B? Having stuff to wear?

So let's sum up. That means:
- Loads of time to do what I like
- Oodles of money
- Endless parties
- Lots of chances to make new friends
- Chicken Tikka every night
- What's not to love?

Social Life

10,000 students in one place – it will be one big party!

Reflection	Life at Uni

How close are these comments to your own fantasy of what student life would be like in higher education?

Activity	My picture of life at Uni

Complete Resource Sheets 20a and 20b to help clarify your current thinking about life as a student in higher education.

20.2 True or false?

For each of the statements below, circle the answer you think applies.

1 Every Uni or college offering higher education is the same.
True / False

2 If you don't have any money, then you can't study for a degree at Uni or at college.
True / False

3 If you go to Uni, you have to live in halls of residence.
True / False

4 There are servants at Uni who collect your washing and return it to you clean and ironed.
True / False

5 At some Unis and colleges, all your meals can be provided for you.
True / False

6 At Uni, if you want to live in halls of residence, this is always provided.
True / False

7 When you arrive at Uni, there will be events and socials organised there to help you meet people and make friends.
True / False

8 You can study for a degree without leaving your own home, even for classes.
True / False

9 British students who want a degree have to study for this at a Uni or college in Britain.
True / False

10 All students spend all their time partying and drinking alcohol.
True / False

11 In higher education, there is a dean of students, chaplain or similar officer who checks in individually with all the students to see that they are generally healthy and happy and keeping up with their studies.
True / False

12 You can choose exactly what you want to study and whether you turn up for classes once you are at Uni.
True / False

Want to know more?
Read the Reality Check pages that follow, to see how far these are true or false. You can also see pages 301–2 to check your answers.

20.3 Reality Check: Year 1 students

My Uni is absolutely fantastic. We do get a lot of study done but I get involved with nearly everything – student rag week, helping out at the student union, the college choir, I've learnt karate. I go to the film nights run by the students' Japanese society as they show amazing animated films, luckily with sub-titles. I am thinking of going to Japan for a year after I finish college.

About 300 students live in this building, but in groups of 6–8. Sometimes, it gets a bit lively but mostly we are out and about a lot. We have this little kitchen on our landing. It's pretty basic for 8 of us. At night, we take it in turn to cook for anyone who is around – usually 4 or 5 people. We all contributed pots and pans and bits and pieces like spices or cooking oil. It's a bit anarchic and the cooking isn't exactly Jamie Oliver but it is all good fun.

I decided to start to study for a degree at my local college and if I get the right grades, there is a scheme that lets me do my final year at the local Uni. I liked the vocational degrees it offers as I thought it would help me get a job. We do meet up as students and have a laugh, but it is nice to go home to my family, and my dad's cooking, and my own bed every night.

Our student union organises millions of things for us. Mainly, I do sports coaching with local kids. This year, I did over 100 hours of support for community projects. Next year, I am going to help with an environmental project overseas – the union helped us raise the money to pay our expenses. It will be a fantastic experience.

My Uni doesn't have much student accommodation but its Accommodation Office helped me to find a place in a privately rented student house – five us live there – very cosy! We cook for ourselves at the house – and for anyone who drops in – but if we wanted we could eat all our meals in the Student Refectory.

Student meals can be a bit hit and miss …

I thought everyone at Uni would be amazingly clever and that I would have to study all the time and have no social life. I did struggle a bit in the first year but my marks are OK. I go to loads of student events and a bunch of us go to 'gym-and-swim' several times a week. A load of us meet up to do street dance.

I looked into studying in the USA or India for my degree. I nearly did, but then I decided to do a degree in England that let me study for just one year abroad. Next year, I will be studying in Spain on an exchange programme and then I'll come back here for my final year.

I have set up an online business and that takes up a lot of my time outside of college. It's only small now but I want to build it so I know I have a job when I finish my degree. I am thinking I might switch to part-time study so I have more time to think about my studies and to put into my business. There are five of us involved so we hang out together most of the time.

I have to do a foundation degree as part of my job. I go into college one or two days a week, and the rest of the time I am at work. I occasionally get to an event on campus, and I have a big network of friends from my course. We work and study for quite a lot of the week so I don't have time for student things. It isn't a problem for me because I love my course and my job and I have met some great people.

I do an on-line course from home. I do get out to some events organised for students that live in the area – and we communicate on-line too.

We are organising an expedition to the South Pole. I never thought one of the big costs of being a student would be thermal underwear!

Post your thoughts

How, if at all, do these students' reflections on their experiences (pages 205–6) change your picture of what life might be like at University?

A rewarding experience?

Higher education offers fantastic opportunities. Most students have a great time and, when they leave, they look back on their days at Uni with fondness.

> I finished my degree a year ago. I see the first years just starting out now and I know the wonderful years that lie ahead of them and all the new friends they will make. I feel really envious and wish I could start out all over again.

Are students satisfied with higher education?

Most students are very happy in higher education. On average, around 4 out of 5 students rate the student experience as good or excellent. Behind those statistics, are people who think their time at university or college was brilliant, and others who didn't have a good time.

You create the experience

To a large extent, having a really great time as a student depends on what you put into the experience. That is true of the study, the social life and how equipped you are for the career you want. Look out for:

- an active student body that provides events, clubs and societies, whether face-to-face or virtually;
- good opportunities for meeting, or communicating with, other students;
- opportunities for you to get involved in the life of the Uni or in the local community;
- the range of opportunities provided, such as work placements, overseas study, or the chance to learn something outside of your main course.

There isn't a typical 'Uni'

All Unis have their own characters so the experience can be very different from one to another. This is one reason why it is so important to visit before applying.

How much independence?

Depending on how independent you want to be – and how much you want to pay for services – you can find a university or college that:

- provides some, all or none of your accommodation;
- provides all meals – or none;
- organises many social activities – or very few;
- provides everything you need on campus – or very little.

20.6 Things I can do now

Picture yourself at Uni …

Imagine what you think your life as a student would be like. Consider the details of day-to-day life. For example, picture the following.

- How might you spend your time outside of class – in the day and also during the evenings, weekends and holidays.
- How will you make friends? What will you and your friends do together?
- What will you eat, and where?
- What travelling is involved? How will you get from A to B?
- What kinds of surroundings form part of that world? City streets? Small town life? Living at home? Views of the sea? Green fields? A location overseas?

And mind the gaps …

Look for gaps in your picture, or those aspects that are harder to imagine than others, especially if you haven't yet visited the institution. These are areas that you need to check out further so as to avoid nasty surprises later.

Make lists; find answers

Use your thoughts from the activity on page 209 to draw up a list of things you want to find out in order to gain a clearer picture of student life. Look for answers using the sources listed in chapter 4, 'Be fully informed'.

Write a list of questions

Many questions will occur to you apart from those you listed above. Be organised about writing these down, either as a long list of general points, or on separate sheets for each HEI that you are considering.

Get better informed

Read chapter 4, 'Be fully informed'. Find out about the range of information sources available to you and follow up those that are most relevant to the questions you have now. If you cannot find the information, then phone the contacts given on HEI websites or ask to speak to their Admissions tutors.

Student voice

If you can, do not rely only on the HEIs' marketing material. Find out what current students think about being at Uni, in general and at the HEIs that interest you.

Listen to what students say

Get a feel for what interests current students. Find out what they say about Uni, the issues relevant to them, and about applying to Uni. See

- the NUS website at www.nus.org.uk
- the Student Room at www.thestudentroom.co.uk

Visit a local HEI

Even if you want to study elsewhere, visit at least one university or college that provides higher education near where you live. It will help you to get a feel for the lifestyle.

20.7 Make it happen

Which strategies will I use?

Decide which of the strategies outlined in the chapter above could help you to gain a better sense of the reality of life in higher education. Tick all that apply.

1. ☐ Check my assumptions: Resource 20a.
2. ☐ Aim to separate out false assumptions from the facts.
3. ☐ Think through what lifestyle I want as a student – and the facilities or environment I would need.
4. ☐ Find out which HEIs are most likely to offer the lifestyle I want.
5. ☐ Think through how much independence I really want at Uni. What is right for me?
6. ☐ Picture myself at Uni – and check out the 'gaps'.
7. ☐ Make lists; find answers.
8. ☐ Get better informed.
9. ☐ Visit the NUS website.
10. ☐ Visit the Student Room website.
11. ☐ Visit a local Uni.
12. ☐ Visit a local college that provides higher education.

Prioritise

Choose between one and three of the strategies listed opposite to try out first. Enter the number given beside each strategy into the box below.

My first 3 priorities	
First choice	
Second choice	
Third choice	

Plan

Decide when you will give time and thought to your priorities.

- Jot those times into your planner or diary – or your timetable for planning towards Uni.
- In your planner, mark in a date within the next month to check that you are keeping to your plan.

Give and take support

Share your ideas with others in your group. Post comments about what you find out.

Give serious thought to other people's views about life at Uni, considering whether these might be helpful to you too.

Jot down your thoughts!

What is your picture of what life is like as a student at university or college?	Where does that picture come from?

In what ways is it likely to be realistic?

In what ways is it likely to be inaccurate?

Share your thoughts

- Discuss your thoughts and opinions with others in your group, or post them for discussion.
- Do you all hold the same fantasies about life at university or college?
- How and why do your opinions vary?

21 Managing your money

Budgets | Bargains | **Costs** | Shopping | **Part-time** | **Debts** | **Jobs** | **Loans** | Repayments | **Spending** | Cash | Savings | Accommodation | **Credit** | Rents | **Income** | **Council Tax** | **Debit** | **Expenditure** | **Interest** | **Expenses** | Enterprise | Business | Earnings | **Spending** | Phone | **Comparison websites** | **Luxuries** | **Earning your own money** | **Essentials** | Planning | **Bills** | Housing | Water | Gas | **Electricity** | Calculating | **Books** | **Accounts** | **Estimating** | **TV licence** | **Rent**

This chapter

In this chapter you can:

→ identify some of the issues that face students in managing their money in higher education;

→ find out some things that students wish they had known about managing money before they went to Uni;

→ learn how to balance your budget so that you will be in control of your finances once at Uni;

→ identify things you can do now to develop skills in managing your money as a student.

Here, our future Einsteins are sketching out their financial plans for student life …

Three years later, and our impecunious heroes are busy sharing tips on how to fund their next big ventures …

◁ **Soraya** *I have to look after my spending money now, so I will just do the same at Uni but on a bigger scale.*

◁ **Soraya** *Yeah, I thought I had the money thing sussed. I just didn't know how many things you were responsible for paying for when you are a student. I'm trying to find a job …*

◁ **Kian** *I am worried about the fees, and how much debt I will have as a student.*

◁ **Kian** *I find it weird the way we use money – it isn't like at home. At my Uni, we pay loads for expensive electronic devices and brands, and then spend our time talking about where we can save pennies on food, cheap socks and washing powder.*

◁ **Keira** *I plan to have at least one job while I am a student, so I think I will have plenty to spend.*

◁ **Keira** *I had to cut back on one of my jobs as my marks were being affected. Some days I live on breakfast cereal or whatever is cheap – until I get paid. But I have a separate bank account for saving up to go to Greece this summer.*

◁ **Lionel** *My parents should be able to help me out a lot so I don't think there will be any real money issues for me.*

◁ **Lionel** *Go away! I am trying to add up how many pennies we have in the penny jar in case we can buy some wine!*

What can you learn from them?

- Jot down a list of the things that strike you about how these students get by financially.
- How is this different from what you might have expected?

21.2 Being in charge of the money

Managing your own money

Once you are a student in higher education, you will be in charge of your personal finances. For most students, this can come as a challenge at first.

I never had to look after so much money at once. It didn't mean much to me.

I never had to keep track of my spending so I didn't know where to begin.

I thought my parents would pay for a lot of my costs but my dad said it would be good for me to find my own way. I was thrown in at the deep end and wasn't mentally prepared.

I ran out of money and hadn't paid all my library fines and money I owed the college. They won't let me back to study until I do. It was such a shock.

I didn't have much idea of what I would need to spend the money on.

I wasted loads of money early on – and then spent over a year trying to save every penny.

I kept buying what I thought I needed as I went along – and then ran out of money.

There is a lot of pressure at my Uni to spend money on certain items. It is hard to say no sometimes.

I was never very clear how much money I had at any one time.

A lot of my friends use their money really smartly buying bargains and they don't have any money to waste. I don't feel comfortable taking money from my parents because it would set me apart from the rest.

I am treated as an adult – if I mess up, I have to find a way out of it. That means finding ways of earning more money, or going hungry.

Activity	Students' experiences

What initial thinking about managing your money is stimulated from reading about these students' experiences?

Managing money doesn't have to be difficult. It usually gets hard if you don't have a plan from the outset about how you will go about managing your finances. If you get that right, it is much easier.

Balance

The key thing you will need to learn is how to balance the money you have available against how much you actually spend. This means balancing income versus expenditure.

If you have £7,000 as combined income from earnings, loans, grants, jobs and other sources, then you need to keep within that limit. If you have only £500 a year to spend, then you need to spend no more than £500.

It becomes more important to plan your finances under the following conditions – all of which can be true of student life in higher education.

When you don't know how much you might have to spend in total.

When you may run out of money if you don't watch carefully what you are spending.

Your spending is uneven across the week, month or year.

There are many things to buy.

Large items or bills could land several times a year, or at the end of the year.

£6000 Income

£10000 Expenditure

£5500 Income

£5200 Expenditure

21.4 Planning your finances now

As a student, you need to be skilled at managing money and planning your finances. You can get useful early practice by starting to think about your money now in ways similar to those you will use as a student.

Reflection	Your current financial planning

In what ways do you plan your money now? For example, are you saving towards a holiday or other large item – or even just to pay for your phone?

How do you go about planning what to spend and what to save, in order to achieve your goal?

Keeping it private

For the next activity, 'Work out your income', keep the actual details private. You can copy the resources pages to work this out accurately for yourself when you are not in class.

Money IN

(A) Work out your income

Use resource sheet A on page 220 to keep track of all the money you expect to gain in the next year from these sources:

- allowances or spending money;
- loans from parents or others;
- part-time jobs such as baby-sitting;
- presents of money and gift tokens;
- any other sources of income.

This is your projected income. Keep this up to date.

If you get a few hours' additional work, for example, or receive money as a present, add it to your list so you know exactly how much money you have available to spend.

Money OUT

(B) Keep track of expenditure

Use resource sheet B on page 221 to keep track of **everything** you spend across the year.

Work out your essentials

Start by writing down the things you have to spend money on – the essentials. Include things you may have to spend money on later in the year, such as presents or phone bills. How much do you need to put aside for these essentials?

Reflection	What if … ?

What will happen if you don't have money for those essentials?

(C) Money remaining

Use resource sheet C on page 221 to work out how much money you are likely to have left to spend on everything else, once you have paid for all the essentials.

(D) Weekly spend

Divide the total amount of money you have left by 52, to find out how much money you will have left to spend each week once all essentials are covered.

Divide the total by 12 to give you your monthly spend.

(E) Write your total shopping list

Use resource sheet E on pages 222–4 to make a list of everything you think you will need to spend money on in the year ahead *apart from the essentials* (as you have already listed these). You will probably find it easier to do this in broad terms such as 'bus fares', 'cosmetics' and 'snacks' rather than listing every single item separately.

Work out roughly what you will spend for each line of your shopping list over the year. If you have no idea of the cost of some items, use Google or another search engine to check these costs. Add them to your list.

If your list is longer than a single page:

- Add up the costs column for that page.
- Write this down as a sub-total.
- Copy that sub-total onto the line provided on the next page.

(F) Total expenditure

Use resource sheet F on page 224 to add together:

- the costs of the essentials;
- the cost of your total shopping list.

This total amount is your projected expenditure – the amount you expect to spend.

Will you be in profit?

Look again at how much money you have available to spend – your income. Compare this with how much you think you are going to need to spend (your total projected expenditure).

If you end up with more money at the end of the year than you started with, then you have made a profit. Any new money you were able to put into a savings account, for example, would be profit.

(a) Is your expected income bigger than your expected expenditure?

(b) If so, what will you do with the money you have over? Will you save it for Uni?

If you are out of balance …

If you are planning to spend more money than you think you will have available, your finances are out of balance. It is time to think about what you will do to balance your spending with your expected budget.

Will you:

- Spend less than planned?
- Find other ways of earning money?
- A mixture of both?
- Wait for money to fall from the sky?

Reflection	Balancing my budget
<ul><li>What could I do differently so that I spend less money?</li><li>How could I earn additional income?</li></ul>	

(G) Keep a running total

You can copy and use resource sheet G on page 225 to keep a record of ALL money coming in and ALL you spend – whether by cash, phone, on-line, or other means such as standing order.

Keep track of how much £ is left

When you spend money, use resource sheet G to subtract that from your previous total. So if you had £100 and you spent £10, your total would be reduced to £90.

Do it every day

Use resource sheet G regularly to maintain an up-to-date record of your finances. If you lost track of your spending as a student, you could run out of money and not be able to continue with your degree.

Forgot all about it?

If so, just catch up as best you can:

- Jot down a list of all the items you forgot to include.
- Add these to your list.
- Work out how much money is left.

Develop the habit

If you put time aside regularly to check your finances, it is easier to remember to do so. This becomes easier to do with practice.

Look for trends

When you have kept your list for a while, check whether you are spending much more (or less) on some items than expected. If so, update your projected expenditure (resource sheet F, page 224). Consider whether you are spending your money the way you really want to.

We spent far more on Not Noodles than I could ever have imagined possible.

Understand the costs

Most students need to contribute towards a set of shared bills – such as gas, electricity, water, council tax, TV licence, broadband and rental costs.

It helps if you can get used to how much such bills cost, and what adds to the costs, before you go to Uni.

- Ask to see household bills at home.
- Read the notes on these and see how the amounts are calculated.
- Experiment to see what makes your household gas or electricity meter work more quickly or slowly. Get permission first!

21.7   Make it happen

Which strategies will I use?

Decide which actions you can take now to help you to manage your disposable income once you arrive at Uni.

1 ☐ Think about how well I plan my money now.

2 ☐ Identify the strengths and weaknesses in how I manage my money now.

3 ☐ Take more responsibility for my own money.

4 ☐ Work out my annual income more precisely.

5 ☐ Work out more precisely my essential spending.

6 ☐ Work out what I want to spend money on – and what all this would cost me.

7 ☐ Work out where my money goes from one week to the next.

8 ☐ Plan ways to bring in more money.

9 ☐ Plan ways I could cut back on how much I spend.

10 ☐ Consider whether my money is going where I want it to.

11 ☐ Develop the habit of checking my finances regularly.

12 ☐ Understand the costs related to basic household bills I will have as a student.

Prioritise

Choose between one and three of the strategies listed opposite to try out first. List these below.

First 3 choices	
First choice	
Second choice	
Third choice	

Plan

Decide exactly when you will make use of each strategy. Set times that help you to build up a routine and that won't clash with other things you want to do.

- Jot the times into your planner or diary.
- Jot down a date within the next month to check what is working.

Experiment

Once you have used your first set of strategies, have a go with a new set. See which ones suit you best.

> **Give and take support**
> Think about who you would trust to discuss your money matters with, such as a responsible family member. How might they be able to advise you?

© Stella Cottrell (2012) *You2Uni*, Palgrave Macmillan

Resource 21a:
Personal finances

Use the table below to work out your likely total income for the year ahead. Keep this up to date, so that if you take on a part-time job, or receive money as a present, you keep a running total of your income and exactly what you have to spend.

(A) Total income	
Source of income	**Amount per year**
Part-time job 1* (See below.)	
Part-time job 2*	
Part-time job 3*	
Allowances or spending money	
Loans from parents or others	
Present/Gift of money 1	
Present/ Gift of money 2	
Gift tokens	
Savings account	
Any other sources of income	

Working out annual earnings from part-time jobs

For each part-time job you have, work out:
(a) How much you earn each week (after any tax and national insurance).
(b) How many weeks will you work?
(c) Multiply (a) x (b) to find your annual earnings from each part-time job. Enter the sum above.

Personal finances (continued)

(B) List of essential outgoings	
Daily travel	
Phone bill	
Presents for family	
Stationery	
Items for school/college	
Contributions to household expenses	
Other essentials	
Total known outgoing on essentials	
(C) Money remaining	
Total income (A)	
Total essentials (B)	
Total remaining to spend on everything else (C)	
(D) Spending per week and month	
Weekly spend: divide (C) by 52 weeks:	
Monthly spend: divide (C) by 12 months:	

(E) My total shopping list

List all the things you are likely to buy over the year ahead – apart from the essentials you have already listed. Use broad categories (e.g. chocolate bars/confectionery x 60 bars). Work out as accurately as you can what you are likely to spend for each line of your shopping list.

Items to buy	Number	Estimated total cost
Sub-total for the page		

(E) My total shopping list (continued)

Items to buy	Number	Estimated total cost
Sub-total for the page		
Sub-total carried across from previous page		
Total expected costs so far		

(E) My total shopping list (continued)

Items to buy	Number	Estimated total cost
Sub-total for the page		
Sub-total carried across from previous page		
Total expected costs of my shopping list		

(F) Total expenditure

On the table below, note down:

- The total costs of your essential outgoings (B)
- The total expected cost of your shopping list (E)

Add these together to find the total amount you expect to spend over the year (your projected expenditure).

Total expenditure	
(B) Essential outgoings	
(E) Total expected cost of shopping list	
(F) Total projected expenditure	

(G) Personal finances – running total

Date	Item purchased/money withdrawn	Money to start (funds available/money carried over)		
		Amount paid	**Income**	**Money left**
	Financial balance to carry forward			

Date	Item purchased/money withdrawn	Money to start (funds available/money carried over)		
		Amount paid	Income	Money left
	Financial balance to carry forward			

(G) Personal finances – running total

Date	Item purchased/money withdrawn	Amount paid	Income	Money left
	Money to start (funds available/money carried over)			
		Financial balance to carry forward		

22   Shopping for food

Buy-one-get-one-free | Campus
Shop | **Supermarket** | Pasta | **Brands**
| **Price** | **Special offer** | **Value brand**
| **Bargains** | **RICE** | Bulk-buy | **Eggs**
| Home delivery | **Sale** | Corner shop
| **Dry goods** | **Weekly shop** | **Market**
| **Milk** | **Compare** | **10% extra free**
| On-line | **Premium range** | Salt |
Convenience stores | Chocolate |
Coffee | **Baked beans** | **Lists** | **Storage**
| **Taste** | **Quality** | Freeze | **Savings**
| Meals | **Snacks** | Pepper | **Student**
Union | **Local** | **BREAD** | **Wastage** |
Stock | **Vegetables** | World foods

This chapter

In this chapter you can:

→ understand why food shopping can be a big issue for students in higher education;

→ find out things that students wish they had known about shopping before going to Uni;

→ consider some of the ways in which you could develop your skills as a 'smart shopper';

→ identify things that you could do now to start developing your shopping skills.

22.1 What students wish they had known …

Three years ago our fab four were innocent in the ways of shopping …

◁ **Mila** *I only eat brand-name food. Anything else makes me ill.*

◁ **Femi** *I shop each day – can of drink and bar of chocolate – sorted!*

◁ **Sarah** *Buy-One-Get-One-Free – that's the way to go. My cupboards will always be full.*

◁ **Jack** *I know supermarkets exist – I've heard my mum talk about them.*

Here they are today, and our industrious purchasers have shopped till they have dropped, rooting out the bargains …

◁ **Mila** *I only eat 'value' brand food. Anything else makes me poor. I found out that I can't actually tell the difference.*

◁ **Femi** *I never realised how much I actually eat in a week and how heavy it is to carry it home. I plan my shop much more carefully now.*

◁ **Sarah** *B.O.G.O.F.s can bog-off! There's only so much of something that I can stand eating and I've ended up chucking loads of it in the bin. Now I only buy the things I know I can use.*

◁ **Jack** *I've now had a number of close encounters with supermarkets – too close. All that choice, all those bright lights, all those people – scary!*

What can you learn from them?

- In what ways were these students' experiences of shopping different from what they expected?
- What do you think it will be like to shop for food when you are at Uni or college? Is your thinking similar to that of any of these students?

Saving a few pence here and there might not feel worth the effort now but many students find that this becomes an important part of everyday life once at Uni. You can make consistent savings week by week which, over the course of your studies, can make a difference to how much you have to spend on clothes, books, holidays or nights out. The following tips can help you save money.

Know how much things cost

Before going to Uni, build up your sense of what things cost. If you are not used to buying food on a regular basis it can be a shock to realise exactly how much the total bill can amount to.

Shop around

The price of items such as a loaf of bread can vary substantially from shop to shop. Get a feel for which shops are best for which kinds of product that you might want to eat.

Find out the price of brand loyalty

Shops want your custom and will lower prices or offer bargains and incentives for you to switch to them from brand labels. If you are willing to shop around and try new things, you can save a lot of money. Most supermarkets now offer 'value' brands at lower prices than mainstream products. The packaging is generally plain so they may look less appetising, but the taste can be the same.

Bulk buy

Some items, such as tinned and dry goods, lend themselves well to bulk buying. This is a good option as long as storage is not a problem.

Buy only what you can use

It can be tempting to do huge shops to get it all out of the way in one go, especially when you are taking advantage of special offers.

However, if you end up throwing food away, it is a waste of money. Fresh foods, such as meat, fish, dairy products, fruit and vegetables, need to be used fairly soon after you have bought them.

Activity

Plan out a meal for yourself, using the tips on page 247. Of the things that you would need to buy, work out which could be stored, and which it would be better to buy in small amounts.

22.3   Know your shopping options

There will be a range of shopping options available to you. If you become familiar with these now, you will develop a sense of where you can save money when shopping for yourself as a student.

> Your choice of shop will depend on:
> * what you want to buy;
> * how much you are willing to pay for it;
> * the range of outlets in your area;
> * how far you are willing to travel to them;
> * whether you can shop on-line.

Convenience stores

Convenience stores often cluster in areas where there is a large student population. These stock 'essential' items such as bread, milk and tinned goods. The range of items and brands tends to be limited. In general, these are slightly more expensive than bigger stores but it is worth keeping an eye out for special offers.

Depending on where you study, your local convenience store may be a good place to buy international products. Pre-packaged spices sold in Indian and South-East Asian convenience stores are often much cheaper than in supermarkets.

Markets

Many people never venture to their local market so they miss the opportunity for some real food bargains. You generally can't buy everything in one place, which makes them less convenient, but they can be great places to buy fruit and vegetables much more cheaply than at a supermarket. Especially at the end of the day, you can get lots for your money when produce is sold off very cheaply.

Supermarkets

These generally offer the widest choice of products, usually at the cheapest prices. Large chains have the purchasing power to discount many products or give special offers such as 'Buy One, Get One Free' (BOGOF).

If you have more than one supermarket chain to choose from, it is worth shopping around to see which one is consistently cheapest for the products that you buy most often. Use websites such as www.mysupermarket.co.uk to compare prices across a range of supermarkets.

Campus shops

Most Unis have a campus shop. It is a convenient option and likely to stock the sorts of things students want to eat when they are in a hurry – plenty of pies, pasties, ready meals and tinned food.

These can be less good for fresh fruit and vegetables and you might pay more for products, depending on who runs the shop. This can be a good option for emergencies or days when you can't face cooking.

22.4   Things you can do now

You may already be an experienced shopper, helping with the family shop. If so, you will have developed skills which will serve you well at Uni. If not, the following information and activities will help you prepare for food shopping as a student.

Guess the prices

Students often get caught out in their first year of living away from home because they don't have a good sense of what things cost for everyday living. Your first step to becoming a 'smart shopper' is to gain knowledge of the price of everyday food items.

Activity	Guess the price of the list

Opposite, is a list of things that might appear on a student's shopping list for a week.

1   Make a quick, 'gut-instinct', guess at what the total spend would be.
2   Jot down your guess in the box below.

Initial guess at total cost of list:

'The price is right'

Now choose ONE local shop or supermarket where you could buy all of these items.

1   Estimate how much each item on the list would cost at that retailer. Jot down your guess on page 236.
2   Next, visit the shop and jot down the actual prices. Compare these with your estimates.
3   If you do this with friends or as a group, see who is best at estimating prices.

Shopping list

1   loaf of white sliced bread
2   4 pint bottle of semi-skimmed milk
3   250g pack of Cheddar cheese
4   440g tin of baked beans
5   2 baking potatoes
6   4-pack of fruit yoghurts
7   multi-pack of 6 packets of crisps
8   4 apples
9   packet of digestive biscuits
10   packet of spaghetti
11   tin of tomatoes
12   250g minced beef
13   200g closed cup mushrooms
14   bag of salad leaves

Reflection	How good was I?

• Which items did you guess accurately?
• Were there any items where the actual cost surprised you?

Activity	Cost your favourite meal

Write a list of items you would need for your favourite meal. Use Resource 22c (page 238) to work out the cost of buying all the ingredients.

22.5   Things you can do now (2)

Can you tell the difference?

If you are convinced that you only like one specific brand of a product, try the 'Taste the brand' activity below. See if you can really taste the difference between costly and cheaper brands.

Activity	Taste the brand

Work in a group of 5 people. For each item below, you will need a product from a major brand and one from a cheaper or value range.

- Baked beans
- Cola
- Tomato ketchup
- Cornflakes
- Digestive biscuits

1 Label the bottom of 10 identical plastic cups or containers with its intended contents – each one will contain a different item and brand. Make sure that this cannot be seen.
2 One person puts a small amount of each product into the container that carries its label, keeping a record of which is which, and the order in which each person tastes each item.
3 The rest of the group takes a taste of both versions and rates each out of 5 for taste. Use resource sheet 22d to record the scores.
4 How well do the products compare? Is there much difference in the scores of expensive and cheaper brands? If so, is this for all items?
5 Which cheaper brands are a good option? Are there any brands for which you would not be willing to make a compromise?

Students generally become excellent at searching for bargains, but often not before they have spent more than they need or dealt with fridges full of festering products that they bought in bulk but couldn't use. Start developing your bargain hunting skills now – in pairs, small groups or as a whole class.

Activity	Bargain Hunt League

How long? Decide how many weeks you will run the activity.

When? Decide on which day of the week you will meet to compare prices.

Choose ONE product a week. Be specific about the brand of product and the weight.

Search for the cheapest. Each week, each player must search out the cheapest possible price for that week's item. You can look in any shop or on-line site.

The day of reckoning. On comparison day, each player writes down the cheapest price they have found and where they found it. The other players must be able to verify your price.

Record it. Make a note of everyone's prices using the resource sheets on pages 240–1.

Winner. At the end of the agreed time, players add up the total of all the prices they found each week. The winner is the one with the *lowest* total score.

Reflection	Best and worst?

What have you found out about the best, and worst, places to find food bargains?

22.6 Things you can do now (3)

Write the family's shopping list

If you are not a regular food shopper, it can be hard to know exactly how much food you need to buy each week. You can start to learn this by thinking about your own family or household's weekly shop.

List

Jot down all the food items that you think your own household needs to buy this week.

Check the cupboards

Do this by looking through the cupboards to see what you think might be needed.

Plan

Consider what kinds of meals you eat across the week. What ingredients and products are needed for these? Make sure that everything you need is available already or on your list.

Estimate

When you think your list is complete, have a go at calculating how much it is likely to cost to do that shop. Don't cheat by asking your parents or carers for the price of items, and don't let them give you tips at this stage.

How good were you?

When you are happy that you have put the full list together and priced it, check with whoever usually does the shopping to see how accurate your list was for:

- contents;
- pricing.

Reflection | **What would I do differently?**

Jot down the following:

(a) Things you had on your list that were not needed this week. What would they have cost you if you had gone out and bought them?
(b) Things that are needed but were not on your list. When you add these up, how much do they add to your costs?
(c) What proportion of the cost of the shopping went on essential items and what went on items that are good to eat but not a key part of meals – such as chocolate, crisps, biscuits, fizzy drinks?

Do the shopping?

As a next step, you may find it helpful to do the shopping yourself. If this seems daunting, you could just take on a part of the shopping list. When doing the shop, notice the following.

Navigation: How easy is it to find your way round the shop or on-line site that you chose?

Distractions: Are you easily distracted by special offers or things that you don't need but which look particularly tasty?

Weight and bulk: How easy is it to carry your shopping back home? Did you have to walk far with heavy bags?

Transport: How did you get it all home? Did you need a lift or taxi? Did you, or could you, manage it all on the bus?

When choosing your Uni: These will be considerations when you are a student and have to do your own shopping.

22.7   Make it happen

Which strategies will I use?

Decide which actions you can take now to help you develop the skills to be a 'smart shopper' at college or Uni.

1 ☐ Consider how my attitudes towards shopping might help or hinder me.

2 ☐ Get to know the shopping options available to me in my local area.

3 ☐ Visit a range of these to learn about the range and prices of their goods.

4 ☐ Play 'The Price is right'.

5 ☐ Cost out my favourite snacks (22b).

6 ☐ Cost out a favourite meal (22c).

7 ☐ Get to know the price of food items that I am likely to buy regularly.

8 ☐ Identify which shopping option allows me to buy these items at the cheapest price (p. 231).

9 ☐ Test out both branded and 'value brand' versions of essential items to see if I can really tell the difference (p. 233).

10 ☐ Take part in a 'Bargain Hunt' League (p. 233).

11 ☐ Plan and cost the household shopping for a week (p. 234).

12 ☐ Do the household food shop to get a sense of how easy or difficult this is (p. 234).

13 ☐ Identify the shopping options available in 3 of the places where I am considering going to Uni.

Prioritise

Choose between one and three of the strategies listed opposite to try out first. List these below.

First 3 choices	
First choice	
Second choice	
Third choice	

Plan

Decide exactly when you will make use of each strategy. Set times that help you to build up a routine and that won't clash with other things you want to do.

- Jot the times into your planner or diary.
- Jot down a date within the next month to check you have done what you had planned.

Experiment

Once you have used your first set of strategies, have a go with a new set. See which ones suit you best.

Give and take support

Think about who might be able to advise you on food shopping, such as family members.

What kind of help would you find most useful?

Resource 22a:
'The Price is right' record sheet

- Jot down one participant's name at the top of each column below.
- Write each person's estimate for the price of each item in the column below their name.
- Write the actual shop price in the final column.
- For each item, highlight the estimate closest to the actual price. Then see whose column has the highest number of highlighted items: to see who made the best overall set of estimates.

Shopping list items	Person 1's estimate:	Person 2's estimate:	Person 3's estimate:	Person 4's estimate:	Actual price
1 loaf of white sliced bread					
2 4 pint bottle of semi-skimmed milk					
3 250g pack of Cheddar cheese					
4 440g tin of baked beans					
5 2 baking potatoes					
6 4-pack of fruit yoghurts					
7 multi-pack of 6 packets of crisps					
8 4 apples					
9 packet of digestive biscuits					
10 packet of spaghetti					
11 tin of tomatoes					
12 250g minced beef					
13 200g closed cup mushrooms					
14 bag of salad leaves					

Resource 22b: Costs of favourite snacks

Use the chart below to write a list of items that you like to eat as they are, uncooked, such as biscuits, fruit, cereals, drinks, etc. The chart enables you to work out the cost per helping too. (If maths isn't your thing: this means that to find the price per helping, you divide the price (A) by the number of helpings (B). So, if an item cost 99p and it contained 3 helpings, each helping would cost 33p).

Like to eat	**A** **Price to buy**	**B** **Number of helpings included**	**C** **Price per helping (A divided by B)**
Total costs	**£**		**£**

Resource 22c:
Meal I like

Choose one meal that you enjoy eating, for which you would need to shop for ingredients as a student. Find out the ingredients you would need. Write these into the table and find the best prices you can for each. Add up the cost of the shopping you would need to do to make your favourite meal.

Consider how many helpings are included when you buy each of these ingredients. How many meals could you make with the ingredients you bought?

Meal:			
Things I would need to buy		**Cost to buy ingredients**	**How many helpings included?**
Total cost to buy all ingredients			

Resource 22d:
'Taste the brand' record sheet

- Use this chart to keep a record of the scores that each group member gives to the expensive and 'value' (cheaper) brands of each item. Write in the name of the item being tested.
- The person(s) not tasting the items allocate one of columns A–D to each of up to 4 tasters, to record their individual score for the expensive item and for the value item.
- Tasters can give any items any score from 0 to 5 (5 being 'excellent').
- After the tastings, add up the set of group scores for the expensive brand of each item and write this down under **Total**. Then do the same for the 'value' items.

Item	Expensive Brand					'Value' brand				
	Score A	Score B	Score C	Score D	Total	Score A	Score B	Score C	Score D	Total
Example	*5*	*1*	*1*	*3*	*10*	*2*	*2*	*4*	*2*	*10*
1										
2										
3										
4										
5										
6										
7										
8										
9										
10										
Number of times the group preferred the expensive brand										
Number of times the group preferred the 'value' brand										
Overall winner (expensive or 'value' brand?)										

My record			
Week	Product (including brand, amount, type, etc.)	Supplier (where I found it in shops or on-line)	Best cost I found
Week 1			
Week 2			
Week 3			
Week 4			
Week 5			
Week 6			
Week 7			
Week 8			

Resource 22f:
'Bargain Hunt League': Group records

League record sheet					
Player names	Player 1 Name	Player 2 Name	Player 3 Name	Player 4 Name	Player 5 Name
Price Week 1					
Price Week 2					
Price Week 3					
Price Week 4					
Price Week 5					
Price Week 6					
Price Week 7					
Price Week 8					
Total costs per player					
Winner!					

23 Food at Uni: Famine or feast?

Delicious | Snacks | **Basics** | Economical | **Hungry** | **Cooked** | **Quick** | **Toast** | **Bake** | **Oven** | Meal | **Microwave** | Cheese | **Breakfast** | Temperature | **Toast** | **Grill** | **Beans** | **Recipes** | **Eggs** | **Potatoes** | Tasty | Fresh | Trial and error | **Cereals** | Supplies | **Edible** | **Raw** | **Confidence** | **Tuna** | **Fillings** | **Salt** | Frying pan | Tagliatelle | Planning | **Pepper** | Tomatoes | **Soup** | **Practice** | **Spaghetti** | **Saucepan** | **Rice** | **Favourites** | Sauce | Lunch | Portions | **Dinner** | Spices | **Stir** | **Pasta** | **Meat** | **Combinations** | Bacon | **Mustard** | Butter | Fish-slice | Variety | **Creative** | Yummy

This chapter

In this chapter you can:

→ find out what students wish they had known about eating and cooking before going to college or Uni;

→ learn some basic cooking techniques which you might use at Uni;

→ identify what you could do now to start to develop your confidence and cooking skills;

→ find out how to make a small amount of cooking knowledge go a long way;

→ build your awareness and knowledge of preparing meals, from the most basic steps to more adventurous recipes.

23.1 What students wish they had known …

Three years ago our foodie four had full bellies and few worries about where their next meal was coming from.

◁ **Jasmine** *I can make a decent cup of tea and a slice of toast. As long as I can work out how to microwave meals, I reckon I'll survive OK.*

◁ **Kobe** *I've been cooking since I was a little kid. I can't wait until I can buy all my own stuff and cook what I want when I want.*

◁ **Andrew** *As long as I can get pasties, pies and sausage rolls I'll be fine. One minute in the microwave – meal sorted.*

◁ **Anjali** *My Mum cooks the best food ever. It looks hard so I've never tried cooking. She says if I ever leave home, she'll send me supplies.*

Three years later, here they are, and the cooks are coming into their own.

◁ **Jasmine** *Ready meals cost too much and toast was boring! I worked out how to make something edible with tuna, pasta and tinned tomatoes – at least it is cheap and filling.*

◁ **Kobe** *I still rock in the kitchen but I found out that cooking every single day is less fun than I thought it would be. Some days, you just can't be bothered.*

◁ **Andrew** *I learned that pastry is not a 'super-food' when my jeans buttons started bulging. I had to learn to cook pretty fast and there was a lot of trial and error.*

◁ **Anjali** *Mum did keep up a steady supply of meals. I can't complain but I still don't really have a clue about how to cook. It would be nice to be able to cook a quick snack when I need it!*

What can you learn from them?

- In what ways were these students' experiences of eating and preparing meals at Uni different from what they expected?
- What skills would have helped them? Do you have those skills already?

23.2 Using the microwave

You may already cook on a regular basis and feel confident in the kitchen. If so, you may wish to skip this section. Otherwise, this section can help you start to develop your confidence to cook.

Using a microwave oven

It is good to know how to use a microwave before going off to Uni. Kitchens in student halls usually have these. They are easy to use and cheap to buy if you are in rented accommodation.

What can you do in a microwave?

- Cook ready meals.
- Warm up milk for hot drinks.
- Defrost frozen food.
- Heat soup.
- Re-heat leftover food.
- Cook jacket potatoes.

Microwave savvy

Different makes of microwave vary in their operating instructions, but you will usually need to do the following.

Get the right container
Make sure that the item you want to cook is in a microwave-safe container. Most ready meals come in these already. Never put anything metal in a microwave, including aluminium foil – it bounces the microwaves back against the oven and will break it.

Select the power
Choose the power level you want to use – almost everything can be cooked on the highest level. The only exception is when you are defrosting food, when you should use a lower power level.

Do it!
- Close the microwave door.
- Select a time. This will usually be indicated on the pack of the item you want to heat. To heat up a cup of coffee generally takes about 90 seconds.
- Press the 'start' button. Cooking will start and the time will count down.
- The end of cooking is usually signalled by the oven switching off and making a bleeping or 'pinging' noise.

See page 253 for information about times and temperatures.

Cooking with liquids?

If you have heated a liquid, allow it to stand for 30–60 seconds before taking it out of the microwave. Stir it well and check it is hot all the way through before consuming.

Want it crispy?

Microwaves work well for many foods. However, they don't work well for most 'crispy' foods like pastry or pizza. You can safely cook these products in a microwave but they will tend to be a bit 'soggy'.

23.3　The wonders of toast

Toast is a great starting place for the beginner cook. The worst you can do is burn it – and possibly set the house on fire. It is simple to make, comforting to eat and versatile.

- With butter and jam or peanut butter, it's breakfast.
- With melted cheese, it's lunch.
- With baked beans, it makes a quick and healthy tea.
- Add toppings to suit your mood.

Instructions for how to make cheese on toast are below. You can adapt this basic technique to give you more variety.

I've made you my speciality: pain grillé au fromage.

Cheese on Toast

What you need
2 slices of bread
25g butter
50g hard cheese, e.g. cheddar
Cheese grater
Grill
Plate

Basic method
- Put 2 slices of bread under a hot grill and cook on one side until a light brown colour.
- Turn bread over; butter the untoasted side.
- Grate the cheese – put this on top of the buttered side, covering the bread completely.
- Put back under the grill until the cheese melts and starts to bubble.
- Remove and eat.

To add variety

Before adding cheese: Put ham, tomato, pickle or mushrooms on the toast; then add the cheese.

After adding cheese: Put tomato, dried herbs, salami, chopped peppers or olives on top of the cheese before you put it under the grill, to create a 'toast pizza'.

Mixed with the cheese: Add one teaspoon of wholegrain mustard and one teaspoon of mayonnaise to the grated cheese before grilling.

Beans on toast: Instead of using cheese, use beans. Warm the contents of a tin of baked beans in a saucepan over a low heat on the hob for 5 minutes until hot – or use a microwaveable container and cook the beans for 1–2 minutes on full power. Cook the toast at the same time. Add the cooked beans to the buttered toast.

23.4   Jacket potatoes

Jacket potatoes are cheap, filling, versatile, and simple to make, all things which tend to make them popular with student chefs.

> *What you need*
> - 1 medium to large baking potato
> - Metal skewer
> - Oven
> - Plate
> - 25g butter
> - Salt and pepper

Basic Method

- Heat the oven to 220° C or Gas Mark 7.
- Wash and dry the potato.
- Push metal skewer through potato lengthways – this will conduct heat to the centre of the potato and help it cook more quickly and evenly.
- Leave to cook for an hour.
- When done, the outside will be crisp.
- Remove the skewer – it should have small bits of cooked potato on it.
- Cut the potato in half, add butter and eat.

Quick method

You can cook a jacket potato in a microwave but don't then use a metal skewer. It takes about 10 minutes to cook on full power but it will not have a crispy skin. You will give your potato a crisp skin if you cook it in a microwave for 5 minutes on full power and then put it into an oven (pre-heated to 220 degrees C) for 30 minutes.

> **Toppings to add variety**
> Grated cheese; baked beans; coleslaw; tuna, mayonnaise and sweetcorn; hummus; crispy bacon; fried mushrooms; cottage cheese; prawns and mayonnaise.

Using up leftovers

Jacket potatoes can be a good base for leftover dishes such as chilli, curry or pasta sauces (see Resource 23a, page 250).

Toppings or fillings?

Instead of putting ingredients on top of your potato you can also scoop out the contents of a cooked potato, mix it with other ingredients, put it back into the potato skin and return it to the oven briefly. Cheese works particularly well as a filling, especially when you add some mustard and mayonnaise into the mixture.

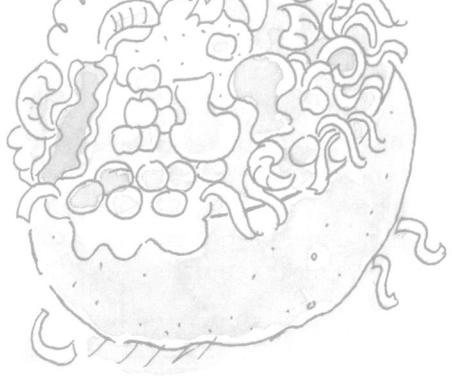

23.5   Planning meals as a student

One of the main challenges of eating as a student is having to consider how you will cover several meals a day, every day, and combining this with study and other life demands. In chapter 22, you looked at how to shop for a week's food. Planning each day's meals is an important part of that shopping. The following tips can help.

Get to know your portion sizes

If you do not cook regularly, you may not know the amounts of food which go into particular meals or recipes. Get into the habit of noting the amounts of food you consume in terms of:

- the amount of different items on your plate;
- how those amounts looked before being prepared and before they were cooked;
- how much you would need to buy to prepare one or more meals.

Give yourself choices

This chapter gives you ideas on how to add variety to basic meals so as to keep these interesting. There are plenty of student cookbooks and websites which will give you ideas of simple cheap meals that you could learn to prepare. See Appendix 4 for details.

I overdid my favourite 2 dishes in my first term until I couldn't face them any more. I found that I needed at least 5 or 6 different meals to stop food from getting really boring.

Have easy meal ideas on standby

There will be some days when you won't feel like cooking. It can be tempting to buy fast food or ready meals at these times, but this can be very expensive and unhealthy. Stock up with ingredients for some easy meal options such as jacket potatoes, beans on toast, and pasta and sauce (pages 250–1) for when you need them.

Cook more than one portion

Many recipes make enough for two people. If you are only cooking for one, most leftovers can be stored in a lidded container in a fridge overnight. Make sure food is cold before putting it in the fridge. Eat it the next day, either cold or ensuring it is heated through thoroughly.

If you have freezer space, you can store leftovers on the day you cook; these will keep for one month. Having leftovers available to re-heat is helpful for busy days when you don't have time to cook from scratch.

23.6   Things you can do now

If you are very inexperienced at cooking, learn some basic skills now to help for life at Uni. You can start by doing one or all of the following.

Observation: Watch others cook

Being around other people when they are cooking can help you develop your own skills, especially if you take good notice of what they do, ask questions and help out.

This gives you a sense of how long it takes to prepare different food, the types and amounts of ingredients used, where ingredients were stored, how much attention to pay food whilst it is cooking, the amount of seasoning to use, the equipment to use, the temperatures to cook at (see page 253), and the equipment needed. You may pick up how to multi-task, so that you can prepare meals whilst keeping other tasks going at the same time.

Become familiar with recipe books

Get used to reading recipes from different sources such as books, internet or magazines. Look for:

- The level of detail: do they assume a basic level of skill or talk you through each step?
- The measurements used for ingredients: are these given in formal amounts such as grams and kilograms or looser measurements such as spoonfuls and cupfuls?
- Illustrations: some recipe books provide a picture of the finished dish whilst others might show you what the dish should look like at different stages of preparation.

Have a go at the practice recipe on 23a as a start.

(see page 253)

Activity	Which recipes?

Read and try out recipes from several different sources. You will notice that these vary in how they are set out and how much detail and background information they provide.

Jot down the names of those books or sources that you prefer to work with.

Reflection	Recipe formats

Which kinds of recipe formats do you find it easiest to work with?

Build your confidence

Practise the simple cooking tasks in this section. The more you cook, the easier it will get. Get into the habit of making lunch or dinner for yourself at least once a week. Keep a record of dishes or techniques which work particularly well for you.

 Try more complex recipes as your cooking skills develop.

 Create your own recipes – you may develop your perfect meal!

 Vary recipes by swapping or adding ingredients.

23.7 Make it happen

Which strategies will I use?

Decide which actions you can take now to make life easier at college or Uni.

1 ☐ Cook something in a microwave.

2 ☐ Make a meal on toast.

3 ☐ Cook a jacket potato with my favourite filling.

4 ☐ Look at a range of recipes in books, magazines and on-line.

5 ☐ Follow the recipe on resource sheet 23a.

6 ☐ Help prepare a meal at home.

7 ☐ Follow a recipe from a book, magazine or website.

8 ☐ Observe someone else cooking a meal I would like to cook myself.

9 ☐ Cook rice or pasta using resource sheet 23b.

10 ☐ Plan out a meal for one.

11 ☐ Shop for ingredients for a meal.

12 ☐ Cook myself a meal once a week.

13 ☐ Experiment with a recipe by adding or changing an ingredient.

14 ☐ Create my own recipe.

Prioritise

Choose between one and three of the strategies listed opposite to try out first. List these below.

First 3 choices	
First choice	
Second choice	
Third choice	

Plan

Decide exactly when you will make use of each strategy.

- Jot the times into your planner or diary.
- Jot down a date within the next month to check what is working.

Experiment

Once you have used your first set of strategies, have a go with a new set. See which ones suit you best.

> ### Give and take support
> Consider ways in which you and your friends could help each other to develop your cooking skills, such as by cooking together or sharing recipes or cooking tips.

Resource 23a:
Basic sauces

A great many meals are generally based around a relatively small core set of recipes. You can create a number of very different dishes by learning the core recipe and then varying what you add to it. A basic tomato sauce provides an ideal starting place for students.

Basic tomato sauce (makes 2 portions)

What you need
- 1 tablespoon of oil
- 1 small onion
- 1 400g tin of chopped tomatoes
- 1 tablespoon tomato purée
- Salt and black pepper to taste
- Medium-sized saucepan
- Sharp knife for chopping
- Wooden spoon for stirring

Method
- Chop the onion into small pieces.
- Put the oil into the saucepan and cook the onion on a low to medium heat for 10 minutes, stirring every couple of minutes. The onion will soften as you cook it and become 'see-through'.
- Add the tomatoes and tomato purée. Bring the temperature of the sauce up to the point where it starts to bubble.
- Then turn the heat down to the point where it simmers (bubbles gently) and allow it to cook like that for 15–20 minutes. The sauce should thicken slightly as it cooks.
- When it is cooked, add salt and pepper to your own taste.

You can use the basic tomato sauce with pasta (see 23b). You can also vary it as shown below.

Bolognese Sauce

Changes to the basic tomato sauce recipe
Once the onion is softened, add in 250g of beef, lamb or vegetarian mince. Fry the mince for a few minutes so that, if it is meat, it is no longer pink. When you add the tomato, stir in a stock cube (beef or vegetable) and a teaspoon of mixed, dried or frozen herbs.
Serve with pasta (see 23b).

Chilli

Changes from the Bolognese recipe
Swap the dried herbs used in the Bolognese recipe for 2 teaspoons of chilli powder (mild or hot to your taste). When you add in the tomatoes, also add in a drained tin of cooked kidney beans and cook for 20 minutes.
Serve with boiled rice (see 23b).

Mattar Paneer (Vegetarian Indian dish)

Changes to the basic tomato sauce recipe
When the onion is cooked, stir in a tablespoon full of ready-made curry paste. Cut a 250g pack of Paneer (an Indian cottage cheese available in most supermarkets) into 2cm squares and cook with the onion for 2–3 minutes. Add in tomato and tomato purée and a mug full of frozen peas. Cook for 20 minutes on a low-to-medium heat.
Serve with boiled rice (see 23b).

Resource 23b:
Cooking rice and pasta

The recipes on the previous page give you several meal options. These are designed to be served with rice or pasta, both of which are cheap ingredients. Neither is difficult to cook if you follow these methods.

Rice

Half a mug of dried rice is a decent sized portion for one person. The general rule of cooking rice is to use twice as much water as you have rice. So, for one portion, use one mug of water.

First, bring the water to the boil in a medium-sized saucepan with a lid on it. Add a pinch of salt. Once the water is boiling, add in the rice, stir once and bring back to the boil. Then, reduce the heat until it is just simmering (bubbling gently); put the lid on the pan and leave to cook like that.

The length of time that you need to cook rice varies depending on the type of rice.

- Easy cook, long grain rice takes about 15 minutes.
- Brown rice takes about 30 minutes.

Keep checking whilst the rice cooks to make sure that it has not boiled dry. Add a little more water if needed. Don't stir the rice again: this releases starch and will make it sticky. If you have kept your rice on a gentle simmer, it should be done when the water is all gone. The grains should be plump and soft to eat.

Pasta

For pasta shapes such as fusilli (twists) or penne (quills), a mug full of dried pasta makes a generous-sized portion for one person. For spaghetti, a bundle approximately 2cm in diameter provides a portion for one person.

First, fill a large lidded saucepan two-thirds full of water, add a pinch of salt, and bring to the boil (bubbling fiercely). Once the water is boiling, if you are cooking long, thin pasta, you can add a tablespoon of oil to help prevent it sticking to itself. Add your pasta, stir once and bring back to the boil. Then, turn the temperature down until it is simmering (bubbling gently).

Cooking time varies depending on the type of pasta and, for dried pasta, how thick it is.

- Long thin pasta like spaghetti or tagliatelle only takes 6–8 minutes.
- Thicker pasta such as penne: 10–12 minutes.
- Macaroni takes around 15 minutes.
- Fresh pasta takes only 3–4 minutes.

Taste a piece of pasta to see if it is cooked. It should have a little resistance when you bite into it – known as 'al dente'. If it is crunchy, cook for longer. When ready, serve with a sauce of your choice.

Resource 23c:
Cooking with eggs

Buying and using eggs

Check the sell-by date when buying and using eggs; use only fresh eggs.

Scrambled egg

What you need per person
- 2 eggs
- About 20 grams of butter (a tenth of a packet)
- 2–3 dessertspoons of milk or cream
- Salt and black pepper to taste
- Medium-sized saucepan with a thick base
- Mixing bowl (or a mug would do)
- Fork
- Wooden spoon for stirring eggs in the pot

Method
- Break the eggs into the bowl, and check that no shell has fallen in. Add salt and pepper. Beat the eggs until the white and the yolk are well mixed together.
- Add the milk or cream to the eggs and beat in.
- Melt the butter in the saucepan on a medium to high heat, watching it so it does not burn.
- Then pour the eggs into the saucepan. Immediately, start to stir the mixture. Keep stirring until the egg cooks to a thick and creamy consistency and you can see the beginnings of small lumps forming within it.
- Remove from the heat straight away to prevent hard lumps forming.
- Ideally, multi-task so that you cook toast alongside this and can have scrambled egg on toast.

Omelette

What you need per person
- 3 eggs for a substantial omelette
- About 20 grams of butter (a tenth of packet)
- 2–3 dessertspoons of milk, cream or water
- Salt and black pepper to taste
- Mixing bowl (or a mug would do)
- Fillings to taste: grated cheese, cooked bacon, fried mushrooms, diced ham or tomatoes, etc.
- Small frying pan (or omelette pan)
- Fish-slice

Method
- Prepare your fillings so they are ready to add.
- Break the eggs into the bowl, and check that no shell has fallen in. Add salt and pepper and beat until the white and the yolk of the egg are well mixed together. Add the milk or cream to the egg mixture and beat in.
- Melt the butter in the frying pan on a medium to high heat, watching it so it does not burn.
- Once the butter has melted, pour the egg mixture into the pan.
- Allow the egg to begin to set at the base of the pan. Gently sweep this up from around the edges using the fish-slice, allowing the unset egg to run beneath it and cook. Use large sweeping movements from below rather than stirring, so you avoid scrambling the egg.
- Whilst a little of the egg is still slightly runny, put your fillings on top of the egg, on one half only. Use the fish-slice to flip the other half of the omelette over the filling.
- Serve immediately. Good with salad.

Gas	Electric	Effect	Cooks	
	°C	°F		(reduces by 10–20° for fan ovens)
Temperatures below 160°C (Gas 3) are rarely used except for slow cooking				
½	120	250	Very cool/slow	Meringues; slow cooking meat after the first half hour
1	140	275	Very cool/slow	Large fruit cake
2	150	300	Cool/slow	
3	160–70	325	Warm/slow	Fruit cake; roast vegetables
4	180	350	Warm/medium	Sponge cakes; shortbread; turkey
5	190	375	Moderate/medium	Stuffed peppers; meat and poultry
6	200	400	Moderate/hot	Bread; pizzas; stuffed marrows
7	220	425	Medium/high	Frozen chips
8	230	450	Hot/high	Baked potatoes; mixed-grain bread
9	240–60	475	Very hot/very high	Roast pork and beef (for the first half-hour)

Know your power – microwave cooking times

The power of your microwave oven has an impact on the length of time it takes to warm or cook items. The power of the oven is usually expressed in Watts. The following table shows how long it would take to warm an average-sized mug of milk, depending on the power of the oven.

Wattage	Time
1100	1 min 30 sec
1000	1 min 39 sec
900	1 min 58 sec
850	1 min 57 sec
750	2 min 15 sec
650	2 min 33 sec

24 Get on the move

Journeys | Go! | **Freedom** | Choice |
Independence | Travel | **Exploration**
| **Sights** | visits | **Trips** | Buses |
Trains | Boats | **Routes** | Autonomy
| **Adventure** | **Direction** | **Location,**
Location, Location | **Where?** | **Maps**
| **Distance** | Transport | **Outings** |
Underground | **Bicycle** | Timetable |
Return | **Coaches** | **Seats** | **Station**
| **Mountains** | **Go see!** | Daypass |
Ticket | Walks | **Fields** | Travel cards |
Reservations | **Seaside** | **Self-reliance**

This chapter

In this chapter you can:

→ consider some of the travel and transport issues that face many young people, and how these affect their decisions about going to Uni;

→ reflect on your own attitude to travel and your experiences of managing different kinds of journey on your own;

→ check out your 'travel savvy' and develop your travel awareness;

→ consider how the locations of a Uni might affect your own choices and lifestyle as a student;

→ identify things that you could do now to develop your attitudes to travel so that these do not compromise your choice of Uni unnecessarily.

24.1 What students wish they had known ...

The world is just a bus trip away for this so-adventurous four ...

◁ **Maryam** *I can't see myself at any Uni that isn't near home. I would be nervous to travel far on my own – and it's another cost.*

◁ **William** *We do most things round here – we hardly ever travel outside of the area. We have never been into the city centre, even. I bet none of us have.*

◁ **Soraya** *My parents have promised to buy me a car if I do well at my A levels so I will be thinking 'my wheels' not 'transport'.*

◁ **Lionel** *Travel to Uni isn't an issue for me. In fact, the further from here, the better!*

Three years later, and our motley crew are far, far away in the lands of their dreams ...

◁ **Maryam** *I decided to go to college as it was nearby. Then, I found I had to go on work placement in the next town. I got to like the local train, reading and looking out the window. I think I could have managed to go away to Uni really.*

◁ **William** *My teacher persuaded me to apply to this Uni – over 100 miles away. I didn't even know where it was! I was very doubtful about it all, but I got a place. Looking back, it was good for me. I get the coach home a lot, and have got the exploring bug. A bunch of us went round Europe on the train this summer.*

◁ **Soraya** *The university I chose didn't have any parking. Everyone uses a bicycle here. I thought I would drive home every weekend, but actually, I get the train home for holidays and that's it.*

◁ **Lionel** *Go away! I am trying to work out how to get from here to China by the cheapest route.*

What can you learn from them?
- Jot down what strikes you about these students' attitudes to travel before and after Uni.
- How do their attitudes compare with your own?

24.2 Being on the move as a student

Travel means choice

There are hundreds of universities and colleges in Britain where you could study for a higher level qualification – and thousands more overseas. Each has its own character and a different set of programmes. The type of experience you have as a student will depend on your choice of Uni.

The breadth of choice open to you depends on:

- how confident you are about living away from home, and
- your willingness to travel to places you don't know well yet.

The more you are prepared to travel, the more likely it is that you will find the Uni that offers the best fit for what you want to do and the person you want to be.

Many people just don't travel far

Although some students are used to travelling long distances before they go to Uni, there are a great many who have barely travelled outside the area where they live.

When that is the case, it isn't always easy to imagine travelling to Unis that seem far away, whether to check them out in the first place, or several times a year as a student.

It isn't unusual for students to choose a Uni near to where they live simply because they don't then have to travel into the unknown.

There's no place like home!

If you find what you are looking for on your own doorstep, then that is great. There are lots of advantages to studying locally, especially if you want to be close to family and friends or to live at home. However, many people limit their choices simply because they are not used to travelling and staying away from home.

Becoming independent

Feeling confident about travel and living in new environments is an important step in becoming an independent person. The more you travel, the more you become used to using different kinds of transport, planning more complex journeys, and becoming self-reliant in new circumstances.

> **Travel opens up your world …**
> - You see things you haven't seen before.
> - You stumble across new possibilities.
> - You meet new people.
> - You find new shops and items to buy.
> - You find out curious things.
> - You see things in a different way.
> - You gain in confidence.
> - Your options and choices can open up.

24.3   Are you travel savvy?

What is the ...
Furthest you travelled in the last month?
Furthest you travelled in the last year?
Furthest you have ever travelled with others?
Furthest you have ever travelled alone?
Furthest you have ever travelled by bus?
Furthest you have ever travelled on foot?
Who in your family has travelled the furthest?
Who in your class has travelled the furthest?

How many forms of transport have you used this year?
How many forms of transport have you used ever?
How far do you travel in a week?
How far do you travel in a year?
How far would you be willing to travel to go to Uni or college?
What is the most complicated journey you have ever undertaken?
What is your attitude to travel? Adventurous? Want to travel more? Nervous? Reluctant? Confused? Stop-at-home?

24.4 Where's that then? Travel quiz

1 How far is it from Inverness to Exeter?*

2 How far is it from London to Aberystwyth?*

3 How far is it from Birmingham to London?*

4 How much does it cost to travel from York to London:

(a) By train?

(b) By coach?

5 How long does it take to travel from Manchester to Southampton:

(a) By train?*

(b) By coach?*

(c) By plane?*

6 What is the cheapest journey you can find from London to Leeds?

7 What is the cost on-line of the cheapest journey you can find from Bristol to Cardiff?

8 In which cities/towns are the following HEIs?*

(a) De Montfont

(b) Heriot-Watt

(c) Aston

(d) Brunel

* Answers to items marked with a * can be found on page 303.

24.5 Things you can do now

Walk somewhere new

Take a 15-minute detour and walk somewhere you haven't been before. Take two or three friends with you. If you prefer, do this by bicycle.

Take a bus journey

Plan a bus journey to at least one place that is near where you live but to a place you have never visited. Who will you go with? What will be the fare? Note what kinds of things you pass during the journey that you weren't aware were there.

Get to know the area

- Go on-line to find out more about your own wider area.
- Use Google Maps to find out where you are now.
- Zoom out to see where your neighbourhood is in relation to other local places.
- Choose one location on Google Maps that you don't know already.
- Zoom in to see the layout of the streets by using the Satellite View in Google Maps.
- For most places, you can choose to drop a pin on a particular location, and view that place at street level.
- Get used to seeing where places are in relation to each other and what they look like before visiting them, so you feel more comfortable about what to expect when you get there.

Visit a different shopping centre

When you get to Uni, you will need to get used to shopping in new places. This can feel quite disorientating. Finding shops that you are familiar with can help you feel at home, whilst going into new shops opens up interesting opportunities.

- Take a bus or train to a shopping centre other than one you usually use.
- Browse the shops and see which are the same.
- Look out for different kinds of shops. What can you buy in these that you couldn't locally?

Use GPS

When you are on a trip to a new place, if you have GPS on your phone, use this to track your journey. This will help you to gain a better sense of where you are whilst travelling.

Plan a coach journey

Plan a coach journey to at least one place you have never been – such as a nearby city or a trip to the sea. Who will you go with? What will be the fare?

24.6 Things you can do now (2)

Price journeys

- Go onto 'rail enquiries' at www.nationalrail.co.uk. It will open to the 'journey finder' section.
- Enter in a starting point, a destination and a time and date for travel. You will then see details of potential journeys and you can find fares for those journeys.
- Enter the details of the nearest main town or city to a selection of Unis that interest you. Note down what it would cost for a typical return journey to each.
- What is the cheapest journey you could get for each?

Plan a train journey

Plan a train journey of at least one hour to a place you have never been to. If you were to make this trip, what places would you visit on a day trip?

Plan a family/class day trip

- Look for the cheapest journey that you could find on-line for a day trip for your family or class.
- What times would you need to leave and return?
- Identify interesting places to visit in that area. How much would these cost to enter? Are there any bargains available?
- Google the location and download maps of the area. Decide which one looks the easiest to use to find the tourist attractions that you identified.

Visit a local Uni

With a group of friends or family members, visit the Uni nearest to where you live. Explore the campus. Visit the Student Union. Check what facilities are available on campus.

Open day trip

Research HEIs within a twenty-mile radius of where you live. Out of those that would require at least a short train ride to get to, decide which one you like best. Arrange to attend one of their opens days. Take a friend or family member with you so you can bounce ideas off them about the experience, and so that you can travel safely.

Find out where Unis are

Use a map to find out where different HEIs are located. Decide which ones are within the ideal travelling distance for you. To which others would you consider travelling if you liked them once you researched them?

Where in the world?

With your friends or family, jot down a list of places anywhere on earth that you have heard of but don't know where they are. Use Google Maps to find them. Zoom in and out to see where they are in relation to other places.

24.7   Make it happen

Which strategies will I use?

Decide which actions you can take now to help you to develop your confidence and experience of travel for when you become a student.

1 ☐ Walk somewhere new.
2 ☐ Take a bus journey.
3 ☐ Get to know the area (page 259).
4 ☐ Visit a different shopping centre.
5 ☐ Use GPS.
6 ☐ Plan a coach journey.
7 ☐ Price journeys.
8 ☐ Plan a train journey.
9 ☐ Plan a family/class day trip.
10 ☐ Visit a local Uni.
11 ☐ Open day trip.
12 ☐ Find out where Unis are.
13 ☐ Where in the world?
14 ☐ Increase my openness to travelling further afield than I do now.
15 ☐ Develop my independence for travelling safely.
16 ☐ Get used to making journeys that open up my sense of belonging to the world outside of my own neighbourhood.

Prioritise

Choose between one and three of the strategies listed opposite to try out first. List these below.

First 3 choices	
First choice	
Second choice	
Third choice	

Plan

Decide exactly when you will make use of each strategy.

- Jot the times into your planner or diary.
- Jot down a date within the next month to check you have done what you planned.

Experiment

Once you have used your first set of strategies, have a go with a new set. See which ones suit you best.

> **Give and take support**
> What are the travel issues that arise for people in your class? What kind of support could you give each other to travel safely to places, or in ways, that you haven't to date?

Being me | Identity | **Decisions** |
Variety | **Skills** | **Discovery** | **Integrity**
| **New** | **Meeting people** | **Having a
go** | Self-knowledge | **Opportunity**
| Independence | **Experimentation**
| Experience | **Discussion** | **Fun** |
Responsibility | **Confidence** | **Self-
reliance** | **Growing up** | Personal
development | Enjoyment | Self-
understanding | **Self-expression** |
Growth | **Self-concept** | **Innovation**
| **Taking a chance** | **Lifestyle** |
Employability | **Caterpillar –
butterfly** | Individuality | **Trying out
new things** | New friends | **Potential**
| Personal statements | **Friendships**

This chapter

This chapter helps you to:

→ think through how open you are to
new experiences now;

→ consider what opportunities are open
to you, of which you are not taking full
advantage;

→ understand the importance of personal
development to your application to
Uni;

→ consider how you might develop
habits now that will put you in the
best place to make the most of what is
on offer once at Uni.

Three years ago, this almost perfect foursome were focused on their studies and their applications to Uni …

◁ **Lorna** *I am expecting great grades and that will get me into Uni. I haven't time to do anything else.*

◁ **Anjali** *I am so excited at the idea of meeting lots of new people at Uni and making millions of friends.*

◁ **Kwame** *I won't have time for messing about as a student – I want a good degree and that will get me a good job.*

◁ **Jack** *I am sure that the Uni will see I am just what they want. My mum says I am lovely as well as brilliant. My gran says they may think I am a couch potato – I don't know what she means …*

Now they are at Uni, and our heroes are busy as bees self-developing all around the campus …

◁ **Lorna** *My first choice of Uni turned me down because they said they didn't think I would make the best use of the opportunities they offered.*

◁ **Anjali** *I think it would have been easier to mix in when I got here if I had tried out more things at school. I didn't have a sport, play an instrument, or do drama or anything. At Uni, I started karate and filmmaking and made loads of different friends that way.*

◁ **Kwame** *When I got to Uni, they told us to take part in activities to develop skills employers look for. I started to do loads of things: student rep, politics, sports coaching, Wii club – it made Uni a million times better – and helps my CV.*

◁ **Jack** *My mum says I am even more lovely since I started doing community volunteering. She says to volunteer at home once I come back for the holidays …*

What can you learn from them?

- Jot down a list of the things these students may wish they had known about before going to Uni.
- What kinds of ideas does this give you about things you could do now?

Choosing the right path to your goals

So that you start to plan as early as possible towards the kind of future life you want for yourself.

So that you can identify whether the qualifications you are taking now are the right ones for your developing career plans.

To help ensure that you make the right choices of HEI and programme for the kinds of careers you might want to have after Uni.

To identify whether you need to take any steps to change direction if your decisions to date are not going to help you achieve what you want.

Keeping yourself motivated

The qualifications you are taking now require a certain amount of dedication and hard work. You have to study at times when you would rather be doing other things. It helps to keep motivated if you can see a purpose or goal as an end-point for all that effort.

Having a sense of what kind of life you are aiming towards can help carry you through your study now and in the future.

Reflection	A pathway to what kind of life?

Jot down your thoughts about the following.
- What kind of person do you want to be?
- What kind of life do you want?
- What do you want to contribute to the world?
- What kinds of jobs, and qualifications, do you need, to achieve this kind of life?

Knowing your own mind

In making decisions about higher education, it helps if you have a sound sense of:
- what you can stick with for several years, and what you can't!
- the challenges you are prepared to take on – and the ones you would not;
- how you need to plan in order to make use of the broader opportunities available through higher education.

Getting to know yourself: Why does this matter?

To discover what you are really capable of achieving – and where your limitations might lie.

To understand more about what you are willing to do in life and why.

To learn more about the kinds of things you could enjoy, or find an interest in, based on as broad a base of experience as possible.

To gain a deeper sense of the kind of person you want to be, and how you want your life to turn out.

What kind of person am I?

One way of getting to grips with what kind of person you really are is to decide what kinds of things you value the most in life – or what matters most to you.

What matters to me ...?

(a) Circle any of the following that apply.

(b) Then highlight the ONE thing that matters the most to you personally.

Friendship? Family? Honesty? Learning?

Kindness? Helping others? Money? Travel?

Achievement? Seeing the world? Recognition?

Doing my best? Changing the world?

Being trustworthy and reliable? My faith?

Winning? Health? Creativity? Community?

Trying out new things? Other things?

Reflection and discussion

- Jot down your thoughts about what really matters most to you.
- Discuss your responses with friends or with others in your group. Consider how far you share, or differ in, your views.

25.4 Planning towards your career

Most students continue into higher education because they feel it will improve their career or job prospects. It is worth you giving thought to your career path, even if you have no idea yet what this might look like.

What kind of working life is for me?

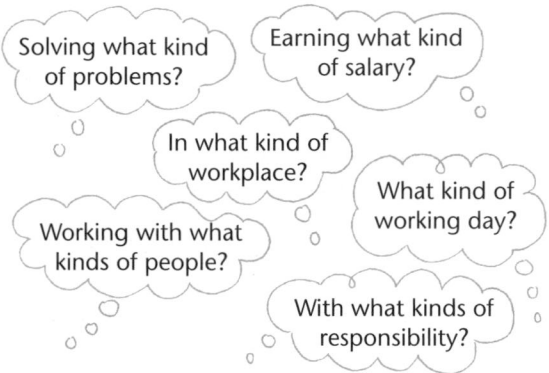

- Solving what kind of problems?
- Earning what kind of salary?
- In what kind of workplace?
- What kind of working day?
- Working with what kinds of people?
- With what kinds of responsibility?

Reflection	Working environment

Give thought to the questions above. They will help you to formulate the kind of career or job that would suit you.

Know what career you want?

If so, talk to a careers adviser about the qualifications and experience that you will need. Identify HEIs that specialise in that career route.

No idea of the career for you?

This is the case for many students. If you cannot decide on a career before you go to Uni, there are many jobs that do not require a specific degree. Even if you do not know what career you want, it is worth reflecting on the broad areas that interest you and selecting subjects now and in higher education that align with the kinds of jobs you might find interesting. For example, if you like creative arts, performing or caring professions you are likely to enjoy degrees, and need skills, that are different from those of people thinking of careers in areas such as marine sciences or engineering. See chapter 5.

Start to plan towards your career

Explore. Begin to gain a feel for the kinds of jobs and careers that might suit you best.

Talk. Ask different professionals about their work. See whether it sounds interesting to you.

Try it. Try out a range of different work placements and part-time jobs. Use the experience to tease out what you like or dislike about different kinds of working environments.

Investigate. Read up about different careers. Look at the kinds of jobs advertised on graduate job websites such as Prospects.ac.uk. Read HEIs' programme websites to see the kinds of jobs that their graduates go on to, and the vocational/professional courses on offer.

Think through. Imagine what the working day would be like for people in different kinds of career. Consider whether you would feel energised by, bored by, or dread that kind of day.

25.5 Preparing for 24-hour student life

For choosing the right HEI

If you try out lots of different things at school or outside of school, you gain a better sense of: what you enjoy, what you don't, and the sorts of things that you would want to continue with as a student. You can use this self-knowledge to help choose the right HEI for you.

If you love football, debating, karate, rowing, music or dance, look out for HEIs where students already engage in these. Consider which HEIs will provide the environment that would best enable you to take part in activities that you would enjoy.

For making friends as a student

Being at Uni offers fantastic opportunities to make new friends. One key way of meeting people is by joining student societies, clubs and activities – or you can start your own. In most cases, you don't need to be brilliant at the activity, and some are tongue-in-cheek ways of getting people together. Typically, you just need to be willing to turn up and join in.

It is much easier to settle into student life, join in and get to know other people if you have already developed the habit of getting involved in things.

I'm just browsing to see which HEIs have a Crisps Appreciation and World Peace Society

- This provides a good starting point for choosing clubs and societies.
- You will feel more confident joining in groups and trying out new things.
- You will have things to talk about easily apart from your studies.

Achieving the entry requirements

Make sure you are working towards the right qualifications for the programmes that you want to take in higher education. See chapter 11.

Selecting the right degree

Research carefully the degrees that you need to take for the professional areas that you want to enter. Speak to your careers adviser or teacher. Use the information on the UCAS website. See chapter 5.

Making a strong application to Uni

Your exam grades will be just one of many things that Admissions staff at HEIs will be taking into account. Most also look closely at what you do outside of class. They consider what these say about you as a person and whether you will benefit from what their HEI has to offer. In particular, they will look at the personal statement that you are required to submit as part of your application.

Personal statement

Admissions staff will read your personal statement to find out:

- why you want to study this subject at this Uni, and how committed you are to their course;
- more about you, your interests, motivations, academic potential, and anything that has had an impact on your education;
- whether you are someone who will really make good use of the opportunity of being a student in higher education;
- what you can contribute to the life and culture of the university or college and the wider community around the Uni;
- whether you show qualities such as initiative, leadership, motivation, endurance, ethical awareness, creativity, teamwork, or others that add to the life of HEI;
- whether you are likely to be the kind of future graduate that would reflect well upon the institution – by gaining a good job, becoming a good employer in your own right, contributing to society, culture, or scholarship in the subject.

Showing your potential

It is helpful to start thinking early about what kinds of things you will include in your personal statement to best reveal your potential. Get involved in activities, reading and thinking that demonstrate such things as the following.

- How you make use of the opportunities open to you – using your initiative and generally participating.
- Skills and personal qualities, especially those that show self-reliance and ability to take on responsibilities.
- An understanding and genuine interest in the subject that you want to study.
- Anything in your educational background or life which has had a significant positive or negative impact on your achievements to date.

25.7 Make it happen

Which strategies will I use?

Decide which actions you can take now that will help you later when you come to make your application to higher education.

1 ☐ **Life goals.** Put time aside to think about what I want from life and which programme or HEI would best contribute to those goals.

2 ☐ **Career understanding.** Investigate the kinds of careers that are available, and the qualifications required.

3 ☐ **Working environments.** Give thought to the kind of environment that I want to work in after I finish my studies.

4 ☐ **Work experience.** Get a feel for what I like and dislike about different kinds of working environments.

5 ☐ **Entry requirements.** Check carefully that I will be able to meet the entry requirements of programmes that interest me.

6 ☐ **Get involved.** Where feasible, get involved in activities outside of the taught curriculum at school or college, to help my personal statement.

7 ☐ **24-Hour student life.** Get used to joining in and making acquaintances in new contexts.

8 ☐ **Demonstrating responsibility.** Consider things I do already that demonstrate self-reliance and responsibility. What else could I do now that would develop such qualities?

9 ☐ **Personal statement.** Draft an initial personal statement to see how well I can present my case for a place on programmes that interest me. Consider what I could do to strengthen my statement.

Prioritise

Choose three of the strategies listed opposite to try out first. List these below.

First 3 choices	
First choice	
Second choice	
Third choice	

Plan

Decide exactly when you will make use of each strategy. Set times that help you to build up a routine and that won't clash with other things you want to do.

- Jot the times into your planner or diary.
- Jot down a date within the next month to check that you are working to plan.

Experiment

Once you have used your first set of strategies, have a go with a new set. See which ones suit you best.

> **Give and take support**
> Talk through with friends or classmates how you are preparing for your personal statement. If you have ideas about how others could develop their profiles, consider whether that advice could also apply to yourself.

26   Looking after yourself

Independence | Safety | **Risks** | Security | **Parties** | **Healthy eating** | **Vitamins** | **5-a-day** | **Self-esteem** | **Confidence** | Food | Fruit | Laundry | **Clean clothes** | Sleep | **Sports** | **Fitness** | **Exercise** | **Protein** | Carbohydrates | **Fats** | Vitamins | Health | Peer Pressure | **Minerals** | Balance | **Cooking** | **Vegetables** | **Sociability** | **Friendship** | **Self-reliance** | **Intregrity** | Energy | Diet | Swimming | **Relaxing** | Chocolate biscuits | **Fun** | **Exercise** | **Enjoyment**

This chapter

This chapter helps you to:

→ take on board considerations and behaviours that, though relatively basic, are essential to well-being and social life as a student;

→ consider what you would need to do for yourself once you are a student;

→ recognise the importance of having your own opinions, and the self-confidence to carry through on these, in order to support your safety and peace of mind once at Uni;

→ consider how you might start to take on approaches now that would help you to look after yourself once at Uni.

Three years ago, life was organised, nutritious and sweet-smelling for this well-favoured four …

◁ **Akiko**　*I eat a balanced diet, loads of fruit and veg. I'm at the swimming pool twice a week. I'm sorted.*

◁ **William**　*Fish and chips. Steak. Rice and peas. Pizza and curry. Watching telly. I know what I like and I'm sticking to it.*

◁ **Soraya**　*I like to look good when I go out. I don't wear anything that isn't newly washed and ironed.*

◁ **Ricky**　*My social life is about my mates. I just want to be part of the gang.*

Three years later, and here they are, mostly looking like hungry, spotty, stinky slobs. Whatever happened?

◁ **Akiko**　*I realise how much my mum was the driving force behind my fitness regime and good diet. After ten weeks on chocolate biscuits, I am now working towards eating more fruit and veg, maybe starting out with 5-a-term …*

◁ **William**　*I found love on the tennis court. I had never played before but there was this very cute girl I needed to impress. Now I work out every day and eat to a strict regime. I am a reformed man.*

◁ **Soraya**　*I finally ran out of anything vaguely clean and had to spend Saturday night in the laundrette. I couldn't work out how to start the machine and then put in way too much detergent. I had to wash everything 3 times.*

◁ **Ricky**　*I am so tired. My mates want to be out all night, every night, partying. I fell asleep in lectures every day this week. I can't wait for the holidays – and to go to bed early with a mug of cocoa.*

What can you learn from them?
- What do you think these students may wish they had known before going to Uni?
- What could you learn from their experiences?

26.2 Why does it matter?

Being independent

If you go away to Uni, you will be in charge of the everyday business of keeping yourself fit, fed, watered, clean, healthy, safe and secure. Whilst this isn't always fun, it does make you feel more of a capable adult, able to look after your own life.

A sense of satisfaction

There can be a sense of satisfaction and security in knowing that you are able to look after yourself, as and when needed.

Being in charge of your life

If you know that you can take care of yourself well, you are likely to have a wider range of HEIs from which to choose. You will be less concerned about living at home and having parents and carers nearby to look after you.

Well-being affects academic performance

Your academic grades as a student can be affected by the basics of good well-being such as:

- sleep;
- healthy eating;
- feeling safe;
- having a social life.

Sociability and friendship

Being able to look after yourself can come across to others as an attractive quality. This can help when it comes to forming friendships and to being included within student groups.

Keeping fit

Undertaking some physical exercise every day is good for physical health, helps you manage your weight, provides a focus for socialising, and can help with a sense of mental well-being.

Sense of self

When they are in new surroundings, separated from everything that has been familiar to them, students can be more susceptible to influences that can do them harm. You may be open to many such influences when you are at Uni.

This is easier to manage if:

- you have a strong sense of who you are and what you believe;
- you have a clear sense of what is right and wrong for you;
- you are well-informed about what is safe and what can do you harm;
- you are able to form friends and recognise good friendships.

Reflection
<ul><li>How do you take care of your health, well-being and fitness at the moment?</li><li>How far do you take charge of this, and how much are you still reliant on others to organise this for you?</li></ul>

26.3　Are you a healthy eater?

Eating well at Uni is important to keeping healthy and to feeding the brain so that you get good grades. This can seem a challenge for some students. However, healthy eating is manageable if you:

- understand what makes a balanced diet;
- plan your shopping;
- indulge yourself in moderation.

Getting a balance

Your diet needs the right mix of protein, fats, carbohydrates, roughage, vitamins and minerals.

Protein: You need about 1g per kilogram of your weight in protein per day, to build and maintain muscle. Good sources are meats, fish, quorn, dairy products and eggs. Vegans can get protein from tofu, beans, pulses and grains such as quinoa.

Carbohydrates: Carbohydrates give you energy. Whole grains and unprocessed foods such as wholemeal pasta and breads, and brown rice, generally keep you feeling full. Processed carbohydrates (white rice, flour, pasta, sugars) give you a quick but short energy burst. The unprocessed sugars found in fruits and vegetables are kinder on your body than processed sugars such as those in sweets and fizzy drinks, which give you a quick 'sugar rush' but leave you feeling tired once this wears off.

Fats: The body needs fat and you shouldn't seek to exclude it from your diet. However, you don't need much of it and it is high in calories. Your diet will be healthier if you get your fat from sources such as nuts and avocados rather than fried food and pastry-based products.

Fruit and vegetables: This is the food group that students most often miss out on. This means they lose out on roughage that helps digestion, as well as vitamins and minerals the body needs. It is recommended that we eat at least 5 portions of these a day. See the next page for more details.

Most things in moderation: Eating a healthy diet doesn't mean you can never eat chips, pizza or chocolate. You can eat any food you like but you will do better if you go easy on high-fat and high-sugar processed foods and keep them as a weekly treat. Bulk up on fruit and vegetables as much as you like.

Things you can do now

- Choose healthy options for meals at school or college.
- Use sweet snacks, crisps and fizzy drinks as weekly treats.
- Eat each of the food types outlined above every day.
- Be aware of how much processed food and sugar you eat.
- Learn to cook, so you can make your own healthy meals.

Reflection

- How balanced is your diet now – are you a healthy eater?
- If so, is this because of your own actions, such as choosing healthy food options?

26.4 Things you can do now: 5-a-Day

It is recommended that everyone eats at least 5 portions of fruit and vegetables every day. These are a good source of fibre and of anti-oxidants (thought to be important in preventing cancer). Research suggests that most young people eat fewer than 3 portions of fruit and vegetables a day.

What counts as one portion? A portion is about 80g or roughly a handful of most fruit and vegetables. Approximate measures for different fruit and vegetables are listed below.

What does not count? Baked beans and canned soups generally don't count, unless the manufacturers can prove they meet strict nutritional guidelines.

Things you can do now

- Eat a variety of fruit and vegetables to get a good range of vitamins and minerals.
- Eat fruit and vegetables of different colours, to gain a better range of essential vitamins.
- If you don't enjoy these, have a go at making a smoothie for one portion.

One portion size of the most commonly consumed fruit and vegetables

Fruit
Apple – 1 medium apple
Apricot (dried) – 3 whole
Avocado – half an avocado
Banana – 1 medium banana
Blackcurrants – 4 heaped tablespoons
Blueberries – 2 handfuls (4 heaped tablespoons)
Fruit juice – 1 x 150ml
Grapes – 1 handful

Mango – 2 slices (5cm or 2-inch slice)
Kiwi fruit – 2 Kiwi fruit
Orange – 1 orange
Pineapple – 1 large slice
Plum – 2 medium plums
Raspberries – 2 handfuls (20 berries)
Strawberry – 7 strawberries

Vegetables
Aubergine – 1/3 aubergine
Broccoli – 2 spears
Brussels sprouts – 8 Brussels sprouts
Cabbage – 1/6 small cabbage or 2 handfuls sliced
Carrots (sliced) – 3 heaped tablespoons
Cauliflower – 8 florets
Celery – 3 sticks
Chick peas – 3 heaped tablespoons
Courgettes – half a large courgette
Cucumber – 5cm or 2-inch piece
Lentils – 3 tablespoons
Tomato – 1 medium, or 7 cherry

Lettuce (mixed leaves) – 1 cereal bowl
Mushrooms – 14 button mushrooms or 3 handfuls of slices
Onion – medium onion
Peas (frozen) – 3 heaped tablespoons
Pepper – half a pepper
Sweetcorn (baby) – 6 baby corn
Sweetcorn (canned) – 3 heaped tablespoons

The college or local laundry is sometimes an unexpected aspect of student life.

What do you mean, 'that there isn't a laundry fairy'????

Things you can do now

- Get used to separating white items of clothing from other colours – the colours may run in the wash.
- Get to know how a washing machine works.
- Become familiar with laundry symbols. Match these to labels on some items of your own clothing.
- Get used to doing some or all of your own laundry. Check the laundry symbols first.
- Take your washing at least once to a local laundry so that you have had the experience of this before going to Uni.

Laundry symbols

Symbols and their meaning can vary around the world. Always double-check if unsure.

Wash

Best washing temperature for the item

Hand wash

Do not wash

Medium to gentle wash

Gentle wash

Do not wring

Spin

Bleach/dry clean

Chlorine bleach

Chlorine bleach

Non-chlorine bleach

Do not bleach

Dry clean

Do not dry clean

Symbols for dry-cleaner

Iron

Cool

Warm

Hot

Steam

No steam

Do not iron

Dry

Can be tumble dried

Cool tumble dry

Hot tumble dry

Do not tumble dry

Dry flat

Line dry

Drip Dry

Security

When considering which Uni or college to choose, give thought to safety and security issues for the kinds of accommodation in which you would live. Take a close look at the general area where the HEI and its student accommodation are located.

Accommodation

- Visit the options for student accommodation. How safe, secure and pleasant are these as places to live?
- Who can get into the residences and at what times of day and night?
- Are there night porters?
- How far is it to local shops if you needed to pop out at night for milk or food?

The area

- Walk around the area: how does it strike you?
- Would it be safe to walk home at night?
- What are the facilities in the area? Are they well looked after?
- How far are you from the campus?
- Does the HEI provide a safe night bus?

Party culture and wild rumpus?

There is a stereotype of student life as one of endless parties and excess alcohol. Although it is true that there are students who respond to independence in an excessive way, most don't. They find ways of joining in and having a good time, whilst knowing and sticking to their limits.

Before you go to Uni, it is worth thinking through what kind of student lifestyle you want. Weigh up the issues such as costs, the impact on health, and the risks of getting into dangerous situations.

If you feel pressurised now to do things that you don't want, this may become even more difficult once you are at Uni. Now is the time to speak to a student counsellor or someone you trust. Develop the confidence to make the decisions you feel are right for you.

Reflection	Attitude to safety

Risk averse?
- Are you too risk averse?
- If so, what does this prevent you from doing that you could benefit from with little real risk?
- What could you do differently?

Too high risk?
- Do you take too many risks with your own safety and security?
- If so, where do you take greatest risks?
- What could you do differently to manage these risks more sensibly?

Discussion point: Student life
- What do you think would be the key risks to students' safety, security and well-being at Uni?
- How would you protect yourself from things you consider ill-advised?

26.7 Make it happen

Which strategies will I use?

Decide which actions you can take now to help you to take good care of yourself as a student at Uni/college.

1 ☐ Choose healthy options for school/college meals.
2 ☐ Use sweet snacks, crisps and fizzy drinks as weekly treats.
3 ☐ Eat each of the food types every day.
4 ☐ Become more aware of how much processed food and sugar I eat.
5 ☐ Learn to cook, so I can make my own healthy meals.
6 ☐ Eat a variety of fruit and vegetables to get a good range of vitamins and minerals.
7 ☐ Eat fruit and vegetables of different colours, to gain a better range of essential vitamins.
8 ☐ Have a smoothie for one of my '5-a-day'.
9 ☐ Find out more about what makes a balanced diet.
10 ☐ Develop a routine for getting exercise into my day.
11 ☐ Get used to doing my own laundry.
12 ☐ Visit the student accommodation to check for safety and security.
13 ☐ Consider further my own attitudes towards personal safety.
14 ☐ Decide what kind of student lifestyle is right for me.
15 ☐ Give thought to aspects of student life I would find ill-advised and how I would avoid or manage these.

Prioritise

Choose between one and three of the strategies listed opposite to try out first. List these below.

First 3 choices	
First choice	
Second choice	
Third choice	

Plan

Decide exactly when you will make use of each strategy. Set times that help you to build up a routine and that won't clash with other things you want to do.

- Jot the times into your planner or diary.
- Jot down a date within the next month to check what is working.

Experiment

Once you have used your first set of strategies, have a go with a new set. See which ones suit you best.

> **Give and take support**
>
> Consider ways that you and your friends could support each other in becoming more aware of issues of health, safety and well-being that are relevant to your lives now.

What next?

As you prepare for Uni, you may wish for more information on some of the topics you have covered in this book.

More information about Uni

Appendix 4 provides detailed information about a range of sources that you can follow up to pursue your interests.

More about Study Skills

You can access free resources from Palgrave Macmillan at www.skills4study.com. The following study skills materials are, typically, recommended for first year students at Uni.

- Cottrell, S. M. (2008) *The Study Skills Handbook*, 3rd edn (Basingstoke: Palgrave Macmillan).
- Cottrell, S. M. (2011) *Critical Thinking Skills,* 2nd edn (Basingstoke: Palgrave Macmillan).
- Cottrell, S. M. (2010) *Skills for Success: Personal Development and Employability*, 2nd edn (Basingstoke: Palgrave Macmillan).
- Cottrell, S. M. (2012) *The Exam Skills Handbook: Achieving Peak Performance*, 2nd edn (Basingstoke: Palgrave Macmillan).
- Cottrell, S. M. (2012) *The Palgrave Student Planner* (Basingstoke: Palgrave Macmillan).

Appendix 1:
Timeline for applications

Timeline for applications		
September a year prior to entry	UCAS accepts applications to Uni for entry the following year.	Apply via UCAS for full-time places.
Before 15 October	If you are applying for medicine, veterinary medicine and veterinary science, and dentistry, look at the Entry Profiles for your chosen courses for details of admissions test. See the UCAS website for details.	Apply direct to the college or Uni for part-time places.
15 October	Final date for receipt, by UCAS, of applications for Oxford, Cambridge, and courses in medicine, veterinary medicine and veterinary science, and dentistry; a reference must be included.	See www. direct.gov.uk for applications to universities overseas.
15 January	Last date for receipt, by UCAS, of applications for equal consideration. References should be included. NB this includes some arts courses.	
16 January to 30 June	UCAS will forward your applications if submitted during this period but universities and colleges can opt not to consider them.	You can apply and then defer entry if the university or college agrees.
24 February	UCAS service, Extra, opens for your use if you haven't yet gained a suitable place.	
24 March	Deadline for receipt by UCAS of applications, including reference, for those arts and design courses that do not have a January 15th deadline.	
31 March	Universities and colleges complete decisions for applications received by January 15th.	You can wait several years before applying to Uni or college.
30 June	Applications received after this date would be dealt with through clearing.	
6 July	Last date for using the UCAS service, Extra, if you haven't been offered a suitable place.	
31 August	Last date for meeting all conditions for offers if you are deferred.	Courses that require Admissions tests may set these at any time. They tend to fall between November and August.
20 September	Final date by which an application can be received for this year's entry via UCAS for full-time places. Part-time places may still be considered by some colleges and universities, through direct application to the institution.	
August/September of the year of entry: not got a place?	You may be able to gain a place through clearing, or apply directly to the university or college for a part-time place. Decide whether you want to apply for the following year's entry.	

Appendix 2:
Countdown to Uni: Action Plan

It is useful to start the following action plan as early as possible, preferably 18 months to 2 years or more before you would start your course at Uni. If you start the process later than that, don't worry but do plan carefully to fit in the necessary steps. This is especially important for courses that have October 15th deadlines.

Countdown to Uni: Personal Action Plan	
Action	**For me this means (what and when)**
1 **Keep others informed** Let your school or college know of your plans as and when these develop, so that they are prepared for their role in supporting your application. Give plenty of notice for them to prepare a reference. Check arrangements for paying the application charge. (For 2012, this was normally £22 in total.)	
2 **Ask for advice** Use the advice and guidance available. Ask where you can get advice if none is offered. You can also contact careers services, colleges and universities for information.	
3 **Qualifications** Check you will have the qualifications you need if you decide to go to Uni and for the kind of programmes that would interest you.	
4 **Organisation** Set up folders or files to hold together all the information you need.	
5 **Early consideration of personal statement** Find out about the requirements of your personal statement. Consider which activities and responsibilities you can take on now so that you can write a good statement.	
6 **Check work experience requirements** Some programmes, especially those related to medical, caring and veterinary professions, like to see that you have undertaken some work experience or volunteering in their area or, in some cases, in a related field that demands similar skills and qualities. Check the course details for information.	

Appendix 2:
Countdown to Uni: Action Plan (continued)

Countdown to Uni: Personal Action Plan	
Action	**For me this means (what and when)**
7 Prepare for independent living Consider the range of life skills and attitudes that you will need at college or Uni, and how you will develop these (chapters 20–26).	
8 Investigate universities and colleges (see chapters 3–11) Find out as much as you can about universities and colleges and the range of subjects on offer. Check their websites, UCAS website and materials outlined in chapter 4.	
9 Check for admissions tests See the UCAS website for those courses that set separate admissions tests, and for when these take place.	
10 Open days and visits Find out the details of open days at colleges and universities that interest you. Each may hold several of these across the year. You may also be able to arrange a visit at other times. (See pages 42, 45 and 289.)	
11 Conventions Find out from your school or college the details of conventions being held in your area, and whether they have places. You can also check and book on the UCAS website, or turn up on the day.	
12 Consider financial and other practicalities Look into the details of fees, financial support, bursaries and fee waivers, accommodation, disability arrangements, as relevant to you. (See chapter 9 and pages 284–6 and 288.)	
13 Choose a course Make a decision on a subject to help focus your searching and choices. Check the final application dates for your chosen courses.	
14 Choose universities or colleges Decide on up to 5 choices for your application. Check carefully that you meet the entry requirements for the courses selected.	

Appendix 2:
Countdown to Uni: Action Plan (continued)

Countdown to Uni: Personal Action Plan	
Action	**For me this means (what and when)**
15 Register with UCAS on Apply Your school or college will give you a 'buzzword', which you will need in order to register with UCAS through them. Then go to **www.ucas.com** and follow the instructions on how to apply.	
16 Complete your application on Apply Read carefully the details and follow these exactly.	
17 Personal statement Word-process following the requirements detailed on the UCAS website. Fine-tune and paste into Apply. (See chapters 11 and 25.)	
18 Student finance section Completing this helps UCAS process any claims you make later for loans and grants. It does not mean that you have yet made a claim for financial support. UCAS will contact you later when that process is open so that, if you apply for a loan, they can forward your details, making the process easier.	
19 Send your application to your referee Your referee will check this for approval and attach the reference.	
20 Submission of your application Your referee submits the application to UCAS.	
21 Check the UCAS acknowledgement UCAS will send you an acknowledgement of your application. Check this carefully.	
22 Calculate costs and loans Work out how much you would receive in loans and how much you would pay back for your course depending on your circumstances, using the calculator on moneysavingexpert.com	

Countdown to Uni: Personal Action Plan	
Action	**For me this means (what and when)**
23 Student Finance Go to **www.studentfinance.direct.gov.uk** to register online with Student Finance England. This will take you through the process of applying for loans and grants. Once the process opens, early in the year, you can apply at any time before going to Uni or for several months after your course starts.	
24 Acceptance and commitment • UCAS sends the applications to the university or college. Universities make their decisions. UCAS informs you of the details of these. • You reply to each offer using Track on **www.ucas.com** or by calling UCAS Customer Service Unit. • An acceptance means you have made a commitment to that university or college. • However, if you receive better grades than expected, you can look for a place that wanted higher grades if they still have places open, without forfeiting your original choice. If you are then offered a place by the alternative Uni or college, this acceptance is now your commitment.	
25 Deferred places If you want to take a year out after school you need to check that this will be acceptable to the university. You still need to meet the conditions of their offer by 31 August (i.e. BEFORE you go).	
26 No suitable offers: Extra and Clearing If none of your applications were successful, if you contact the UCAS services Extra and Clearing, these may match you to an unfilled place.	
27 Part-time places Obtain an application form direct from each university or college, and also return these direct to the university or college.	

Appendix 3:
Costs, financial support and repayments

Arrangements vary depending on where in the UK you live and where you plan to study. The following information is a broad summary. If you wish to study overseas, you would need to find your own funding for study. Similarly, if you have not been resident in the UK or EU within the last few years or are aged over 60, the arrangements would be different. Many sources of additional support are available, such as for students with a disability, or from charities.

Home address and study will be in England

What if we have no money?

From 2012 onwards, if you gain a place at Uni, the Student Loan Company will pay the fee. It does this *automatically* once your application is processed so you will not need to apply for it separately. This is the case both for full-time courses and for eligible part-time courses. You can also opt to pay upfront but you don't have to. This means that lack of funds, in itself, should not prevent anyone from studying.

Loans and grants for living costs

Loans

If you will be studying full-time, you will be able to take out a loan to cover the costs of living such as accommodation, food, travel and books. All full-time students are eligible for some of the loan. Some aspects of the loan are means tested. Part-time students are not eligible. The maximum loan available in 2012 is:

- £4,375 if you are living with your parents;
- £5,500 if you live away from home;
- £7,675 for London;
- £6,535 for study overseas.

Grants

If you are from a household where the residual income is less than £42,000 a year, you will be entitled to a grant, though the amount of loan you could apply for would be reduced. You would never have to repay this grant, unless you left your course without completing it.

If your household income is £21,000 or less, you would normally be eligible for a non-repayable grant of £3,250 and a maintenance loan of £3,875, or £7,125 in total.

If the household income is between £21,001 and £42,000 you would get a smaller amount of grant, depending what that income is.

How would I work out what I would owe?

You can use the student finance calculator, an on-line tool available via moneysavingexpert.com. Before using this, find out the amount of the fee you would pay at your preferred universities as you will be asked to type that in.

Fee waivers, bursaries and scholarships

Your university may offer you a reduced fee or a cash bursary or scholarship that you can put towards living costs. The amounts, eligibility and conditions for payment will be different at every Uni. If you have the choice, it is usually better to go for the bursary/scholarship rather than the waiver, as you have that to spend now and you may never repay the fee in full.

You can find out about what each Uni offers as financial support via either:

- www.direct.gov.uk/en/ – go to Education and learning / University and higher education / student finance / Student Finance A–Z; or
- university and college websites. These will also have details about the full range of scholarships and bursaries on offer and how to apply for them. Some of the scholarships will be restricted according to academic ability, geographical location, programme or year of study.

No repayment until you are earning

You would not repay the loan until after you have graduated and you start to pay tax. It would come out of your future pay packet automatically if you earned enough to pay it. This means that it is not like other debts where debt collectors can be involved.

No repayment if you earn under £21,000

Repayments are scaled to match how much you earn. If you never earn over £21,000, then you would never pay back anything. After that, you pay nothing on the first £21,000 of what you earn. Your repayments would be set at 9% of the difference between what you earn and £21,000.

If you are not able to repay, you would accrue interest, so the longer you take to repay, the more you will pay. This is just spread over a long time. At the end of 30 years, if you haven't repaid the loan, it will be written off. Many people will never pay it all back and there would be no penalty for that.

How much will I repay?

This will depend on such things as how much you borrow and how much you earn. You can work out how much you would pay, for different kinds of scenarios, by using the calculator on moneysavingexpert.com. Select the Student tab.

Monthly repayments will be the same whatever the fee

Whether the university or college of your choice charges £5,000 or £9,000, when you start to make repayments, the amount you pay each month would be the same.

When do I apply for grants and loans?

- Full-time students can apply for grants and loans at any time from early in the calendar year in which they will start their course until up to nine months after the start of the academic year.
- Part-time students can apply for loans from early in the calendar year they will start their course until up to six months after the start of the academic year.

How do I apply for loans and grants for living costs?

- Go to www.studentfinance.direct.gov.uk or type 'Student Finance England' in your search engine.
- Once on the site, you will be asked to register on-line with Student Finance England.
- Their website then takes you through the application process step by step.
- This will help you to set up a student finance account and ask you to complete an application form.

Appendix 3:
Costs, financial support and repayments (continued)

- You will be asked to send in evidence such as proof of your identity and household income. If you are applying for means-assessed loans and grants for maintenance, childcare, or Adult Dependants' Grant, this is dependent on household income. Your parents and partner may also have to provide information.

Home address in England; study will be in Scotland, Wales or NI

English students studying in Scotland, Wales and Northern Ireland will be responsible for paying fees and eligible for financial support, just as they would if they were studying for a degree in England.

Scottish universities will set their own fees for non-Scottish students, up to a maximum of £9,000 a year.

Home address and study in Scotland

You will not be asked to pay for tuition fees. Student loans are available. For 2012–13, these are offered at a maximum of £5,417 a year. Bursary support up to £2,640 a year is also available for young people from low income families.

Home address in Scotland; study outside of Scotland

If you study outside of Scotland, you are entitled to a non-income-assessed loan of up to £3,375 a year towards the cost of tuition fees.

Home address and study both in Wales

- Fees will rise to up to £9,000 as in England.
- The Welsh Assembly will pay fee costs above £3,465 a year for Welsh students studying at any UK university or college.
- The maximum loan will be £4,745.
- Maximum grant for students from low income households will be £5,000. The income threshold for the maximum grant is £18,370.
- Part-time student fees in Wales for 2012–13 will be the same as for 2011–12: that is, students pay £1,600 for the equivalent of a full year's study. New arrangements will be introduced for 2013–14.
- Details are available from studentfinancewales. co.uk.

Home address and study in Northern Ireland

From 2012–13, Northern Ireland students studying in Northern Ireland will pay tuition fees of £3,465 a year. Loans towards living costs are payable up to a maximum of £3,750.

Home address in Northern Ireland; study in UK

If you study outside of Northern Ireland but within the UK, you could pay up to the full £9,000. If you study elsewhere in the UK, you can get a loan of up to £4,840 a year.

Appendix 4:
Where to get more information

1 Applying to Uni/Admissions

University and Colleges Application Service www.ucas.ac.uk

This provides information, links, tools and resources to help with all aspects of the application process.

Admissions policies

Each HEI should have this accessible from their website.

2 Comparison of HEIs: Data, information and League Tables

Key Information Sets (KIS)

To be provided from 2012–13 on every HEI's website.

www.Unistats.com

Provides means of comparing HEIs and programmes on a range of indicators. Includes details of the National Student Survey.

League Tables

A number of League Tables compare HEIs. These tables are not directly comparable with each other as they include and provide ratings for different items. They cover, variously, entry requirements, amount spent on resources, student ratings, research ratings, income, ratio of staff to students, etc. You would need to look carefully at the categories included to see how far the overall rating was a reflection of student experience rather than other aspects such as research.

3 Employment

The Destination of Leavers from Higher Education (DLHE) www.hesa.ac.uk

This provides the official statistics on graduate employment. Most other data sets on graduate employment refer to this. It provides a range of data on the kinds of jobs graduates enter, and provides this information to Unis. Unis can find out the data for each of their programmes and for different kinds of students. The KIS data on university websites will use these statistics.

Appendix 4:
Where to get more information (continued)

Office for National Statistics (2011) www.ons. gov.uk/ons/dcp171776_233872.pdf

Provides information about graduate earnings over the last decade.

www.Prospects.ac.uk Information about graduate employment.

www.jobs.ac.uk Guidance and jobs for school leavers and graduates.

www.insidecareers.co.uk Career guidance and jobs for students.

www.milkround.com Career guidance for students.

www.companieshouse.gov.uk Lists all UK public companies.

http://vault.com What it is like to work for named companies.

4 Finance and money

See Appendix 3 additionally.

Student Support

Student Loans 0845 300 50 90 **www.slc.co.uk**

Student Awards Agency for Scotland 0300 555 0505 **www.saas.gov.uk**

Student Finance Wales 0845 602 8845 **www. studentfinancewales.co.uk**

Department for Employment and Learning Northern Ireland 0845 600 0662 **www. studentfinanceni.co.uk**

Student Support for Ireland **www.studentfinance. ie**

Financial Advice

www.adviceguide.org.uk Finance advice from the Citizens Advice Bureau.

www.direct.gov.uk/en/EducationAndLearning/ UniversityAndHigherEducation/StudentFinance Information on student finance.

www.cccs.co.uk Consumer Credit Counselling Service, which includes the Student Debt Line.

www.moneysavingexpert.co.uk Independent finance advice for students, on bank accounts, savings, credit cards etc.

www.nus.org.uk Includes guidance on student finance.

www.rbs.com/media/news/press-releases/2010- press-releases/2010-08-27-universtiy.ashx Nat West Student Living Index. Information on the most cost-effective cities for students to live in.

5 Gap years

www.gap-year.com Website and guidebook available. Includes information on preparing for a gap year.

http://igapyear.com Provides information and guidance about work, trips, courses, sports, expeditions, tours, travel around the world.

www.projects-abroad.co.uk Provides information for students planning to undertake volunteering work abroad during their gap year.

www.realgap.co.uk Provides information on a range of work opportunities, trips, destinations and experiences.

www.gapwork.com Provides information on work and volunteering opportunities abroad during your gap year.

6 Open days

www.opendays.com
www.ucasevents.com Information about events, exhibitions and conventions for prospective students and their parents.

7 Quality

Quality Assurance Agency for Higher Education
www.qaa.ac.uk

The QAA has responsibility for reviewing each HEI and making judgements about the quality of provision. Its reports are publicly available on its website: these are long and detailed reports, but include a summary of aspects they commend as well as recommendations for action, and a general statement about whether they are confident that the university can ensure the quality of its provision. You might like to check the latest QAA report for the Uni that you are thinking of selecting, using this in combination with other information.

8 Student perspectives and organisations

www.nus.org.uk National Union of Students (NUS) website.
www.thestudentroom.co.uk Articles and forums on all aspects of student life.
www.interstudent.co.uk Lots of useful general information for students.
www.studentuk.com Lots of useful general information for students.
www.nistudents.org The student movement in Northern Ireland.

www.usi.ie Union of Students in Ireland.
www.ukcisa.org.uk Website for the Council for International Student Affairs, with advice on studying abroad.

9 Universities and other Higher Education Institutions

www.ucas.ac.uk University and Colleges Application Service. Provides detailed information about each course and HEI.
www.guardian.co.uk/education/datablog/2010/jun/15/university-tables-spreadsheet
University League Tables produced by *The Guardian* newspaper.
www.timeshighereducation.co.uk/world-university-rankings League Table produced by the *The Times Higher Education Supplement*, listing the top 400 universities in the world.

10 Student life

Shopping

www.studentfreestuff.com Freebies and special offers available to students.
www.mysupermarket.co.uk Price comparison website which allows you to compare the prices of groceries at different supermarkets.
www.supermarket.co.uk Price comparisons and information about special offers and money-saving vouchers on offer at UK stores.

Food

www.studentrecipes.com Simple recipes – updated regularly with new suggestions from students.

www.studentnosh.com Simple recipes and cooking tips for students. You can also buy the 'student nosh' books from the site.

www.sortedfood.co.uk Simple recipes for students. You can also buy the 'sorted' cookbook from this site.

www.bbcgoodfood.com/content/recipes/ favourites/student BBC website with plenty of suggestions of easy-to-make meals.

www.studentcook.co.uk Lots of recipes and advice on eating healthily on a student budget.

Travel

www.tfl.gov.uk London Travel Information 0843 222 1234.

www.nationalrail.co.uk National Rail Enquiries: information about times and costs of train journeys 08457 48 49 50.

www.raileurope.co.uk Rail Europe: information about train travel across Europe 08448 484 064.

www.nationalexpress.com National Express: information on coach travel across the UK 08717 81 81 78.

www.buseireann.ie Bus Eireann (Ireland): information on bus travel across Ireland 01836 6111.

www.citylink.co.uk Scottish Citylink: information about coach travel across Scotland 0871 266 33 33.

www.fco.gov.uk Foreign and Commonwealth Office travel advice.

www.railcard.co.uk National Railcard website, with details on how to purchase a Young Person's Railcard.

www.statravel.co.uk Provides discount student travel.

www.travelhealth.co.uk Provides useful health advice for travellers.

www.yha.org.uk International Youth Hostels Association: information about cheap accommodation in the UK and abroad.

Taking care of yourself

www.nhsdirect.nhs.uk NHS Direct online health advice 0845 46 47.

www.studenthealth.co.uk Good health advice for students, written by doctors.

www.talktofrank.com National Drugs Helpline ('Talk to Frank') 0800 77 66 00.

www.suzylamplugh.org/personal-safety/ personal-safety-tips/student-safety Suzy Lamplugh Trust: information for students on personal safety and security.

www.relate.org.uk Relate: advice and support on relationships for people of all ages, including young people.

www.nhs.uk/livewell/studenthealth/Pages/ Studenthealthhome.aspx NHS website, with advice on living and eating healthily as a student.

www.samaritans.org Samaritans: support for those in crisis or feeling suicidal 08457 90 90 90.

Answers and Feedback

2.3 Do I want to go to Uni?

Statement	Feedback
1 I'm definitely going to study in higher education.	National surveys such as NSS show that most students value their time at Uni and the opportunities it offers, so your decision is likely to be a sound one. It is certainly good to be firm in this as it is such a big commitment. However, make sure that you have sounded out all of your options even if you believe you know what you want to do. This is especially important if there is any possibility that you will not receive the grades that you will need. Make sure you have a back-up plan if you don't get onto the course you want, or don't get into Uni, the first time around.
2 I want to go on to higher education straight from school.	Most students make this choice. There are advantages in that you will probably settle more easily into academic study. The study skills and habits you are developing whilst working for your current qualifications will be still fresh in your mind; these can sometimes lapse after a gap year. There will be many students of the same age and with similar interests, which isn't always the case if you return to study after several years. However, you may find living independently to be more challenging. Also, many people find that their interests and career ambitions change within the first few years of leaving school. The degree you choose now may not be the one you would wish you had chosen in a few years time.
3 I want to go to Uni – but I think I want to have a gap year first.	Find out as much as you can about taking a gap year before deciding for or against one. What is it that you want to gain from that year? Remember that you could opt to take a gap year after Uni as well as beforehand.
4 I want to go to Uni one day but probably not for a few years.	It can be a sensible decision to gain more experience from work and life generally before deciding on a programme of study and a career. There are many ways of returning to study one or many years after school.
5 I want to go on to higher education but still have to decide what to study and which Uni to choose.	You need to be strongly committed to studying a subject in depth for three years or more. If you have not yet committed to a subject, this suggests that you may not have thought through sufficiently why you want to go to Uni and what you want to gain from it. The job or career that you choose may not need a degree.
6 I am interested but they probably wouldn't take me.	If you have the motivation and a genuine interest in studying a particular subject or for a particular degree, then there is a good chance that a Uni will take you. If you have the interest, it is up to you to put in the time to make sure you get the grades you need. If your grades are low, it may be worth planning a longer route to Uni. This may mean taking time out to develop your academic skills further and build your understanding of that subject, or to work in a related area and return as a mature student.

Answers and Feedback (continued)

Statement	Feedback
7 I have to go – there's a lot of pressure to go on to higher education straight from school.	The pressure to go to Uni can sometimes feel overwhelming, especially if your friends are all going, or your teachers or parents feel this is right for you. However, it is such a big commitment in terms of time, money, and energy that you need to be clear for yourself why this is right for you, and not just submit to the pressure. Taking one or more years away from study can help clarify what you really want.
8 Probably, but I need to know more before I can make up my mind.	This is the position that many people find themselves in. You are absolutely right to find out as much as you can to make a decision of this magnitude.
9 Possibly. I think I want to go to Uni but other things interest me too so I keep changing my mind.	It is good that you are aware of a range of options and the need to keep an open-mind about the possibilities that each might offer you. It is important that you weigh up the pros and cons of the various alternatives and feel that you are sure of your choice before committing to Uni. If you try something else first, this doesn't preclude you from going to Uni later.
10 Don't know. I haven't a clue whether I want to go to Uni.	You are clearly not yet ready to make this decision. If you haven't found out much about Uni, now is the time to start as, if you suddenly find that going to Uni straight from school is what you really want, you will have more time to prepare and to make a strong application if you start now.
11 Don't know – I might like it but it sounds like a lot of work and I don't know if I would cope.	There is a lot of work to do at Uni. That will feel OK at Uni if you genuinely enjoy the subject or are very strongly motivated to enter a particular profession. Most students can cope if they are prepared to put in the hours, develop their study skills and maintain a good balance between study and enjoying the fantastic opportunities of student life. You do need to be ready to make that commitment.
12 I do want to go but I probably won't try as I'd probably fail anyway.	If you really wanted to go to Uni, you would pull out all the stops. If you have given up before you start, you may well fail, as attitude, and strong motivation, are essential. If you think you really want to go to Uni, then start to plan now. Consider how you will develop your skills – and your attitude. What do you need to do to get the grades you need? What will you need to manage at Uni? Ask your teachers or the careers service for advice if you feel you need it.
13 Uni? Don't know much about it. You don't think about things like that round here.	Break the mould. Do think about it. You may decide that it isn't for you but at least that will be your choice based upon sound information. If you know hardly anyone else who went to Uni, and the thought interests you at all, then be reassured that there will be many other people who are in the same position. There are schemes and summer schools to help.

Answers and Feedback (continued)

Statement	Feedback
14 No. I absolutely do not want to go to Uni.	It sounds as if not going to Uni is the right choice for you at the moment. However, don't entirely discount it as an option for the future – or burn your bridges. For example, gaining good grades in your current qualifications could help to gain a place at Uni if you did change your mind later.

2.4   Why I do – or don't – want to go to Uni

Statement	
Because of other people	
Because other people say it is great.	It is good to take that on board – but find out more about what you would find great about it yourself.
Because most of my friends are going.	That can put pressure on you to decide the same way, but to stay the course you will need better reasons than that. If you don't go to Uni, it is highly likely that you will make new friends who took the same decisions as you.
Because it is expected in my family.	Pause to consider whether these are really good grounds for spending many years of your life in an activity, and the costs involved. It may feel difficult to disappoint other people if you think they really want you to go to Uni. However, they will probably want what they feel is best for you – whatever you choose – once they understand your reasons. If you are not ready for Uni, or not willing to put in the amount of study required, you are less likely to complete your studies.
Because it is expected at my school.	
Because I don't want to disappoint my parent(s).	
Because I don't want to disappoint my teacher(s).	
Because I have to be a role to my brother(s)/sister(s).	That is an admirable aim. However, you could be a role model in other ways, such as by being true to your personal goals and wishes, and through the ways you lead a responsible life.
Because everyone goes to Uni these days.	This isn't the case. Fewer than half of school-leavers go to Uni. Also, about 40% of students are part-time and/or mature students, so there are many different paths that people take after leaving school, including returning to Uni later in life when they know what they really want to do, or combining work with study.

Answers and Feedback (continued)

Statement	
For study reasons	
Because I enjoy studying.	These are ideal starting places for deciding to go to Uni. If you are highly motivated by love of study, you will find a way of enjoying the experience and have a better chance of gaining a place and achieving your qualification.
Because I love the subject(s) I want to take at Uni.	
Because I want to study a subject in depth.	
For career reasons	
Because it will help me get a good job.	These are good reasons for considering going to Uni. If your choice is associated with a longer goal such as a career or taking on new experiences, your motivation should see you through. However, if career and income are your main reasons, it is worth checking carefully that there are not alternative and cheaper routes to the career you want. Graduates, in general, make far more money over their lifetimes than those without degrees, live healthier lives, are more likely to have improved life chances. However, a degree is not a guarantee of these things nor is it the only route to them. Studying at Uni can be a fantastic and life-changing experience, and people generally say they are glad they made that choice even when they don't earn more as a result.
Because it will broaden my career options.	
Because I'll earn more money if I have a degree.	
Because I can't enter the profession I want without a degree.	
Because I want to go on to postgraduate study or a research career, and need a degree first.	
For personal reasons	
I don't know what else to do after school.	These are not good reasons in themselves for the cost and effort involved.
It's like a 'rite of passage' when you leave school.	
I am doing this for me – because I feel it is something that I will enjoy.	These reasons are likely to motivate you to succeed and make the experience worthwhile.
I want to prove I can do it.	
I want the student lifestyle for a few years.	
There will be lots of opportunities to try new things.	
I'll get to meet interesting people.	

Answers and Feedback (continued)

2.5 Reasons I don't want to go to Uni

Statement	
I don't want to leave my family/boyfriend/girlfriend.	This can be a really hard decision. If you would like to go on to higher education otherwise, then there may be ways that you could both study or work in the same area. If not, term times are relatively short and you may be able to travel home for vacations and weekends even if you go away to Uni. You can communicate using a service such as Skype so that the distance seems reduced. Alternatively, you could get your qualifications now so that you can take up a place at Uni in a few years time if your situation changes. There are ways that people can manage their relationships at a distance, but it is wise to plan together a number of strategies for managing this. Be prepared for this to be a struggle at first, and avoid rushing into rash decisions once you start at Uni.
I don't want to spend all that money on a qualification.	That is a reasonable position to take. Before making a final decision, find out the relative benefits financially, over a lifetime, of gaining a qualification in the kinds of careers and work that interest you. Also, make sure you are well-informed about when, and how much, if anything, you would ever need to repay. For example, you don't pay anything at all up front for most programmes in the UK. If you were to be on a low income after gaining your qualification, then you would not make any repayments towards this until you were earning over £21,000 per annum. If you remained on a low income, eventually the loan would be written off. There are also grants and bursaries to which you may be entitled and which do not have to be repaid. Also note that your monthly repayments would be the same no matter what fee the university charges.
I want to get a job straight after school.	If you are clear what you want to do, that is fine. Bear in mind that you can decide to work full-time or part-time and study part-time for a degree. Also, consider whether it is worth gaining the entry qualifications now so that, if you did change your mind in a few years, you would have the option to enter higher education as an adult student – many people do.
I have had enough studying. It doesn't interest me.	That is probably a very good reason not to carry straight on to Uni. Before making your final decision, consider whether a practical, creative or vocational subject in a new area might capture your interest. For most jobs, it is likely that some training and study will be involved. You may be over-focused on your current study, and find that your interest returns after a break. If so, if you have your qualifications, there will be opportunities to return to study if you change your mind.

Answers and Feedback (continued)

Statement	
I don't know anyone who has been to university.	In that case, going to university may seem rather a bizarre thing to do. Before making up your own mind, take time to find out what Uni is about, the variety of programmes and vocational and professional areas available to you, and the potential life and financial benefits. Weigh these up for yourself. If you still feel Uni is not for you now, be aware that there may well be opportunities to go to Uni later on.
I don't think there will be anyone else like me there.	There may not be anyone exactly like you, but there will probably be others who feel the same way, and who share your interests and concerns. Universities are big places, even the smaller ones, so it is likely that you will find people you can get on with. If you are very anxious about this, look at Uni and college websites to gain a feel for the ones that are most likely to attract people like you. Also, consider whether there may be advantages to being different from other people at the place you really want to study. Universities generally value diversity of all kinds and want people with different personalities, backgrounds and beliefs to apply.
I am scared I won't be clever enough.	There is a lot of competition for places at Uni. If you gain a place, then you have a good chance of being clever enough. If you don't gain a place, this in itself does not necessarily mean you couldn't do extremely well at Uni. You may need to select a different Uni or subject, or you may benefit from waiting a few years and gaining more life experience. Be realistic. If you really struggled to pass your level 2 or 3 qualifications, then it is likely that you will struggle even more at Uni. However, people mature at different rates academically and some of the mature students who do best at Uni did not do well at school.

You2Uni Quiz

True or false?

1 **You can take other qualifications at Uni apart from an honours degree.**
   True. You can study for a range of qualifications at Uni such as Higher National Certificates, Higher National Diplomas, Foundation Degrees, and postgraduate degrees.

2 **You can study for a higher qualification at a college as well as at a university.**
   True. You can study for a degree at a college. This will usually be validated by a local university.

3 **Some students start studying for a degree at college and then complete it at a university.**
   True.

4 **British students can only study for a higher qualification in Britain.**
   False. British students can, and do, study all over the world. The number of British students

Answers and Feedback (continued)

studying for degrees overseas in 2010 was 22,000. The most popular destinations are the US and Germany.

5 You can study for a degree at almost any age, even if you are 80.
True.

6 If you don't complete your degree, then you can't come back to finish it later.
False. You can generally return to a degree that you have started, or gain recognition for that study if you start a new programme. However, HEIs vary in their approaches and some will require you to start and complete a degree within a set time limit.

7 People from state schools don't go to Uni.
False. In 2010 nearly 90% of first degree entrants to Uni came from state schools.

8 There is no longer financial support available for students from low income households.
False. There are grants and loans available (see Appendix 3). In addition, universities and colleges offer reduced fees, scholarships and bursaries to students from low income households.

9 Universities make arrangements to support students with disabilities.
True. HEIs are required to make arrangements to support students with disabilities. Depending on your needs, this might include specialist support or equipment, or adapted student accommodation.

10 Most students rate their time at Unis in Britain as good or excellent.
True. Around 85% of students rate their experience as good or excellent.

11 A degree always lasts for 3 years.
False. The length a degree takes depends on the type of course you are taking and whether you are studying full- or part-time; 3 years is the most common length for full-time degrees but a degree in medicine takes 5 years and some UK Unis now offer 2-year degree courses.

12 You don't have to pay for your study at Uni up front – you only pay later and if you personally earn over a certain income.
True. Those commencing their studies at Uni from 2012 will only start paying for their degree once they earn more than £21,000 per year. This would be subtracted from their salary.

Multiple choice questions

13 According to the Sodexo University Lifestyle Survey (2008), which of the following is the top reason people give for going to university?
(a) To improve job opportunities (74% of respondents).

14 What does UCAS stand for?
(c) UCAS stands for University and Colleges Admissions Service.

15 Which subject received the most applicants to Uni through UCAS in 2011 (by Feb. 2011)?
(a) Nursing (over 145 thousand applications).

16 Which subject had the highest ratio of applications to acceptances in 2010?
(d) Dentistry (10.3 applications for every student accepted).

17 Which Uni had the highest ratio of applications to places in 2010?
(a) Brighton and Sussex Medical School (19.5 applications per place).

18 Which Uni received the highest number of applications for degree programmes in 2010?
(a) The University of Manchester.

19 Russell Group Universities are all universities that:
(c) The Russell Group Universities are all research-intensive universities.

Answers and Feedback (continued)

20 **For the following four subjects, match the subject with the % that goes on to graduate jobs within 6 months of graduating (according to the HESA Survey for 2009/10)?**
The % that goes on to graduate jobs within 6 months of graduating:
(a) Law 18%
(b) Social work 66%
(c) Italian 37%
(d) Maths 28%.
The proportion is likely to go up after 6 months, as some students will be taking a gap year, doing an internship, doing a postgraduate qualification or trying out different jobs.

21 **What proportion of graduates are unemployed 6 months after graduating (according to the HESA Survey for 2009/10)?**
(b) Around 9% of graduates are unemployed 6 months after graduating.

22 **What is the NSS?**
(a) NSS stands for National Student Survey. This is an independent survey of English universities completed by students in their final year. It looks at student satisfaction with over 20 aspects of their experience on their programme.

23 **What proportion of students live at home with parents or family (according to the HEFCE report *Living at Home* 2009)?**
(b) 20%

24 **What is the most popular subject for international students?**
(d) Business and Administrative Studies is the most popular subject for international students studying in the UK (The Complete University Guide 2009); www.thecompleteuniversityguide.co.uk (downloaded 5 Jan. 2012).

Fact finding

25 **What proportion of students in each of the following subjects is unemployed 6 months after graduating (according to the HESA survey for 2009/10)?**
The proportion of students in each subject unemployed 6 months after graduating is
(a) History 9%
(b) Law 6%
(c) Architecture 14%
(d) Aeronautical and Manufacturing Engineering 15%
(e) Celtic Studies 6%
(f) Accounting and Finance 12%.

26 **According to the National Student Survey ratings for 2010–11, these Unis got the highest overall satisfaction ratings of any university or college for each of the following subjects.**
(a) **Electronic and Electrical Engineering**: King's College London (97%)
(b) **Art and Design**: Liverpool Hope (100%)
(c) **Food Science**: University of Nottingham (98%)
(d) **Business Studies**: University of St Andrews; St Mary's University College Twickenham (both 97%)
(e) **History**: Brunel University; University Campus Suffolk; University of Chichester; University of Derby; University of Dundee; Liverpool Hope University; Teesside University (all 100%)
(f) **Other Subjects Allied to Medicine**: Lancaster University (100%)
(g) **Social Work**: Glasgow Caledonian; University College Plymouth St Mark and St John (both 96%)
(h) **Sports Science**: University of Glasgow; University of Ulster (both 100%)

Answers and Feedback (continued)

Part A: Choices and decisions

11.4 Who would you choose? (1)

The first thing to note is that each university and college, and even courses within those HEIs, will value different things in candidates. This is why it is important to get to know as much as you can about HEIs from their websites and visits, so that you choose a good match with your own interests and values.

- The two most likely to be chosen on the strength of their personal statements are Marcus and Harjinder. They come across as having the most genuine interest in the subject. We can see how this developed, how this impacts upon their current thinking and/or activities, and where they want to specialise when they get to Uni.
- The most likely to be rejected would be Arlene, because of the weaknesses detailed in the **Strengths and weaknesses of each candidate** below.

11.6 Who would you choose? (2)

In this instance, the HEIs are looking more at the predicted grades in the subject. The candidates who are projected to achieve these are: Chelsea, Harjinder and possibly Ben.

- Harjinder is likely to be offered a place.
- Marcus is predicted a B. However, he is from a social economic background that the HEI may be seeking to attract, so he may still be offered a place.
- If Marcus was not given the second place, and if Ben achieved A in the subject, he would be the most likely candidate to gain the second place. He would get this ahead of Chelsea because he demonstrates a stronger love of the subject.

Who would you choose? (3)

In this instance, the admissions tutor is looking for those who would contribute to the life of the HEI. The two most likely to be offered places are:

- Chelsea, because of her excellent sporting record.
- Marcus, because of his evident track record in contributing to the life of the school through the history club.

Strengths and weaknesses of each candidate.

Chelsea

- Strengths: She says why she is choosing this particular college and how it matches her own interests. She makes clear what she has to offer to the HEI. She is expected to get an A in her preferred subject.
- Weaknesses: Her flexibility about choice of subject sounds as though she doesn't have a real commitment or interest, and would be looking for easy routes in study rather than rising to academic challenge.
- Other considerations: Chelsea's sporting interests are likely to be seen as an asset, but her lack of a keen subject interest combined with the impression that her sport matters more than her study, could be off-putting to some HEIs.

Ben

- Strengths: He indicates a clear interest in a particular aspect of history, with future plans for investigating it further, suggesting more than a passing interest in the subject discipline. His statement suggests that he has investigated the university, as he refers to its research record. His love of reading would be an advantage for a subject such as history where this will be needed.
- Weaknesses: His statement is reasonable but may

not stand out if other candidates are strong. He doesn't give a sense of what he would contribute more broadly to his HEI or to the community, or what he might do with his degree.

- Other considerations: Ben's opening comments about a society understanding its past may not sound very original – see similar comments from Arlene. Given his opening statement, he misses an opportunity to comment on the link between his interest in the Second World War and contemporary society – and the relevance of this to him or his future.

Arlene

- Strengths: A certain amount of enthusiasm and energy comes across from the application. A B in history would be a relative strength if she chose the right HEI.
- Weaknesses: The tone of her application is likely to irritate many admissions tutors – it sounds superficial and as if she has an inflated sense of her own achievement. They are awarding places on the grounds of academic merit combined with such things as evidence of strong motivation – 'really, really wanting' something doesn't count as such evidence. Her projected grades for A level do not suggest a student in a position to assume that she could get a first class degree – that sounds silly. Arlene doesn't come across as a very credible candidate.

Marcus

- Strengths: Marcus demonstrates an especially strong interest in the subject. It is evident where that comes from, how he lives out that interest now, and where he intends to develop his interests into new areas if he is offered a place. He shows an interest in different aspects of the subject, in a specialist area,

and based on reading within the subject.
- Weaknesses: His grades are respectable but not high enough for some universities that offer history.
- Other considerations: As he is the first in his family to go to university, and from a family on an income of £25,000, and with a very strong statement, he may be offered a place at a university that usually requests high grades.

Harjinder

- Strengths: Harjinder's statement indicates that her interest in history is based on her experiences and the way she thinks about these, linking the present to the past. It suggests that she feels passionately about the subject and that it forms part of the way she lives her life, even though she doesn't state that explicitly. She demonstrates that this isn't just a subject that she studies at school. Her projected high A level grades in History will also be an advantage.
- Weaknesses: The focus of her statement is purely academic. She doesn't provide any information about what she contributes more broadly or would bring to the life of the HEI.

Part B: Academic skills for Uni

14.3 How good is my vocabulary?

1 'elucidate' is a verb which means 'to clarify, explain or make clear'. Sentences (a) and (b) both use the word correctly. Sentence (c) treats the word as an adjective, which is an incorrect usage.

2 'paradigm' is a noun which means a typical example or model of something or a worldview underlying the theories and methodology of a particular subject or discipline. Sentence (b) uses the word correctly. Sentences (a) and (c) are incorrect, referring to a paradigm as a type of building and a mode of transport respectively.

Answers and Feedback (continued)

3 'pastiche' can be a noun or verb and means an imitation of a particular artistic or literary style. None of the sentences use the word correctly – it is not something to eat, an item of clothing or a route.

4 'tacit' is an adjective meaning 'silent, implied or unsaid'. All of the three sentences use the word correctly.

5 'aggravated' is an adjective which means 'to make something worse or more serious'. Sentences (b) and (c) use the word correctly. Sentence (a) makes a common misuse of the word, confusing it with the word 'irritate', meaning 'to annoy'.

6 'infer' is a verb which means 'to deduce or conclude' something from evidence rather than from explicit statements. Sentences (a) and (c) use the word correctly. Sentence (b) confuses infer with 'inter', which means 'to bury'.

14.4 How good is my vocabulary? (2)

7 'deferential' is an adjective meaning 'respectful'. Only sentence (c) uses the word correctly. Both sentences (a) and (b) confuse deferential with 'differential', which means differing or varying according to circumstance.

8 'salient' is an adjective meaning 'most conspicuous' or 'important'. Only sentence (a) uses the word correctly.

9 'anodyne' can be both an adjective and a noun. As an adjective, it means something which is inoffensive or uncontentious, often deliberately so. As a noun, it means something which relieves pain or distress. Sentences (a) and (b) use the word correctly. Sentence (c) confuses anodyne with 'anode', a terminal in an electrical circuit.

10 'synchronous' is an adjective meaning 'occurring at the same time'. All three of the sentences use the word correctly.

11 'obviate' is a verb meaning 'to avoid, remove or prevent' a need or difficulty. Only sentence (b) uses the word correctly.

12 'serendipity' is a noun meaning a fortunate accident or development of events by chance. None of the sentences use the word correctly.

Part C: Uni-life

20.2 True or False

1 **Every Uni or college offering higher education is the same.**
False. Each has its own character and ethos. Reputations, programmes, resources and facilities, prices and admissions criteria vary immensely.

2 **If you don't have any money, then you can't study for a degree at Uni or at college.**
False. For most programmes in the UK, there are no up-front fees. Maintenance grants and loans are available for full-time students. Many universities and colleges offer support packages to help with living costs and/or to reduce fees for those from households on lower incomes. See chapter 9 and Appendix 3.

3 **If you go to Uni, you have to live in halls of residence.**
False. Accommodation requirements vary from one Uni to the next. Some do require you to live in Halls for one or more years, but many others do not.

4 **There are servants at Uni who collect your washing and return it to you clean and ironed.**
False. Some universities do provide cleaners for halls of residence and college rooms. These generally keep communal areas clean and may do some general cleaning. As a rule, you are required to look after your own clothes, washing up and personal belongings.

Answers and Feedback (continued)

5   **At some Unis and colleges, all your meals can be provided for you.**
   True, but check carefully as requirements vary. You may be required to eat all your meals in some colleges or Unis but, in others, no meals may be provided. Most HEIs have a student refectory of some kind where meals are available at reasonable rates.

6   **At Uni, if you want to live in halls of residence, this is always provided.**
   False. The availability of accommodation varies a great deal. Many universities provide accommodation only in the first year, but that is not always the case. Some have no accommodation. Others can provide accommodation for certain students, such as those with disabilities. Many HEIs offer accommodation services to help you find local accommodation.

7   **When you arrive at Uni, there will be events and socials to help you meet people and make friends.**
   True. Induction week, or 'Freshers' Week' usually offers many opportunities to meet and mingle. It can feel as if there is too much to do. However, these are not generally continued at the same level after the first week, so it is wise to make full use of the chance to meet people early on.

8   **You can study for a degree without leaving your own home, even for classes.**
   True. There are programmes of study that you can take on-line or through distance learning materials. If this interests you, check the details, as many still require you to attend certain sessions or a summer school. You may be required to meet other students virtually, on-line, for interactive learning.

9   **British students who want a degree have to study for this at a Uni or college in Britain.**
   False. You can study at universities and colleges all over the world if you choose, either in English or in other languages. Depending on where the university is based, study overseas can be an excellent way of perfecting your use of another language, learning about other cultures and widening your personal network. On the other hand, it could be a lonely and isolating experience if not planned well and if you are not relatively outgoing. Check carefully for the full cost, including fees, living costs, travel costs, insurance and other potential hidden costs.
   You may not be eligible for grants and financial support from UK sources if you study overseas but there may be scholarships or other support available from the overseas university that accepts you. Note, too, that many HEIs provide opportunities for you to study abroad for a year or semester.

10 **All students spend all their time partying and drinking alcohol.**
   False. The bulk of students cannot afford to do this, and have too much invested in their studies to party all the time. However, there are good opportunities for socialising and students tend to be creative in finding ways of celebrating. Some students go a bit wild once they are away from home for the first time, especially in the first few weeks. There are so many students at Uni and college that you can organise groups that enjoy socialising in ways that suit you, whether you are the party type or not.

11 **In higher education, there is a dean of students, chaplain or similar officer who checks in individually with all the students to see that they are generally healthy and happy and keeping up with their studies.**

False. Although there may be staff who hold the role of chaplain or dean of students, their job is not to check in with individual students. Once at Uni or college, you are considered to be an adult who can take care of yourself. However, you may have a personal tutor or similar who will make contact with you and may wish to see you for 10–15 minutes several times a year. There will also be student services that you can make use of, but usually it will be up to you to take the first step.

12 **You can choose exactly what you want to study and whether you turn up for classes once you are at Uni.**

False. You will be on a programme of study which will carry particular requirements about what you study, the hours you attend and what you have to do for assignments. Typically, there is very little room to manoeuvre on assignment hand-in dates, unless there are very strong mitigating circumstances. However, for some programmes and Unis, there will be more flexibility about attendance and choices than for others. If flexibility and independent learning are important to you, check carefully for programmes that allow this.

24.4 Where's that then? Travel quiz

1 How far is it from Inverness to Exeter?
The distance between Inverness and Exeter 'as the crow flies' is approximately 475 miles. However, to travel between the two cities by road you would have to travel a distance of approximately 600 miles.

2 How far is it from London to Aberystwyth?
The distance between London and Aberystwyth 'as the crow flies' is approximately 180 miles. However, to travel between the two locations by road you would need to travel a distance of approximately 236 miles.

3 How far is it from Birmingham to London?
The distance between Birmingham and London 'as the crow flies' is approximately 102 miles. However, to travel between the two cities by road you would need to travel a distance of approximately 118 miles.

5 How long does it take to travel from Manchester to Southampton:
(a) By train?
The quickest direct journey between Manchester Piccadilly and Southampton Central stations is around 4 hours and 15 minutes.
(b) By coach?
The fastest direct coach journey between Manchester and Southampton coach stations is 5 hours and 55 minutes with Mega Bus. The fastest journey with National Express is 7 hours and 20 minutes and requires a change of coach at London Victoria.
(c) By plane?
The average flight time between Manchester and Southampton airports is 55 minutes.

8 In which cities are the following HEIs?
(a) De Montfort
De Montfort University is located in Leicester.
(b) Heriot-Watt
Heriot-Watt University is located in Edinburgh.
(c) Aston
Aston University is located in Birmingham.
(d) Brunel
Brunel University is located in Uxbridge in West London.

Glossary of terms and acronyms

Acronyms

CIPD	Chartered Institute of Personnel Development
HEI	Higher Education Institution
HNC	Higher National Certificate
HND	Higher National Diploma
KIS	Key Information Sets
NUS	National Union of Students
UCAS	University and College Admissions Service

Glossary

Admissions The formal processes through which applicants are selected for an HEI place.

Admissions Tutor At many HEIs, there are one or more Admissions Tutors allocated to each programme. These tend to be teaching staff so being an Admissions Tutor may be only one of many things they have to do – in other words, they may not be able to get back to you immediately, so not hearing back from them at once does not necessarily mean they are not interested. Some HEIs have centralised Admissions run by administrative staff. These may be able to get back to you quickly for general enquiries, but may take longer to find out the responses to some enquiries if they need to check the details with specific programme staff.

'Apply' The online system you use, via the UCAS website, to apply for full-time programmes of higher education.

Brochure Some HEIs provide a short outline of information about the university/college as a supplement to their full prospectus (see below).

Bursary Financial support offered by HEIs is often called a bursary. Each HEI decides how much financial support they give as bursaries and to whom. At some universities these are referred to as scholarships.

Campus The site on which the majority of a university's or college's buildings are located. Some HEIs have several campuses, sometimes spread across a single city, sometimes in different towns and cities.

Classification Typically, degrees in the UK are classified as first class, 2.1, 2.2, 3rds and fails.

Clearing Once the A level results are announced, and it is known who has gained the grades required to take up places that have been offered, HEIs then check to see whether there are any unfilled places. If so, these are offered through a process known as 'Clearing' to those who haven't secured the places they wanted.

Conditional offer If an HEI makes you a conditional offer, this means that they are offering you a place provided you gain particular grades or qualifications or experience prior to the start of the academic year.

Confirmation Once you have received your exam results or qualifications, you can confirm a conditional offer.

Course Short-hand for your 'programme of study'.

Course Search A useful means of finding out information about full-time and most part-time courses; accessible via the UCAS website.

Credit In Britain, each full year of study is the equivalent of 120 credits. A three-year undergraduate degree is the equivalent of 360 credits. Each credit is assumed to be roughly the equivalent of 10 hours of study.

For some degrees, you can take larger or smaller modules or units of study, each equivalent to different amounts of credit. You would need to check that the total amount of credits achieved at each level was appropriate.

Deferral If you have been offered a place at an HEI, you may be able to opt to hold this open for a year. For example, you could take a gap year and take up that place a year later.

Degree A qualification gained through higher level study. These may be at undergraduate or postgraduate level. There are other qualifications that you can gain in higher education that are less than a full honours undergraduate degree, such as a Certificate of Higher Education or HNC (equivalent to one year of full-time study) or a Foundation Degree, HND or Diploma (equivalent to two years of full-time study).

Direct entry Applying directly to the university or college rather than via UCAS.

Dissertation A longer piece of work, usually based on your own research, typically undertaken in your final year of study.

Elective Some HEIs allow you to make up part of your year's study through a free choice of units or modules. Their subject matter may be unconnected to the rest of your programme.

Enrolment Once you have registered for a programme, you may also have to enrol on particular modules or units.

Entry profiles (about HEIs and programmes) These can be found through Course Search on the UCAS website. They provide detailed information about each HEI and programme, including their entry requirements.

Essay A typical assignment in higher education. These have a particular structure and are used to check students' ability to present reasoned, written argument and demonstrate their understanding of the subject.

Extra If you have used all five choices open to you when applying to an HEI and not gained a place, you can use Extra to apply for another course.

Firm offer The offer of a place that you accept as your first choice.

Foundation Degrees A two-year qualification in its own right and an alternative route to gaining a degree. These are the equivalent of the first two years of full-time study of an Honours degree, usually with a strong workplace element. Students can then opt to take a 'top-up' year to complete an Honours degree.

Foundation years These programmes prepare students for higher study and are pitched at the same level as 'A' level study. These provide useful bridges between school and higher education if you didn't achieve expected grades or left several years' gap between school and starting at Uni. Foundation level programmes are common for some subjects, such as Art. They are also helpful if you decide late, at school, that you want to study a subject for which you have not taken the right qualifications.

Freshers' Week A week that is used to welcome new students, typically the week before formal teaching begins.

Gap year A year taken out either between school and Uni, or between Uni and employment or further study.

Graduate Once students have been awarded their qualification, they are referred to as graduates.

Glossary of terms and acronyms (continued)

Graduation The ceremony at which students who have successfully completed a qualification are awarded their degree.

Hall; halls; halls of residence Many HEIs refer to student accommodation as 'halls' or 'Hall'. Some also refer to their formal dining space as 'Hall'.

Honours degree Most full-time three-year undergraduate degrees (or part-time equivalents) lead to Honours, provided you earn 360 credits at the appropriate levels. There may also be Ordinary degrees awarded if you gain fewer than 360 credits.

Insurance offer Your second choice of the conditional offers made to you – in case you don't meet the requirements for the first choice when you get your exam/qualification results.

Internships HEIs often have arrangements with employers for their students or recent graduates to undertake a workplace project or placement so that the student gains experience of that kind of work. Sometimes employers pay for the work undertaken but this is not always the case. There is usually a lot of competition to gain each internship, even if not paid, as students want work experience that can help them to find a job later.

Labs Short for 'laboratories'. Laboratory work is a typical feature of science programmes.

Lecture A method of teaching typical in higher education. These usually consist primarily of a lecturer talking to the class about the subject, often providing an overview of a topic, and students listening and making notes. Often, these are followed up by smaller group teaching such as seminars or workshops, where the issues raised can be discussed.

Lecturer The name given to teaching staff at Uni. These may also be referred to at some Unis as 'dons'.

Masters A postgraduate qualification, normally taken only when you have received a degree in higher education already.

Matriculation Formal admittance to the HEI. There are usually minimum requirements for previous qualifications in order to matriculate. The grades that you are required to achieve to gain a place on your programme would usually be higher than that minimum. For example, the HEI may require a minimum of a grade C maths at GCSE whereas the entry requirement for your programme might be an A or B.

Module At some HEIs, the year's study is divided up into sections; these may have different names depending on the HEI; typically they are referred to as modules or units.

Option As part of your degree programme, as well as compulsory units, you may be able to choose some optional units/modules.

Oxbridge Shorthand for 'Oxford and Cambridge'.

Personal tutor Many HEIs provide each student with a named personal tutor who is their main point of contact for the programme. Generally, these offer academic advice and may also be required to offer pastoral support.

PhD (or D.Phil) Doctor of Philosophy. A postgraduate qualification, typically involving original research, normally taken only once you have a degree in higher education and after starting on a Masters level programme.

Placement year A year structured into your programme of study during which you spend all or most of your time in a placement at work or overseas.

Programme Your programme of study may be referred to as either your 'programme' or your 'course' for short.

Prospectus The formal full brochure of the university or college that provides an outline of all programmes, services, and key information about the university.

Registration If you have been accepted as a student at the HEI, you usually have to register for the programme in order to be recognised as a student for that year. You would normally register each year. You may need to enrol separately onto individual modules or units of study.

Sandwich course A course that includes a set amount of time out of study where you undertake a period of employment. This might be for a whole year on placement, or for shorter work placements.

Scholarships 'Scholarships' are usually awarded to recognise academic achievement or excellence; depending on the HEI, scholars may be awarded money, accommodation rights or other privileges. At some HEIs, the term is also used to refer to bursaries offered to support those on low incomes.

Semester Many universities and colleges organise study over two longer semesters rather than three terms.

Seminar A taught session typical at many HEIs. These can vary in size from small groups through to 60 students or more. They tend to involve more discussion and student input than traditional lectures.

STEM subjects Subjects in Science, Technology, Engineering and Maths.

Tariff/UCAS Tariff In order to help HEIs compare candidates, a points system is used with different points awarded for different kinds of qualifications and grades. You and the HEI can work out the total number of points that you are expected to get for your qualifications and projected grades as well as those you already have. This includes qualifications such as music exams and key skills. When you look up a programme on a university website or the UCAS website, you can see the number of points – or the 'tariff' – normally required for entry to that programme. HEIs can offer places below that tariff if they choose. Having the right number of points does not mean you would automatically gain a place.

Term Some universities and many colleges organise study in three terms, similar to the school system. At Oxford and Cambridge, the terms are named Michaelmas, Hilary and Trinity.

Top-up year The final level of an Honours degree, taken by students who have previously successfully completed a Foundation Degree.

Track An on-line system you can access via the UCAS website and use to keep track of your application and the offers made to you.

Tutorial Teaching or support offered in a relatively small group. In some HEIs, these are short sessions on an individual basis, with your personal tutor or year tutor.

Unconditional offer If you already meet the entry requirements of a programme, the HEI can make you an unconditional offer – as there are no further 'conditions' you have to meet.

Undergraduate Students are known as undergraduates or postgraduates. When you first go to Uni/college, you are usually an undergraduate. Postgraduate study is at a higher level, such as Masters degrees.

Unit At some HEIs, the year's study is divided up into sections; these may have different names depending on the HEI; typically they are referred to as modules or units.

Vice Chancellor Usually, the chief executive officer, or equivalent, of a university. Names vary, so at some HEIs, these may be referred to as the Provost, Rector, Principal, etc.

VLE Virtual Learning Environment. Online learning space provided for organising learning resources for the university, typically with dedicated space for each programme of study.

Year tutor At some HEIs, there is a designated tutor to provide oversight of the programmes and support for all students in a given year of each programme.

References

BBC News (2010) *Uni fees subsidy for Welsh students.* www.bbc.co.uk/news/uk-wales-11878033

Coates, A. (2010) *Applying to University: The Essential Guide* (Peterborough: Forward Press)

Chartered Institute of Personnel and Development (CIPD) (March 2010) *Focus on graduate jobs.* www.cipd.co.uk/pressoffice/_articles/290310+EOGgraduate.htm

Connor, H. and Brown, R. (2009) *Value of graduates: employers' perspectives.* Council for Industry and Higher Education (CIHE). www.cihe.co.uk/wp-content/ themes/cihe/document.php?file=0911VoGsummary.pdf

Cottrell, S. M. (2008) *The Study Skills Handbook*, 3rd edn (Basingstoke: Palgrave Macmillan)

Cottrell, S. M. (2011) *Critical Thinking Skills*, 2nd edn (Basingstoke: Palgrave Macmillan)

Cottrell, S. M. (2010) *Skills for Success: Personal Development and Employability*, 2nd edn (Basingstoke: Palgrave Macmillan)

Cottrell, S. M. (2012) *The Exam Skills Handbook: Achieving Peak Performance*, 2nd edn (Basingstoke: Palgrave Macmillan)

Cottrell, S. M. (2012) *The Palgrave Student Planner* (Basingstoke: Palgrave Macmillan)

HEFCE Report (2009) *Patterns in Higher Education: Living at Home* (June 2009). www.hefce.ac.uk

HESA Statistical First Release (2011) *Destinations of Leavers from Higher Education in the United Kingdom for the Academic Year 2009/10*, SFR 162 (June 2011) www.hesa.ac.uk/index.php?option=com_content&task=view&id=2150&Itemid=161 (accessed 29 April 2012)

Lebus, S. (2011) 'Higher Education ensuring access through partnerships with schools'. *Higher Education Futures Forum, London, 11 May 2011.* From the video of the conference at

www.policyreview.tv/video/561/3621 (accessed 1 October 2012)

London Higher (2006) *Attitudes to part-time study: The perspective of London employers* (Feb. 2006). www.londonhigher.ac..uk/fileadmin/documents/PT_EmployerAttitudes.pdf (downloaded 28 Aug 2011)

Mason, G. and Hopkin, R. (2011) *Employer perspectives on part-time students in UK Higher Education.* BIS Research paper 27. www.bis.gov.uk

Office for National Statistics (2011) *Graduate earnings over the last decade.* www.ons.gov.uk/ons/dcp171776_233872.pdf (downloaded 11 Dec. 2011)

O'Leary, J. (2011) *The Times Good University Guide 2012* (London: Times Books)

Piaget, J. and Inhelder, B (1958) *The Growth of Logical Thinking from Childhood to Adolescence* (New York: Basic Books)

Prospects (2011a) *What do graduates do?* www.Prospects.ac.uk/assets/assets/documents/WDGD_2011.pdf (downloaded 11 Dec. 2011)

Prospects (2011b) *Beyond the financial benefits of a degree.* www.prospects.ac.uk/cms/ShowPage/ (downloaded 11 Dec. 2011)

Sodexo University Lifestyle Survey (2008) http://uk.sodexo.com/uken/media-centre/releases-2008/university-lifestyle-survey.asp

Thomas, G. (2011) *The Daily Telegraph Guide to Student Money*, 16th edn (Richmond: Trotman)

www.studentfinance.direct.gov.uk

See also: Appendix 3.

Index

Notes

Notes

Notes